Modern Christian Spirituality

ÆR

American Academy of Religion
Studies in Religion

Editor
Lawrence S. Cunningham

Number 62
MODERN CHRISTIAN SPIRITUALITY

edited by
Bradley C. Hanson

MODERN CHRISTIAN SPIRITUALITY
Methodological and Historical Essays

edited by
Bradley C. Hanson

Scholars Press
Atlanta, Georgia

MODERN CHRISTIAN SPIRITUALITY

edited by
Bradley C. Hanson

© 1990
The American Academy of Religion

Library of Congress Cataloging in Publication Data

Modern Christian spirituality : methodological and historical essays /
    edited by Bradley Hanson.
    p. cm. -- (AAR studies in religion ; no. 62)
    Includes bibiographical references.
    ISBN 1-55540-557-6 (alk. paper) ISBN 1-55540-558-4 (pbk. : alk. paper)
    1. Spirituality--History. 2. Spirituality--Study and teaching.
I. Hanson, Bradley. II. Series.
BV4490.M62 1990
248'.09'03--dc20   90-20586
                                                    CIP

Printed in the United States of America
on acid-free paper
∞

CONTENTS

CONTRIBUTORS

Diogenes Allen is Stuart Professor of Philosophy at Princeton Theological Seminary. He has published 11 books, including *Philosophy for Understanding Theology* (1985), *Christian Belief in a Postmodern World* (1989), and *Quest: The Search for Meaning Through Christ* (1990).

Annice Callahan, R.S.C.J., is Assistant Professor of Spiritual Theology at Regis College, Toronto. She has written *Karl Rahner's Spirituality of the Pierced Heart* (1985) and edited *Spiritualities of the Heart* (1990).

Ewert Cousins is Professor of Theology at Fordham University. Besides being general editor of *World Spirituality: An Encyclopedic History of the Religious Quest*, he has written *Bonaventure and the Coincidence of Opposites* (1978) and edited and translated *Bonaventure: The Soul's Journey Into God, The Tree of Life, The Life of St. Francis* (1978).

Carlos M. N. Eire is Associate Professor in relgous studies and in history at the University of Virginia. He is author of *War Against the Idols: The Reformation of Worship From Erasmus to Calvin* (1986).

Robert L. Fastiggi is Associate Professor of Religious Studies, St. Edwards University in Texas. His book *The Natural Theology of Yves de Paris O.F.M.Cap. (1588-1678)* is soon to be published by Scholars Press.

Charles E. Hambrick-Stowe is Pastor of Church of the Apostles, UCC, in Lancaster, Pennsylvania. He has written *The Practice of Piety: Puritan Devotional Disciplines in Seventeenth, Century New England* (1982), *Early New England Meditative Poetry: Anne Bradstreet and Edward Taylor* (1988), and coedited *Theology and Identity* (1990).

Bradley C. Hanson, editor of this volume, is Professor of Religion at Luther College in Iowa, and chaired the AAR Seminar on Modern Christian Spirituality 1984-1988. Among his publications are *The Call of Silence* (1980) and *Teach Us To Pray* (1990).

Contributors

Eric Lund is Associate Professor of Religion at St. Olaf College, Minnesota. His publications include "Lutheran and Reformed Spirituality 1550-1700," in *Christian Spirituality III: Post-Reformation and Modern* (1989) and "The Impact of Lutheranism on Popular Religions in Sixteenth Century Germany," *Concordia Journal* (1987).

Bill Pitts is Professor of Church History and Director of Graduate Studies in Religion at Baylor University. Among his publications is "The Priesthood of All Believers in the Baptist Tradition," *Southwestern Journal of Theology* (1988).

Sandra M. Schneiders, I.H.M., is Professor of New Testament Studies and Spirituality, Jesuit School of Theology/Graduate Theological Union, California. She is author of *New Wineskins* (1986), *Women and the Word* (1986), and numerous essays on biblical hermeneutics, spirituality, and feminism.

Edward L. Shirley is Assistant Professor of Religious Studies at St. Edward's University, Texas. He has written "Raimundo Panikkar and Bede Griffiths: A Comparison of Approaches to Inter-Religious Dialogue," *ASSR Proceedings* (1986) and a twelve-part series on Mary and the Rosary in *Catholic Spirit* (1987-1988).

David Trickett is Executive Director of the Washington Theological Consortium and Professorial Lecturer in Theology and Ecumenics. His publications include "Holiness of Heart and Life," *Doxology* (1987) and "A Step in the Reception of *Baptism, Eucharist, and Ministry*," in *Mid-Stream* (1987).

Wendy Wright is Assistant Professor of Theology at Creighton University. She has written *Bond of Perfection: Jeanne de Chantal and François de Sales* (1985) and *Sacred Dwelling* (1989), and has co-edited *Francis de Sales and Jane de Chantal: Letters of Spiritual Direction* (1988).

Introduction

BRADLEY C. HANSON

All the authors represented in this volume participated in the Seminar on Modern Christian Spirituality during the 1984-1988 Annual Meetings of the American Academy of Religion, and all but one of the essays in their original form were presented to that seminar. The AAR Seminar on Modern Christian Spirituality had two basic goals. The first was to reflect on the nature of our enterprise—what is spirituality and how is it to be studied? Although this issue comes first logically and is taken up in Part One of this volume, the seminar actually took it up last; after studying particular cases of Christian spirituality, we were in much better position to address the more general question. The second goal was to be a forum in which scholars with diverse interests in the modern era could discuss their current research on particular examples of Christian spirituality and discover historical connections as well as similarities and differences in substance. Publication of the essays in Part Two permit a wider community of scholars to join this discussion.

Part One

The four essays in Part One address the central question, what is spirituality? Spirituality has become such a popular term that a host of books have been launched under this heading. Many colleges, universities, and seminaries offer courses in spirituality, and a few even give graduate

1

degrees in spirituality. Nonetheless, serious questions need to be asked. What is the subject matter of spirituality? There is great fuzziness here, which might be the sign of either richness or confusion. We must also inquire about the methodology appropriate for study of this phenomenon. A related question is whether the study of spirituality has broad implications for what has become the dominant approach of religious studies in the academy—the study *about* religion? Still another question concerns the position of the study of spirituality among other scholarly studies of religion: Is spirituality a new distinct discipline like liturgics or simply an approach like deconstructionist literary criticism usable in several disciplines? Finally, is the study of spirituality part of a fundamental new step in the human quest for meaning that takes into account the insights of other religious traditions in the world? These are some of the questions addressed directly in the four essays of Part One and, to some extent, in the initial essay of Part Two.

Sandra Schneiders has led the way in reflecting on the nature of spirituality. Her important paper "Theology and Spirituality: Strangers, Rivals or Partners?" (1986) was discussed by the seminar, but her 1989 essay "Spirituality and the Academy" is the opening chapter in this book, for it is a refinement in her thinking. In both essays Schneiders suggests a definition of the phenomenon of spirituality as "the experience of consciously striving to integrate one's life in terms not of isolation and self-absorption but of self-transcendence toward the ultimate value one perceives."[1] Her compact definition has several noteworthy features: 1) This is an anthropological approach that focuses on the human dimension of spirit whereby people transcend themselves. 2) The nature of that toward which a person transcends is left open; it is whatever one perceives as the ultimate value. Thus spirituality can be either religious or nonreligious. 3) Spirituality is understood as a person's experience; ideas and institutions may be generated, but spirituality refers primarily to experience. 4) The particular type of experience of transcendence being considered is that in which a person seeks unity of life rather than, say, escape. When Schneiders shifts from spirituality as experience to spirituality as a formal study, she says its participative methodological style makes spirituality like psychology, for, in both, personal involvement and understanding intertwine.

---

[1] See also Sandra M. Schneiders, "Theology and Spirituality: Strangers, Rivals or Partners?" *Horizons* 13 (1986): 266.

Ewert Cousins also gives mainly an anthropological definition of spirituality as concerned with the inner movements of the human spirit, but unlike Schneiders he speaks of that toward which the spirit transcends as "the real, the transcendent, the divine." When Cousins considers spirituality as a discipline, he emphasizes that spirituality is wisdom intended to help one follow a path, "[T]raditional spirituality contains an enormous amount of wisdom, guiding one on a journey, through the pursuit of virtues and the exercise of prayer and meditation, towards the goal of spiritual realization." So, like Schneiders, Cousins seems to view the discipline of spirituality as a self-involving enterprise. His distinctive emphasis is that, at least for Christians, following the path today should include dialogue with other spiritual traditions in the world, for he believes interreligious dialogue is a new phase in the human spiritual quest.

In my own essay I question whether spirituality has a subject matter distinct from what is studied in other fields of religious studies, for its object is simply faith, religious or nonreligious. The distinctiveness of spirituality in today's academic arena lies more in its method of combining hard reflection with a strongly existential relation with the subject matter of faith. Spirituality is a faith's wisdom for living that faith. It is difficult to fit spirituality into the contemporary academic study of religion. Wisdom no longer functions as wisdom when it is treated as a neutral object. The existential element makes spirituality a distrusted partner in departments of religious studies that stress the more distant relation. Thus in the short run, I believe, it may be necessary to have separate courses and faculty in spirituality alongside those from other fields in religion, but in the long run the sapiential orientation of spirituality should influence scholars in many but not all fields of religious studies.

Diogenes Allen speaks in a similar way about the relevance of spirituality to theology in the final section of his essay on George Herbert. He argues that theology has lost credibility for many, because there is a widespread confusion about how the mind gains access to spiritual truths. The confusion is to think that we can gain access to spiritual realities in the same ways we use to consider scientific or ethical matters, whereas worship and prayer are among the ways we attend to spiritual realities. One result of the confusion is that in many theological centers participation in worship and prayer is regarded as a private, optional concern as though one could do theology perfectly well without it. Allen asserts, though, that the theologian's participation in spiritual practices and reflection is essential to having one's eyes opened to spiritual realities.

In the last essay of Part One Carlos Eire leans more toward the stance of critical reason and dwells on methodological issues which he thinks the study of spirituality must address before it can win acceptance in the academy.   Eire follows Schneiders' suggestion when he says that spirituality studies experiences, "principally those in which individuals claim to transcend the world in which they live." Since the study of spirituality focuses on experiences, he admits it must have renewed contact with them. However, he says that praxis and analysis will each be at their best when detached from each other. Again he seems to take up a suggestion by Schneiders that the immature discipline of spirituality can gain recognition in academic circles only when it has been undergirded by a generalized theory. In particular, Eire identifies three basic questions which must be addressed in such a theory.   First, in order to know how spiritual experiences differ from other experiences, the metaphysical underpinnings of the concept of "spirit" need to be explained.   Second, since spiritual experiences often include claims to know an ultimate reality, what are the epistemological grounds for such claims? "After all, a complete skeptic sees no 'other' in religious experience." Third, there is a cluster of social science questions of how to understand every such experience in relation to its particular historical situation and yet define the characteristics these experiences have in common.

It is clear that this discussion—about what spirituality is and how one studies it—is very much connected with the broader discussion about the nature of religious studies and theology. In his 1989 presidential address to the American Academy of Religion, "Who Will Speak *For* the Religious Traditions?", Robert L. Wilken says that the academy needs some people whose scholarly relation to religion is not limited to the study *of* religion and teaching *about* religion. He argues the scholarly community also needs some scholars who *care for* the religious traditions, because the religious traditions speak about wisdom.   Wilken says, "Inevitably the study of religion, if it is not delivered into the hands of scholarly undertakers, has 'sapiential' features, if not in the mind of the instructor, certainly in the mind of students."[2] Those scholars engaged in the study of spirituality are generally people who care for a religious tradition.

---

[2] Robert L. Wilken, "Who Will Speak *For* the Religious Traditions?" *Journal of the American Academy of Religion* 57 (Winter, 1989): 704.

Part Two

While Part One consists of methodological discussions of spirituality as an academic study, Part Two consists of historical studies of particular persons and movements. Each of these studies has merit and interest on its own, but reading them together has additional value in at least four respects.

First, the essays in Part Two help us think through the questions raised in Part One about defining the subject matter of spirituality. These questions cannot be answered in the abstract; specific cases are needed to test the usefulness of the proposals made in Part One.

For instance, Ewert Cousins' suggestion that spirituality is a pathway toward the ultimate or divine is supported by Diogenes Allen and David Trickett, who independently understand spirituality as a pilgrimage or path. Cousin's proposal gains further support from the fact that each essay dwells on a particular way of understanding and following the Christian path to God. These studies do not focus on the history of an ecclesiastical institution, nor on doctrine, nor on cultural conditions of the time, although all of these factors play a part. Their central theme is a certain vision of the Christian pathway and some practical advice on how to follow it. Although this collection of Christian studies cannot demonstrate the usefulness of Sandra Schneiders' definition for including both religious and nonreligious forms of spirituality, the close link between life and thought in the people treated in the essays verifies her emphasis on spirituality as experience.

A second value in viewing these essays together is that as a collection they are more likely to show up the limitations of a reductionist approach to the study of religion, such as trying to explain religious behavior and thought as purely the result of social and historical forces. No doubt social and historical influences were at work in each of the figures and movements discussed, yet it becomes abundantly clear that all the figures have in common their intent to be faithful to God. Of course, their intent does not refute the reductionist interpretation of religious spirituality, but holding up their intent to follow a path to God is like waving a caution flag to scholars of religion—watch carefully what you are doing, remember what these people thought they were about, don't thoughtlessly follow the reductionist way.

A third value in viewing these essays together is that the culture-wide character of certain social and historical forces becomes more apparent than when one views each figure or religious tradition alone. While all of these figures intend first of all to navigate by what they believe is God's star, they steer in a sea subject to the mighty tugs of Western cultural currents. Some tows like Jansenism were felt only in restricted areas, but during 1600-1900 at least two currents swept across ecclesiastical and national lines. During the early part of this era one very strong tendency was to consolidate and further the reforms initiated in the sixteenth century by Protestants and Catholics. The other and eventually more powerful current was modern culture; shaped by modern science and the Enlightenment, modern culture came on strong in the mid seventeenth century, and by the nineteenth century threatened to sweep religion entirely away.

The figures in the first three essays—George Herbert, Anne Bradstreet, and Jane de Chantal—lived in situations where the influence of modern science had not yet thoroughly transformed the world view. While they chart their own course by the light of God given them, they are living within a church and culture that is still preoccupied with working out the implications of the Reformation. None of the three was a controversialist or made reform their leading concern, but each was tugged along by that larger movement within church and state—to advance either the Protestant or Catholic Reformation.

As some recent interpreters have emphasized, the Church of England clergyman George Herbert (1593-1633) was a Puritan who had moderate views on church ritual and held a thoroughly Calvinist theology in a time when Arminian accomodations were being advanced. This particular blend of Puritanism is the background for what Diogenes Allen concentrates on: Herbert's understanding of the Christian pilgrimage in his lengthy poem *The Temple*. The pilgrimage is a process of being formed as a certain kind of person. The division of the poem into two parts reflects the twofold division of the Christian pilgrimage. First, there is the basic formation of curbing one's desires enough to even have one's eyes opened to the things of God. Second, there is the movement of believers who perceive God's sacrifice in Jesus Christ and seek for an appropriate response to such a love. The pilgrimage is from having stony hearts to having hearts that yield to God's sacrificial love by depending totally upon it.

The Puritan spirituality of American poet Anne Bradstreet (1612-1672) is the subject of the essay by Charles Hambrick-Stowe. He contends that Puritans often used the same methods of meditation and prayer as Catholics, but Calvin's doctrine of sanctification shaped Puritan spirituality into something different. Whereas the prime locus of sanctification for Catholics was in the cloister, Calvin said sanctification takes place in the responsibilities and relationships of ordinary life in the world. The crisis of this householder spirituality comes when a beloved creature is taken away. This happened to Anne Bradstreet when her house burned down, destroying the pages on which many of her private poems were written. Like many other Puritans in grief, Anne Bradstreet turned in devotional acts to offer her lost poems to God. Her loss became the occasion for further sanctification.

In her essay Wendy Wright focuses on the mode of spiritual direction developed by Jane de Chantal (1572-1641), co-foundress with Francis de Sales of the Order of the Visitation of Holy Mary. The order was part of a larger force within the Catholic Reformation—renewal of the church through establishing vigorous new religious orders and revitalizing the old orders. The broad character of the Visitation path was expressed in the order's Rule written by the reform-minded Francis de Sales. The core of this Salesian spirituality was expressed in the order's motto, "Live Jesus." The intent was to let Jesus live within them by surrendering to the will of God, which meant in practice accepting their concrete situation as an arena for service willed by God. This emphasis on serving God in everyday circumstances bears some resemblance to the Protestant doctrine of vocation. Salesian spirituality stressed the little or feminine virtues: humility, simplicity, patience, obedience. This Salesian context influenced the spiritual direction practiced within the Visitation, but Jane de Chantal added her own personality and life experiences as a wife, widow, and mother of four children. From Jane de Chantal's letters of spiritual direction to laity, clergy, and members of her religious order, Wendy Wright shows a style of spiritual direction that manifests and encourages a maternal type of personal attachment and involvement in intimate relationships.

In various degrees, the remaining essays show the effect of modern culture, in which a wedge was driven between the mind and the heart, between reason and faith in God. Modern science, the main driving force of modern culture, tended to push God increasingly out of the mind's picture of reality. It did not happen all at once. Building on the scientific contributions of Copernicus, Kepler, and Galileo, Descartes (1596-1650) pictured a world and human being of two distinct realities—mind and matter. Using a mode of reasoning modeled after mathematics, Descartes still affirmed the existence of God. Soon Newton (1642-1727) portrayed the universe as a vast machine with God as the great manufacturer. The impact of the new science on other aspects of culture was exemplified in English literature: the seventeenth century began with the passion and paradox of Shakespeare and ended with the common sense and clarity of

Dryden. In a similar way those who let scientific rationality dictate the terms of religious faith wound up with an unmysterious universe, a distant architect and lawgiver for God, and a piety that emphasized morality instead of devotion.

Another response to the new science was to largely ignore its implications for religious faith; like twentieth century fundamentalists, many held to most of the old beliefs and selectively adopted aspects of modern science and technology. However, a third type of response was to emphasize that religious faith is principally a matter of the heart. Pascal (1623-1662) showed the way by affirming that the heart has reasons for religious faith which the mind does not know. Soon after Pascal, what flourished in both Catholicism and Protestantism were various forms of heart religion. Thus long before systematic theology broke new ground with Schleiermacher (1768-1834) basing theology on faith as feeling, there were movements in Christian spirituality which emphasized the heart.

Several essays deal with manifestations of heart religion. Eric Lund traces the way Lutherans perceived and reacted to the problem of religious complacency from Luther to Spener. While Johann Arndt had stressed conversion of the heart already in 1605, among Lutherans renewal through heart religion became the widespread movement of pietism only when Philipp Jacob Spener's *Pia Desideria* appeared in 1675. At the same time the drive to maintain the insights of the Lutheran Reformation was still very strong. Some critics of pietistic tendencies saw it as a betrayal of Luther, but Arndt, Spener, and others believed they were only extending the Lutheran Reformation to a new situation.

As the eighteenth century dawned, the cleft between scientific reason and religious faith widened, for British deists argued that the simple truths of rational religion and morality were adequate; the distinctive elements of biblical revelation of God were unnecessary. In France Voltaire in the name of "enlightenment" ridiculed much of Scripture as well as the distinctive doctrines of the Christian tradition.

In Britain another form of heart religion with striking similarities to continental pietism appeared in the 1740s when John Wesley (1703-1791) emerged to lead the Methodist movement that swept Britain and America as part of the broader evangelical movement. David Trickett's essay shows that Wesley's religion of the heart properly went together with the disciplined use of external means of grace within a corporate setting. While Wesley believed divine grace is the prime mover in the work of salvation, he thought grace ordinarily works through certain means, especially prayer, searching the Scriptures, receiving the Lord's Supper, fasting, and small gatherings of Christians. Consecration of the whole self in love to God and to the neighbor involves a discipline of using the means of grace. John Wesley's peculiar genius lay in devising a variety of small Christian groups to meet different needs: society, class, band, penitents, and select society.

At the same time as these developments of heart religion in Protestantism, forms of devotion emphasizing the heart received new impetus in Catholicism. Annice Callahan discusses a contemporary of Spener, the French Visitation sister Margaret Mary Allacoque (1647-1690), whose special way of following the Christian path centered on devotion to the Sacred Heart of Jesus. In 1673 Margaret Mary Allacoque began having a series of visions which eventually propelled devotion to the Sacred Heart of Jesus from a practice of a few to a widespread devotion in modern Catholicism. Her visions urged upon the whole church devotional practices which remained strong among Catholics until the Second Vatican Council (1962-1965), practices such as communion on the first Friday of the month, a weekly holy hour, and making reparation or consoling Jesus for the rejection he has encountered. While her image of the disembodied heart of Jesus with a wound, a crown of thorns, and cross on top appears strange and even repugnant to many contemporary Christians, a closer look at the symbol and the devotion reveals a strong emphasis on the believer's heartfelt gratitude for the merciful, suffering love of God. Keith Luria argues that Sacred Heart devotion tended to receive support from Catholic reformers, for they wanted to foster among the laity decorous forms of devotion which were centered in Christ and the parish church.[3] Thus the current of reform converged with the current of heart religion.

A similar convergence happened a generation later in France when Louis Marie de Montfort (1673-1716) proclaimed another way of following the Christian path: union with Christ through Mary, particularly through devotion to the rosary. Of course, devotion to Mary through the rosary was not new and had received papal approval already in 1495, yet Luria says that Marian devotion in France declined in the latter part of the seventeenth century.[4] Thus it is understandable that the eccentric priest Louis Marie de Montfort received a papal commission to be an itinerant preacher in one of the key programs of the Catholic Reformation—the internal mission. In his chapter Edward Shirley underscores the Christ-

---

[3] Keith P. Luria, "The Counter-Reformation and Popular Spirituality," in *Christian Spirituality III: Post Reformation and Modern*, eds. Louis Dupre and Don E. Saliers. Vol. 18 of *World Spirituality: An Encyclopedic History of the Religious Quest* (New York: Crossroad, 1989): 117-119.

[4] Ibid., 107,108.

centered nature of Father Louis' Marian devotion. Beyond the general devotion which every Christian owes Mary, Louis de Montfort urged perfect devotion of total self-consecration to Mary, becoming "a slave of Jesus in Mary." Relying totally upon Mary for all one's needs and using the rosary in vocal and mental prayer were central for his way to union with Christ.

In the nineteenth century scientific reason and religious faith broke into open conflict when Feuerbach, Marx, and others explicitly rejected belief in God. In Protestantism, heart religion continued to evolve in the latter half of the nineteenth century when the holiness movement appeared among evangelicals and especially Methodists. Bill Pitts discusses the spirituality of the prominent holiness leader A. B. Simpson, who wove several strands of the post Civil War holiness movement into the distinctive fabric of the Christian and Missionary Alliance. While Simpson rejected evolution and higher criticism of the Bible, his positive vision of the Christian path was expressed as the Fourfold Gospel: Jesus present in the believer as Savior, Sanctifier, Healer, and Coming Lord. To these emphases on salvation, holiness, healing, and millenialism, Simpson added a powerful impetus to foreign mission work. According to Bill Pitts, what bound these themes together was Simpson's mystical understanding of Christ taking up residence within the individual believer.

The monumental effort of John Henry Newman (1801-1890) to reconcile mind and heart is the subject of the final essay by Robert Fastiggi. Newman's quest for integration was not just a theoretical undertaking but informed his long life. His mid-life conversion from Anglicanism to Catholicism was motivated primarily by a search for integrity, since his study of the church fathers led Newman to conclude the Anglican middle way was very like the heretical position of the ancient Monophysites.[5] His passion for integration was also evident in his understanding of religious belief as involving an assent in which both the mind and heart are converted, for it is not just "notional assent" to an abstract proposition but "real assent" to a reality which excites the mind through the imagination, touches the heart, kindles devotion, and moves to action.

Recognizing the cultural currents that tugged at these Christians in the seventeenth, eighteenth, and nineteenth centuries gives us a better historical understanding of them, but it may also assist Christians in setting their course today. At a time when the Western world is slowly shifting

---

[5] Louis Bouyer, *Newman: His Life and Spirituality* (Cleveland: World, 1960): 194-196.

from modern to post-modern culture and contemporary churches feel the affects of diverse movements calling for renewal, the core elements of the spiritualities discussed in Part Two may function like landmarks to help contemporary Christians plot their course. For instance, the emphasis on the presence of Christ in believers appears in so many of these diverse persons that it seems to be a bit of wisdom contemporary Christians ought to take very seriously.

A fourth value in reading these chapters of Part Two is that the essays exhibit a range of ways in which scholars may, as Robert Wilken suggests, "care for" a religious tradition. In her essay Sandra Schneiders says that the study of spirituality will always have three objectives:

> [S]pirituality as a discipline seems to have an irreducibly triple finality. While research in the field is aimed first of all at the production of cumulative knowledge, there is no denying that it is also intended by most students to assist them in their own spiritual lives and to enable them to foster the spiritual lives of others.

While the study of spirituality involves all three objectives, the emphasis varies at different points in a project.[6] The essays in Part Two illustrate these different emphases.

The essays by Charles Hambrick-Stowe on Anne Bradstreet, by Eric Lund on seventeenth century Lutheranism, and by Robert Fastiggi on John Henry Newman can be read as strictly historical studies. There is no suggestion by them that their subject might foster the spirituality of themselves or others. It is left up to the reader to make any connections for spiritual life today. Although in fact Hambrick-Stowe cares for the Reformed tradition, Lund cares for the Lutheran tradition, and Fastiggi cares for the Catholic tradition, none openly reveals that commitment to the reader.

Several other authors hint at the contemporary spiritual relevance of their topic. Bill Pitts' paper on A. B. Simpson is straightforwardly descriptive, although in the concluding section Pitts seems to be implicitly appealing to some in the contemporary evangelical community to move beyond a conversion oriented piety to a deeper life centered in the presence of Christ in the believer. David Trickett's study of early Wesleyan spirituality is also solidly historical, but he strongly suggests its relevance for today by often setting the discussion in the universally human issue of character formation. In the final section of her essay, Wendy Wright examines the spirituality of Jane de Chantal's Visitation community using

---

[6] Schneiders, "Theology and Spirituality," 269.

the psychological ideas of Carol Gilligan and others on typical male and female life orientations. Wright suggests that Visitation spirituality holds out to the broader Christian community an example of loving one another that emerges from women's experience.

The three other papers in various degrees make explicit that their subject might foster spirituality today. Edward Shirley caps his descriptive study of the spirituality of Louis Marie de Montfort with three specific suggestions of Father Louis' relevance for contemporary Christian spirituality. Annice Callahan's entire approach to the visions of Margaret Mary Allacoque about the Sacred Heart of Jesus is to assess their significance for contemporary devotion to Christ. Callahan lets us know she and her community have a stake in this endeavor, for she tells us she is a member of a religious community consecrated to the Sacred Heart of Jesus. Whereas Callahan most directly addresses that limited number of contemporaries committed to reinterpretation of Sacred Heart devotion, Diogenes Allen speaks to a wider audience. For instance, when Allen says, "The problem of the Christian life for Herbert is what we can render to God in the face of his sacrifice for us in the person of Jesus Christ", every Christian reader is included in the "we" and "us." In his final section Allen goes even further to address everyone affected by modern Western culture with some insights from George Herbert and others about access to spiritual truth. Thus Allen's form of caring for a religious tradition most directly challenges what Robert Wilken calls "an intellectual climate that discourages, if not prohibits, the scholar from speaking as a member of a religious community."

Spirituality is not yet fully mature as an academic study, but it is growing up. Playing a very important part in this growing up process have been collective publications such as the twenty-five-volume *World Spirituality: An Encyclopedic History of the Religious Quest*, whose general editor is Ewert Cousins, and *The Study of Spirituality* edited by Jones, Wainwright, and Yarnold. This Scholars Press volume can also play a significant role in this development, for this is the first book to provide both a thorough methodological discussion of spirituality as an academic study and chapters on specific historical figures and movements which are integrated with the methodological discussion.

PART ONE:

WHAT IS SPIRITUALITY?

1

Spirituality in the Academy

SANDRA M. SCHNEIDERS, I.H.M.

Spirituality, despite the fluidity of the term's usage and the general confusion about its meaning, is a subject which can no longer be politely ignored either in a church which would prefer a less "emotional" approach to faith or in an academy which would guard its intellectual precincts from "subjectivism." Since Vatican II, both the Catholic and the Protestant Churches have had to contend with an increasing interest in spirituality on the part of their membership; programs designed to foster the lived experience of the spiritual life have multiplied; and the academy is witnessing (not without apprehension) the birth of a new discipline in its midst.

The contemporary interest in spirituality on the part of the laity, seminary students, and ministers has been documented and analyzed repeatedly in the recent past by scholars, publishers, and cultural commentators.[1] The World Council of Churches, increasingly aware of the

---

Originally published in *Theological Studies* 50 (December, 1989). Reprinted by permission.

[1] A Protestant, Bradley Hanson, "Christian Spirituality and Spiritual Theology," *Dialog* 21 (1982): 207-12, attributes the upsurge of interest in spirituality to the crisis of meaning generated by the events of the 1960s. Anglican Tilden H. Edwards, "Spiritual Formation in Theological Schools: Ferment and Challenge. A Report of the ATS-

thirst for spirituality among its membership as well as the importance of spirituality in the dialogue with non-Christian religions, convened consultations on spirituality in 1984, 1986, and 1987.[2]   Academic consultations on spirituality, resulting in published proceedings, have been held at Oxford,[3] Louvain,[4] Villanova,[5] and elsewhere.   The American Academy of Religion, the Catholic Theological Society of America, and the College Theology Society now have ongoing seminars on spirituality.[6]

The increasingly serious attitude toward spirituality in the academy[7] is due in no small measure to the fact that the major theologians of the

---

Shalem Institute on the Spirituality," *Theological Education* 17 (1980): 7-52, reports on the factors accounting for the increased interest in spirituality in seminaries. Among Catholic authors Joann Conn, "Books on Spirituality," *Theology Today* 39 (1982): 65-58, attributes the increased interest in spirituality to the spiritual maturation of Catholics since Vatican II. John Heagle, "A New Public Piety: Reflections on Spirituality," *Church* 1 (1985): 52-55, singles out the increased desire to integrate faith and life, especially the justice agenda. Eugene Megyer, "Theological Trends: Spiritual Theology Today," *The Way* 21 (1981): 55-67, focuses on the factors, especially the biblical and liturgical renewals, on the eve of the council which favored the development of the interest in spirituality. Ewert Cousins, "Spirituality: A Resource for Theology," *Catholic Theological Society of America Proceedings* 35 (1980): 124-37, chronicles the development of interest in spirituality and lists its salient characteristics, while Joseph A. Tetlow, "Spirituality: An American Sampler," *America* 153 (1985): 261-67, notes that 37 million Americans bought books in spirituality during 1985, publishers of spiritual books prospered, and outlets handling publications in spirituality multiplied.

[2] Ans J. van der Bent, "The Concern for Spirituality: An Analytical and Bibliographical Survey of the discussion within the WCC Constituency," *Ecumenical Review* 38 (1986): 101-14, describes the process, beginning in 1948, of the gradual integration of the concern for spirituality into the WCC agenda.

[3] Andrew Louth, *Discerning the Mystery: An Essay on the Nature of Theology* (Oxford: Clarendon, 1983) is the volume on the relation of spirituality to theology which resulted from the Oxford program.

[4] H. Limit and J. Ries, eds., *L'Expérience de la prière dans les grandes religions* (Louvain-la-Neuve: Centre d'Histoire des Religions, 1980) is the acts of a colloquium studying prayer across historical periods and religious traditions, both pagan and Christian.

[5] Francis Eigo, ed., *Dimensions of Contemporary Spirituality* (Villanova: Villanova University, 1982), and *Contemporary Spirituality: Responding to the Divine Initiative* (Villanova: Villanova University, 1983).

[6] The AAR Seminar on Spirituality meeting at the 1988 national convention was centered on the question, "What Is Spirituality?" and discussed unpublished papers on this topic by Ewert Cousins of Fordham University, Carlos Eire of the University of Virginia, Bradley Hanson of Luther College, Sandra Schneiders of the Graduate Theological Union, and F. Ellen Weaver of the University of Notre Dame. The participants were not in agreement about the nature of either the subject matter or the discipline which studies that subject matter, but as the discussions proceed, it is becoming clearer what questions must be answered.

[7] Vernon Gregson, at the 1982 CTSA convention, remarked that "the theological use of spirituality is an obvious and significant change in recent Roman Catholic tradition."

conciliar era have made explicit the roots of their constructive work in their
own faith experience and their conscious intention that their work should
bear fruit in the lived faith of the Church as well as in its speculation and
teaching. Karl Rahner's conviction that "the Christian of the future will be
a mystic or he or she will not exist at all"[8] has its academic parallel in the
evident conviction of such theologians as Mary Collins, Charles Curran,
Margaret Farley, Gustavo Gutiérrez, Monika Hellwig, Hans Küng, Bernard
Lonergan, Rosemary Radford Ruether, Edward Schillebeeckx, and
Dorothee Soelle that only a theology that is rooted in the spiritual
commitment of the theologian and oriented toward praxis will be
meaningful in the Church of the future.[9]

The recognition *that* there exists a vital relationship between faith
and spirituality on the one hand and theology and spirituality on the other
by no means clarifies either what is meant by the term *spirituality* or what
the relationship among faith, theology, and spirituality is. Before
addressing these questions, however, two preliminary observations are
necessary.

First, the term *spirituality*, like the term *psychology*, is unavoidably
ambiguous, referring to (1) a fundamental dimension of the human being,
(2) the lived experience which actualizes that dimension, and (3) the
academic discipline which studies that experience. Some writers have tried
to resolve this ambiguity by reserving the term *spirituality* for the lived
experience while referring to the discipline as *spiritual theology*.[10] For
reasons that will be given below, I think this solution creates more problems
than it solves and I opt for retaining the term *spirituality* for both the
experience and the discipline, even though this requires specification
whenever the context is not sufficiently clarifying.

See "Seminar on Spirituality: Revisiting an Experiential Approach to Salvation,"
Catholic Theological Society of America Proceedings 37 (1982): 175.

[8] Karl Rahner, "The Spirituality of the Future," in *The Practice of the Faith: A
Handbook of Contemporary Spirituality*, ed. K. Lehmann and A. Raffelt (New York:
Crossroad, 1986): 22. This collection of writings by Rahner on topics related to
spirituality includes (313-14) the references to the original location and publication data
of each essay.

[9] See the excellent article by Regina Bechtle, "Convergences in Theology and
Spirituality," *The Way* 23 (1985): 305-14. She discusses the work of Rahner, Lonergan,
Pannenberg, Soelle, and the liberation theologians and concludes that their work makes
clear that unless theology is grounded in the taste of mystery and in search of God
through conversion, it is empty and sterile. But unless spiritual experience is involved in
the search for understanding and thus in the movement of reflection, it remains
inarticulate for itself and for others.

[10] Among the authors who take this position are Hanson, "Christian Spirituality," 212;
Cousins, "Spirituality," 126; Megyer, "Theological Trends," 56.

Secondly, the term *spirituality* (referring to lived experience) has undergone an astounding expansion in the last few decades. Before Vatican II it was an almost exclusively Roman Catholic term. The term is being gradually adopted by Protestantism, Judaism, non-Christian religions, and even such secular movements as feminism and Marxism, to refer to something that, while difficult to define, is experienced as analogous in all of these movements.[11] A singular indication of how universal the term has become is the title of the 25-volume Crossroad series, only three volumes of which are devoted to Christianity: *World Spirituality: An Encyclopedic History of the Religious Quest.*[12]

Furthermore, the term no longer refers exclusively or even primarily to prayer and spiritual exercises, much less to an elite state or superior practice of Christianity. Rather, from its original reference to the "interior life" of the person, usually a cleric or religious, who was "striving for perfection," i.e. for a life of prayer and virtue that exceeded in scope and intensity that of the "ordinary" believer, the term has broadened to connote the whole of the life of faith and even the life of the person as a whole, including its bodily, psychological, social, and political dimensions.[13]

The academic discipline which studies the lived experience of spirituality has developed rapidly in the past 30 years. Although I will examine this development in a subsequent section, I note here two

---

[11] Rachel Hosmer, "Current Literature in Christian Spirituality," *Anglican Theological Review* 66 (1984): 425, captures the vagueness of the modern sense of the word: "Spirituality in the broadest sense defies definition. It refers to whatever in human experience is alive and intentional, conscious of itself and responsive to others. It is capable of creative growth and liable to decay." The descriptive definition chosen by the editors of the World Spirituality series is the following: "That inner dimension of the person called by certain traditions 'the spirit.' This spiritual core is the deepest center of the person. It is here that the person is open to the transcendent dimension; it is here that the person experiences ultimate reality. The series explores the discovery of this core, the dynamics of its development, and its journey to the ultimate goal. It deals with prayer, spiritual direction, the various maps of the spiritual journey, and the methods of advancement in the spiritual ascent." Cf. Ewert Cousins, "Preface to the Series," in *Christian Spirituality I: Origins to the Twelfth Century*, eds. Bernard McGinn and John Meyendorff, vol. 16 of *World Spirituality: An Encyclopedic History of the Religious Quest* (New York: Crossroad, 1985): xiii.

[12] *World Spirituality*, 25 vols., ed. Ewert Cousins (New York: Crossroad, 1985-).

[13] Heagle, "A New Public Piety," 53, succinctly summarizes the major differences between preconciliar and postconciliar spirituality. The former was theoretical, elitist, otherworldly, ahistorical, antisecular, individualistic, concentrated on the "interior life" and "perfection." By contrast, "The emerging spirituality of our age is intensely personal without being private. It is visionary without being theoretical. It is prophetic without being partisan, and it is incarnational without becoming worldly. It emphasizes personal response and interior commitment but it radically changes the context within which this response takes place."

indications of its power and direction. The first is the proliferation in the academy of courses and programs in spirituality.[14] The graduates of these programs are increasingly being invited to teach in their area of expertise, a sign that interest in the field at the undergraduate level is also increasing.

The second indication of the development of the discipline is the extraordinary burgeoning of publications, especially of research tools, in the field of spirituality. The renowned *Dictionnaire de spirtualité ascétique et mystique*[15] has arrived at the letter S and is now joined by the aforementioned *World Spirituality* encyclopedia and a number of single-volume encyclopedic dictionaries.[16] Introductory volumes such as *The Study of Spirituality*[17] and the *Compendio de teologia spirituale*,[18] extensive bibliographical tools such as the *Bibliographia internationalis spiritualitatis*,[19] which annually indexes approximately 500 publications under eight major headings, introductions to classical texts,[20] as well as a number of series of both critical texts and translations of spiritual classics[21] facilitate work in the field.

Given this extraordinarily broad and deep interest in spirituality on the part of laity, ministerial professionals, and theologians, as well as the rapid development of the academic discipline, it is not surprising that there is also an increasing concern about such basic questions as what the term *spirituality* means, how the discipline of spirituality is related to lived experience of the faith, how the discipline is related to theology on the one hand and other fields of inquiry (such as psychology, anthropology, the arts, and history) on the other, and what role, if any, praxis plays in the study of spirituality. These are the types of questions which any emerging discipline

---

[14] E.g., there are doctoral programs in spirituality at the Graduate Theological Union in Berkeley, Duquesne University in Pittsburgh, Fordham University in New York, and at the Pontifical, Gregorian University in Rome.

[15] M. Viller, F. Cavallera, and J. de Guibert, eds. (Paris: Beauchesne, 1932-).

[16] E.g., the *Dictionnaire de la vie spirtuelle*, adaptation française par François Vial (Paris: Cerf, 1983).

[17] Cheslyn Jones, Geoffrey Wainwright, and Edward Yarnold, eds. (New York: Oxford University, 1986).

[18] Charles-André Bernard (Rome: Gregorian University, 1976).

[19] Juan L. Astigarrago, dir. (Rome: Pont. Inst. Spiritualitatis, 1966-). *The Way, Studies in Formative Spirituality*, and *Nouvelle revue théologique* regularly publish bibliographies and review articles in the field of spirituality. *New Review of Books and Religion* devoted the entire issue 4, April 1980, to books in the field.

[20] E.g., Michael Glazier's 12-volume series The Way of the Christian Mystics; Crossroad's Spiritual Classics series; *Christian Spirituality: The Essential Guide to the Most Influential Spiritual Writings of the Christian Tradition*, eds. Frank N. Macgill and Ian P. McGreal (San Francisco: Harper & Row, 1988).

[21] E.g., Paulist Press's 60-volume series *Classics of Western Spirituality* and its new series *Sources of American Spirituality*.

must face early in its development. The purpose of this article is to chart the progress of the discipline in coming to grips with these basic questions, to indicate the areas of continuing confusion, and to suggest directions for further clarification.

THE TERM *SPIRITUALITY* REFERRING TO EXPERIENCE

Preconciliar Development

Several recent studies have explored the development of the term *spirituality* from its origin in the Pauline neologism "spiritual" (*pneumatikos*), the adjectival form derived from the Greek word for the Holy Spirit of God (*pneuma*), to its modern use in pre-Vatican II Catholicism.[22] Briefly, the adjective "spiritual" was coined by Paul to describe any reality (charisms, blessings, hymns, etc.) that was under the influence of the Holy Spirit. Most importantly, he used it in 1 Cor. 2:14-15 to distinguish the "spiritual person" (*pneumatikos*) from the "natural person" (*psychikos anthrōpos*). Paul was not contrasting spiritual with material, living with dead, or good with evil, but the person under the influence of the Spirit of God with the merely natural human being.

This theological distinction continued to govern the term *spiritual* and the derivative substantive *spirituality* throughout the patristic period until the 12th century, when a philosophical meaning developed opposing spirituality to materiality or corporeality. In the 13th century a juridical meaning emerged in which spirituality was opposed to temporality to designate ecclesiastical goods and jurisdiction in contrast to secular property or power. It was in the 17th century, the so-called *golden age of spirituality*, that the term came to be applied to the interior life of the Christian. Because of the primary emphasis of the term on the affective dimension of that life, the term often carried pejorative connotations. Thus *spirituality* came to be associated with questionable enthusiasm or even heretical forms of spiritual practice (such as quietism) in contrast to *devotion*, which placed a proper emphasis on sobriety and human effort even in the life of the mystic. In the 18th century the elitist emphasis which

---

[22] The full-length monograph of Lucy Tinsely, *The French Expression for Spirituality and Devotion: A Semantic Study* (Washington, D.C.: Catholic University of America, 1953) was augmented by Jean Leclercq in his article "'Spiritualitas,'" *Studi medievali* 3 (1963): 279-96, which he wrote in response to the study by Italian historian Gustavo Vinay "'Spiritualità': Invito a una discussione," *Studi medievali* 2 (1961): 705-9. Leclercq's study in turn, has been summarized and augmented by Walter H. Principe, "Toward Defining Spirituality," *Studies in Religion/Sciences religieuses* 12 (1983): 127-41.

has been the object of contemporary controversy attached to the word. Spirituality was used to refer to the life of perfection as distinguished from the *ordinary* life of faith, and the role of the spiritual director as the one who possessed the requisite theological expertise to guide the mystic (actual or potential) assumed great importance. By the 19th and early 20th centuries the meaning common just prior to the council, i.e. spirituality as the practice of the interior life by those oriented to the life of perfection, was firmly established.

Contemporary Meaning and Use

As noted above, the term *spirituality* referring to lived experience, i.e. to the reality which the academic discipline studies rather than to the discipline itself, is being used today to denote some experiential reality which characterizes not only Christianity but other religions as well and which, in some analogous fashion, can be predicated of nonreligious or even antireligious phenomena such as secular feminism or Marxism. Arriving at a definition of a term used so broadly has proven extremely difficult. It is possible, however, to discern among authors discussing this issue two basic approaches: a dogmatic position supplying a "definition from above" and an anthropological position providing a "definition from below."

The former is typified by C.-A. Bernard,[23] who equates spirituality in the full sense of the term with the life of the Christian communicated by the Holy Spirit and governed by divine revelation. (This entails, of course, the dependence of the discipline of spirituality on dogmatic theology,[24] a position against which I will argue in my second main section.) The latter is typified by J.-C. Breton[25] who argues, persuasively in my opinion, that spirituality, i.e. the spiritual life, "could be described as a way of engaging anthropological questions and preoccupations in order to arrive at an ever richer and more authentically human life."[26]

---

[23] Charles-André Bernard, *Traité de théologie spirituelle* (Paris: Cerf, 1986).

[24] E.g., Megyer, "Theological Trends," 611-62, says that spirituality is a theological discipline because it derives its principles from revelation; that it is subordinate to dogmatic and moral theology, but is not merely the practical application of these disciplines because it pays particular attention to the personal, historical, and experiential aspects of faith and action. He says that, in a sense, spiritual theology could be called "supernatural anthropology" because its material object is the human being as he or she lives spiritually.

[25] Jean-Claude Breton, "Retrouver les assises anthropologiques de la vie spirituelle," in *Studies in Religion/Sciences religieuses* 17 (1988): 97-105.

[26] Ibid., 101.

For the dogmatic approach spirituality is the life derived from grace and therefore any experience which is not explicitly Christian can be called spirituality only by way of extension or comparison. Humanity, i.e. the anthropological givens of human being, merely supplies the conditions for the reception of grace. For the anthropological approach the structure and dynamics of the human person as such are the locus of the emergence of the spiritual life. Spirituality is an activity of human life as such.[27] This activity is open to engagement with the Absolute (in which case the spirituality would be religious) in the person of Jesus Christ through the gift of the Holy Spirit (in which case the spirituality would be Christian) but is not limited to such engagement. In principle it is equally available to every human being who is seeking to live an authentically human life.[28]

In a recent article Jon Alexander surveyed the definitions of spirituality given by a number of contemporary scholars in the field[29] and concluded that the term is being used by most in an experiential and generic sense,[30] i.e. in a sense consonant with the anthropological rather than the dogmatic approach. In other words, there is a growing consensus in recognizing that Christian spirituality is a subset of a broader category that is neither confined to nor defined by Christianity or even by religion.

The obvious disadvantage of this approach is that it gives the term *spirituality* such a wide application that it is very difficult to achieve the clarity and distinction requisite for a useful definition. Raymundo Panikkar, for example, defines spirituality as "one typical way of handling the human condition."[31] One is tempted to say, "So is alcoholism." The advantages of the anthropological approach, however, outweigh its disadvantages. First, the term is being used this way by increasing numbers of people, both by lay people interested in spirituality as personal experience and by scholars who regard this experience as a subject of study, and there is no way to control the development of language. However vague it may seem, the term is apparently sufficiently connotative to enable people to communicate about the subject matter, and the scholar who insists on a definition which rules out of consideration most of what

---

[27] Ibid., 100.

[28] Ibid., 103.

[29] "What Do Recent Writers Mean by Spirituality?" *Spirituality Today* 32 (1980): 247-56.

[30] See Sandra M. Schneiders, "Theology and Spirituality: Strangers, Rivals, or Partners?" *Horizons* 13 (1986): 265-67, for a summary of Alexander's position and my criticism of it.

[31] Raymundo Panikkar, *The Trinity and the Religious Experience of Man: Icon-Person-Mystery* (Maryknoll, NY: Orbis, 1973): 9.

ordinary people are talking about will find his or her scholarly world largely irrelevant. Second, in our rapidly shrinking world the importance of cross-denominational and interreligious dialogue is rapidly increasing. Scholars like Thomas Merton and Panikkar are not the only thinkers who have insisted that it is not primarily in the area of theology that such dialogue becomes possible and fruitful but in the area of spirituality.[32]

It would seem that the most practical way to arrive at a usable definition of spirituality as experience is to extract from the plethora of current definitions[33] the notes which characterize the contemporary understanding and to construct a definition which includes them. I have attempted this by defining spirituality as "the experience of consciously striving to integrate one's life in terms not of isolation and self-absorption but of self-transcendence toward the ultimate value one perceives."[34] The generally-agreed-upon characteristics included in this definition are the notions of progressive, consciously pursued, personal integration through self-transcendence within and toward the horizon of ultimate concern. If the ultimate concern is God revealed in Jesus Christ and experienced through the gift of the Holy Spirit within the life of the Church, one is dealing with Christian spirituality. But this definition, while excluding the organizing and orienting of one's life in dysfunctional or narcissistic ways (e.g., alcoholism or self-centered eroticism), includes potentially any spirituality, Christian or non-Christian, religious or secular.

At this point, however, it must be realized that while it is possible and, for the reasons given, desirable to define spirituality in such an inclusive way, there is no such thing as "generic spirituality." Spirituality as lived experience is, by definition, determined by the particular ultimate value within the horizon of which the life project is pursued. Consequently, it involves intrinsically some relatively coherent and articulate understanding of both the human being and the horizon of ultimate value (i.e., in Christian terms, theology), some historical tradition, some symbol system, and so on. In order that the discussion may not remain completely

---

[32] See discussion of this point by Cousins, "Spirituality," 124-25, who calls the interaction between Western and Eastern traditions one of the salient features of contemporary spirituality; William Johnston, *The Inner Eye of Love: Mysticism and Religion* (London: Collins, 1978): 60, who says the mystical experience of the Trinity is the meeting ground for the dialogue between Christianity and the great religions of the East.

[33] Besides the definitions given in Alexander's article (see n. 29 above), descriptions and/or definitions can be found in the following: Antonio Queralt, "La 'espiritulidad' como disciplina teológica," *Gregorianum* 60 (1979): 334; Hanson, "Christian Spirituality," 207; Principe, "Toward Defining Spirituality," 136; Hosmer, "Current Literature in Christian Spirituality," 425; McGinn, "Introduction," *Christian Spirituality I*, xiv-xvi.

[34] Schneiders, "Theology and Spirituality," 266.

formal, through the remainder of this article, unless I specify otherwise, I will be speaking of Christian spirituality. Thus, while theology may not be intrinsic to spirituality as such, it is intrinsic to Christian spirituality and therefore to the academic discipline which studies that experience.

CHRISTIAN SPIRITUALITY AS AN ACADEMIC DISCIPLINE[35]

Preconciliar Development

The use of the term *spirituality* to denote an academic discipline which studies Christian spirituality as lived experience is a fairly recent development, and the use is not yet established beyond competition from other terms such as *spirituality theology* or *mystical theology*. However, as Walter Principe correctly observes,[36] and as the titles of research tools in the field increasingly demonstrate, this usage is rapidly gaining ground against its competitors.

Although the term and the discipline are new, they are not without forebears in the history of Christian theology. Recent studies, in the attempt to diagnose and suggest remedies for the "dissociation of sensibility"[37] in theology as well as the "spirituality gap"[38] in Christian experience, have recalled the premedieval unity of the theological endeavor as an intellectual-spiritual pursuit. Patristic theology would today be called

---

[35] What is said in this section about Christian spirituality as an academic discipline is applicable, in general and with appropriate modifications, to other spiritualities. While nonreligious spiritualities obviously do not have theologies, they do have ideological structures which function analogously.

[36] "Toward Defining Spirituality," 135-36.

[37] This expression of T. S. Eliot is used by Bechtle, "Convergences," 305, for what she calls the post-Enlightenment lobotomizing of Western culture, i.e. the separation of thought from feeling, mind from heart, which was reflected in theology as a separation of theology from spirituality or of Christian thought from Christian living. There came to be two paths to God: the way of knowledge/thought/theory and that of love/prayer/action, the first a journey of the mind and the other a journey of the heart. The same phenomenon is discussed by Louth in *Discerning the Mystery*, 1-3. Harvey Egan, "The Devout Christian of the Future Will . . . Be a 'Mystic': Mysticism and Karl Rahner's Theology," in *Theology and Discovery: Essays in Honor of Karl Rahner*, ed. W. J. Kelly (Milwaukee: Marquette University, 1980): 156, remarks that the deeply experiential character of Rahner's theology is "all the more remarkable when one considers the tradition out of which he comes. He had to overcome the radical divorce between spirituality and theology."

[38] Richard Lovelace, "The Sanctification Gap," *Theology Today* 29 (1973): 365-66, coined this term to refer to the rationalistic process within the evangelical tradition which so overloaded the conversion process that it left no room for the lifelong process of spirituality growth and resulted in a separation of spirituality from both theological discourse and personal witness.

biblical theology or more likely biblical spirituality.[39] It consists principally in an exegetically based interpretation of Scripture for the purpose of understanding and living the faith and/or a biblically elaborated theological exploration of spiritual experience.[40]

The roots of the separation of theology from its spiritual matrix were sown in the Middle Ages as philosophy began to rival Scripture in supplying the categories for systematic theology. At the same time the subject matter of spirituality as Christian experience was placed by Thomas Aquinas in Part 2 of the *Summa theologiae*, thereby making it a subdivision of moral theology, which drew its principles from dogmatic theology. In other words, from being a dimension of all theology spirituality began to appear as a subordinate branch of theology. This situation remained essentially unchanged, despite the elaboration of the discipline of spiritual theology itself, until the 1960s.[41]

In the 17th century we meet the first use of the term *ascetical theology* to denote a branch of dogma dealing with the principles of the spiritual life. In the 18th and 19th centuries, following the development during the 17th century of an intense interest in Christian perfection and especially in the mystical life, the spiritual life became the object of study and teaching in its own right. This field of study was called *spiritual theology* and its object was defined as "the science of perfection." It had two branches or subdivisions: *ascetical theology*, which studied the life of perfection (i.e., the spiritual life that had developed beyond the keeping of the commandments and the fulfilment of the ordinary duties of Christian life) in its active premystical phase, and *mystical theology*, which studied the life of perfection subsequent to the onset of passive mystical experience.[42]

The early 20th century saw the publication of the standard textbooks in spiritual theology,[43] which concurred in specifying the proper object of the discipline as the perfection of the Christian life and in situating it as a

---

[39] Megyer, "Theological Trends," 56, describes it well as reflection on Christian experience, which led to intensified spirituality life, in contrast to scholastic theology, which was "scientific, theoretical and dry speculation."

[40] For a fuller historical treatment of this topic, see Sandra M. Schneiders, "Scripture and Spirituality," *Christian Spirituality 1*: 1-20.

[41] Megyer, "Theological Trends," 58-61, surveys the situation of spirituality under moral theology by such scholars as Congar, Maritain, Vandenbroucke, and Mouroux.

[42] G. B. Scaramelli (1867-1952) was the first, apparently, to establish "ascetical and mystical theology" as one of the sacred disciplines, with the distinction between the two in terms of whether the activity of the spiritual life was acquired or infused.

[43] E.g., Adolphe Tanquerey, *The Spiritual Life: A treatise on Ascetical and Mystical Theology*, 2nd ed. (Tournai: Descléem 1930); Reginald Garrigou-Lagrange, *The Three Ages of the Interior Life*, 2 vols. (New York: Herder, 1948).

subdivision of moral theology which draws its principles from dogmatic theology but is superior to both because of its finality in lived holiness. It consisted in a speculative part which explored the doctrinal principles of the Christian life, a practical part which described and prescribed the means by which to develop this life, and the art of applying these principles and means to the individual.

Until the conciliar era most scholars in the field were in basic agreement about the general outline, basic content, and method of the field of spiritual theology. The only real controversy centered on the question, still being discussed today,[44] of the continuity or discontinuity of the mystical life with the life of Christian holiness to which all the baptized are called. In other words, the question is whether mysticism is the normal development of the life of faith or an extraordinary state to which only some, in virtue of a wholly gratuitous vocation, are invited. The modern discussion, especially since Vatican II's stress on the universal call to holiness, has tended more and more to the former position, and this probably has favored the growing preference for the inclusive term *spirituality* as a designation for the field which studies Christian religious experience over the term *spiritual theology* with its division into ascetical and mystical theology.[45]

CONTEMPORARY DISCIPLINE OF SPIRITUALITY

Vocabulary

Dense terminological confusion surrounds the developing academic discipline which studies what we have defined as spirituality. As already noted, the development of language cannot be controlled by fiat. Consequently, all that can be attempted here is to sort out the confusion, pin down the various uses of terms, and suggest a coherent vocabulary. Whether the latter will prevail depends on factors beyond the control of the written word.

There is a historical connection on the one hand between what was called in the 19th century *the life of Christian perfection* and what is today called *Christian spirituality*, and on the other hand between the 19th-century

---

[44] Karl Rahner takes up this issue in "Everyday Mysticism," in *The Practice of Faith: A Handbook of Contemporary Spirituality*, ed. K. Lehmann and L. Raffelt (New York: Crossroad, 1986): 69-70, and decides in favor of the continuity position. Rahner's position is elaborated by Egan in "Mysticism and Karl Rahner's Theology," 149.

[45] Megyer, "Theological Trends," 58.

discipline of *spiritual theology* and the contemporary academic discipline of *Christian spirituality*. However, there are obvious and important discontinuities as well.

The expansion of the term *spirituality* to include non-Christian and even nonreligious spiritual experience entails an understanding of the discipline which is not necessarily theological. Thus, since the relation, if any, of theology to a particular spirituality is not determined by the nature of the discipline as such, the question of how the discipline of Christian spirituality is related to theology must be addressed. I have elsewhere proposed that Christian spirituality can be called a theological discipline only if theology is understood as an umbrella term for all of the sacred sciences, i.e. for all religious studies carried out in the context of explicit reference to revelation and explicitly affirmed confessional commitment. But if theology is strictly understood, i.e. as systematic and moral theology, then spirituality is not a theological discipline for the same reasons that church history or biblical exegesis would not be called theological disciplines. Although spirituality and theology in the strict sense are mutually related in that theology is a moment in the study of spirituality and vice versa, theology does not contain or control spirituality. In other words, I have proposed that spirituality is not a subdivision of either dogmatic or moral theology.[46]

Those scholars who defend the opposite thesis, i.e. that spirituality is a subdivision of theology in the strict sense, do so for one of three reasons. A few continue to think that spirituality derives its principles from the systematic elaboration of revelation,[47] i.e. from dogmatic and/or moral theology, of which it is therefore a subdivision. Others consider spirituality a theological discipline in the strict sense because, after describing the data of spiritual experience, the scholar of Christian spirituality judges that experience against a normative faith position.[48] The majority of those who see spirituality as a strictly theological discipline take this position because they are convinced that good theology is rooted in religious experience, reflects upon that experience, and nourishes the religious experience of the theologian and the church community.[49]

---

[46] Schneiders, "Theology and Spirituality," 271-73.

[47] This is Megyer's position in "Theological Trends," 61-62.

[48] Principe, "Toward Defining Spirituality," 139-40.

[49] Some who take this position are Bechtle, "Convergences," 305-14; Egan, "Mysticism and Karl Rahner's Theology," 140 and elsewhere; Johnston, *The Inner Eye of Love*, 53, 56, and elsewhere; Alan Jones, "Spirituality and Theology," *Review for Religious* 39 (1980): 161-76; M. Basil Pennington, "Spiritual Theology," *America* 155 (1986): 87.

Some of the scholars who prefer the term *spiritual theology*, especially those in the last-named category, also tend to use the terms *spiritual theology* and *mystical theology* interchangeably. For two reasons this seems to me an unfortunate terminological move. First, both mystical theology and spiritual theology are terms which have specific historical meanings, and using them for something other than what they historically designated introduces unnecessary confusion into the contemporary discussion. Mystical theology, as it was used in the premedieval period, referred not to systematic theological reflection *on* mystical experience, i.e. to what Rahner correctly calls the "theology of mysticism,"[50] but to the obscure knowledge of God experienced *in and through* mystical experience precisely in contradistinction to the knowledge of God arrived at through systematic theology. As the medieval theologian Jean Gerson said, "[M]ystical theology is experimental knowledge of God through the embrace of unitive love."[51] Merton makes the distinction between mystical and systematic theology well when he says:

> Beyond the labor of argument it [contemplation] finds rest in faith and beneath the noise of discourse it apprehends the Truth, not in distinct and clear-cut definitions but in the limpid obscurity of a single intuition that unites all dogmas in one simple Light, shining into the soul directly from God's eternity, without the medium of created concept, without the intervention of symbols or of language or the likenesses of material things.[52]

The difference between mystical theology and systematic theology, in other words, is not in *what* is apprehended (the divine Mystery) but in *how* it is apprehended. Systematic theology remains discursive and categorical even when it reflects on mystical experience, including the experience of the theologian himself or herself. And, as Merton says, even mystical theologians usually have recourse to the categories of systematic theology when they want to explain the knowledge received in contemplation.[53]

Spiritual theology, as has been explained, was the technical term used from the 17th century to our own time to denote that branch of theology, subordinate to dogmatics, which studies the Christian life of perfection in

---

[50] Karl Rahner, "The Theology of Mysticism," in *The Practice of Faith*, 70-77.

[51] Cited by Jones, "Spirituality and Theology," 170.

[52] Thomas Merton, *New Seeds of Contemplation* (New York: New Directions, 1962): 148.

[53] "And yet when the contemplative returns from the depths of his simple experience of God and attempts to communicate it to men, he necessarily comes once again under the control of the theologian and his language is bound to strive after the clarity and distinctness and accuracy that canalize Catholic tradition." Ibid., 149.

its ascetical and mystical realizations. Since we are still very much in the process of trying to liberate the contemporary discipline of spirituality from its tutelage to dogmatics and to broaden its scope to include the whole of the human search for self-transcendent integration and authenticity, it is not helpful to use this historically freighted term to speak of the contemporary discipline.

The second and more serious disadvantage of referring to experientially rooted systematic theology as spiritual (or mystical) theology is that it pre-empts the discussion of the proper relationship between spirituality and theology in favor of subordination of the former to the latter. Obviously, when the spirituality under discussion is religious, Christian or otherwise, theology is integrally involved. But the question of how it is involved is one which must not be decided by a premature subsuming of spirituality under theology.

I find most convincing and clarifying the position that regards spirituality as an autonomous discipline which functions in partnership and mutuality with theology. It is a relationship analogous to that between biblical studies and theology. Theology is a moment within the study of spirituality insofar as it is essential to the full interpretation of Christian spiritual experience.[54] Spirituality, as Keith Egan has explained[55] and William Thompson demonstrated,[56] is a moment integral to theology, both because it raises questions which theology must consider and because it supplies data for theological reflection. Rahner has made this point concretely in relation to the theological study of mysticism. He insists that the empirical mystic supplies data for the theologian which is not available from the traditional sources[57] and that this data is not only useful but necessary for a theological study of the experience.

---

[54] Cf. Harold Hatt, "Christian Experience, Systematic Theology, and the Seminary Curriculum," *Encounter* 36 (1975): 195.

[55] Egan's contribution is recorded by Vernon Gregson, "Seminar on Spirituality: Spirituality as a Source for Theology," *Catholic Theological Society of America Proceedings* 38 (1983): 124.

[56] In his *Fire and Light: The Saints and Theology: On Consulting the Saints, Mystics, and Martyrs in Theology* (New York/Mahwah: Paulist, 1987), Thompson uses specific problems in theology and in spirituality to demonstrate the mutual relationship between the two disciplines.

[57] Rahner says that nothing in his position implies that the "theology of mysticism can only be constituted from the same sources and via the same methods as those employed by traditional dogmatic theology (Scripture, the magisterium, Church tradition, and so on)." "The Theology of Mysticism," 74.

Naming the Discipline

Throughout the preceding sections I have indicated my conviction that, despite its inherent polyvalence, the term *spirituality* is the most useful name for the emerging discipline. I now offer four reasons for this position.

First, if the emerging contemporary discipline which studies what we have defined as spirituality (in the anthropological sense) is to develop freely in terms of its proper subject matter and the appropriate scholarly approaches, especially in the context of Christian theological scholarship, it is crucial that it distance itself from its 19th-century forebears. Spirituality is related to 19th-century spiritual theology in much the same way that experimental psychology since Freud is related to scholastic rational psychology. The discontinuity, at the moment, is at least as important as the historical link, and new terminology is needed to underscore this point.

Second, by eliminating the term "theology" from the name of the new discipline we can avoid a premature resolution of the question of how spirituality (especially religious spirituality) is related to theology. Even more importantly, we can avoid the subordination of spirituality to theology which would foreclose the very contributions which an autonomous discipline of spirituality is capable of making to the theological enterprise itself.

Third, the term *spirituality*, precisely because it has little history in the academy and is not necessarily a theological term, has great potential for facilitating comparative and cross-traditional inquiry and dialogue. It is truly remarkable that a term which only 20 years ago connoted suspect enthusiasm or mindless piety in Protestant circles and was virtually unknown to Judaism, Eastern traditions, Native American religion, the new religious movements, or secular systems of life integration is now used freely within all of these circles. Even those who know that the term is historically Catholic do not seem to feel that it belongs to Catholicism or that to discuss spirituality is to appear on Catholic turf or to accept Catholic ground rules. It is very interesting that the Crossroad series includes a volume on ancient Greek, Roman, and Egyptian spirituality.[58] Although from a strictly historical perspective this use of the term is clearly anachronistic, it functions well for discussion of a particular dimension of the experience of classical antiquity. In short, by using the term *spirituality* for the discipline, we can identify the subject matter without freighting the discussion with disciplinary, denominational, or ideological presuppositions.

---

[58] A. H. Armstrong, ed., *Classical Mediterranean Spirituality: Egyptian, Greek, Roman*, (New York: Crossroad, 1986).

Fourth, spirituality better denotes the subject matter of the discipline than other narrower terms. This is true even when Christian spirituality is the specific area of inquiry. A striking illustration of this occurs in Rahner's essay on the theology of mysticism.[59]   He engages the often-discussed question of whether mysticism is a higher state of Christian life to which only some are called, i.e. a nonconstitutive experience in relation to the Christian vocation.   He answers that theologically there is no essential difference between ordinary faith experience and mystical experience, but then goes on to recognize that empirically there is a marked difference. He concludes:

> When and to what extent such experiences [mystical phenomena of a psychological kind such as altered states of consciousness, paranormal experiences, etc.] occur (to the point of enjoying "essential" differences of a psychological kind), it is the mystic and the experimental psychologist within whose competency an investigation of these phenomena falls, not that of the dogmatic theologian.

In other words, mysticism is the type of subject which, if it is to be studied "in the round" as religious experience, must be explored in an interdisciplinary way.   One of the relevant disciplines is theology, but constitutive elements of the phenomenon are outside the competence of theology. A scholar in the field of spirituality would agree with Rahner that one other relevant discipline is psychology, but would also recognize that comparative religion, anthropology, theory of myth and symbolism, history, literary interpretation, and other disciplines are also relevant. Spirituality better denotes the subject matter of this interdisciplinary field than narrower terms such as *spiritual theology*.

Defining the Discipline

We can now attempt to describe the contemporary discipline which studies "the experience of consciously striving to integrate one's life in terms of self-transcendence toward the ultimate value one perceives." *Spirituality is the field of study which attempts to investigate in an interdisciplinary way spiritual experience as such*, i.e. as spiritual and as experience. I use the expression "spiritual experience" to indicate that the subject matter is not only religious experience in the technical sense but those analogous experiences of ultimate meaning and value which have transcendent and life-integrating power for individuals and groups.

---

[59] Rahner, "The Theology of Mysticism," 73.

Several characteristics of this emerging discipline should be highlighted, because in combination they help to distinguish it from related fields of study. First, spirituality is essentially an interdisciplinary discipline, or what Van Harvey felicitously called "a field-encompassing field."[60] Although theology is an important moment within the investigation of religious experience (as we saw in the case of mysticism), it is precisely because spirituality is interested in the experience *as* experience, i.e. in its phenomenological wholeness, that it must utilize whatever approaches are relevant to the reality being studied. In the case of Christian spirituality, usually at least biblical studies, history, theology, psychology, and comparative religion must be involved in the investigation of any significant subject in the field.[61]

Second, spirituality is a descriptive-critical rather than prescriptive-normative discipline. Unlike spiritual theology, which aimed to apply unquestioned principles derived from revelation and tradition to the life of the Christian, spirituality wishes to understand religious experience as it occurs. As in any field, the scholar in the field of spirituality will make critical judgments about the adequacy of such experience using norms derived from various disciplines including theology.[62] And spirituality as a discipline has, as one of its ends, to facilitate healthy religious experience in much the same way that the study of psychology is directed toward therapy. But spirituality is not the *practical application* of theoretical principles, theological or other, to concrete life experience. It is the critical study of such experience.

Third, spirituality is ecumenical, interreligious, and cross-cultural. This does not mean that every investigation in the field is comparative in nature but rather that the context within which spiritual experience is studied is anthropologically inclusive. Even the study of Christian

---

[60] Van A. Harvey, *The Historian and the Believer: The Morality of Historical Knowledge and Christian Belief* (Philadelphia: Westminster, 1966): 54-59.

[61] Principe, if I understand him correctly, takes a different view of the pluralistic approach to spirituality. Rather than conceive of the discipline of spirituality as itself interdisciplinary, he takes spirituality as the unitary subject matter, which is then studied historically (history of spirituality), theologically (spiritual theology), in terms of its cultural setting (sociology of spirituality), etc. See "Toward Defining Spirituality," 139-40.

[62] Principe distinguishes a history-of-religions approach to spirituality from a theological approach at precisely this point. He says that after describing the spirituality in question, the theologian goes on to evaluate the data against a normative faith position. At this point one is involved in spiritual theology. I believe that the theologically critical moment is integral to the study of the experience under investigation, just as a psychologically critical moment is, without either one translating the study into another field, e.g. theology or psychology.

spirituality as such does not proceed on the assumption that Christianity exhausts or includes the whole of religious reality or that only Christian data is relevant for an understanding of Christian spiritual experience. A study of Christian mysticism, for example, must be carried on within and in terms of the ongoing cross-cultural and interreligious discussion of mysticism, religious and nonreligious, as a human experience.

Fourth, spirituality is a holistic discipline in that its inquiry into human spiritual experience is not limited to explorations of the explicitly religious, i.e. the so-called *interior life*. The psychological, bodily, historical, social, political, aesthetic, intellectual, and other dimensions of the human subject of spiritual experience are integral to that experience insofar as it is the subject matter of the discipline of spirituality.

It is not amiss to remark that the emphasis in spirituality on inclusivity, wholeness, integration, and the validation of experience creates a particular affinity between spirituality and feminism, which embraces as values in both life and scholarship these very characteristics. The volume of writing in feminist spirituality testifies to this affinity.[63] Some authors have even identified feminist sensibility as a characteristic of the contemporary discipline of spirituality.[64]

Aside from these characteristics, the practice of the discipline involves the conjunction of a particular *type of object* (the individual as opposed to the general), a particular *methodological style* (participation), a general "ideal" *procedure* (description—critical analysis—constructive appropriation), and a particular kind of *objective* (plural rather than singular) which further qualifies and distinguishes it.

Paul Ricoeur referred to the study of texts as a "science of the individual,"[65] by which he meant to insist that the logic of probability consisting in the convergence of mutually supportive indices arrived at through a dialectic of explanation and understanding can provide the appropriately scientific knowledge of a reality which is studied and known not as a member of a class or a verification of a principle but precisely as an individual. Spirituality is characteristically involved in the study of individuals: texts, persons, particular spiritual traditions such as

---

[63] For a brief but excellent introduction to feminist spirituality, see Anne Carr, "On Feminist Spirituality," in *Women's Spirituality: Resources for Christian Development*, ed. Joann W. Conn (New York/Mahwah: Paulist, 1986): 49-58.

[64] Keith Egan suggested this in the context of the seminar discussion at the 1983 CTSA convention as recorded by Gregson. "Seminar on Spirituality," 124. See also Hosmer, "Current Literature in Christian Spirituality," 426.

[65] Cf. Paul Ricoeur, *Interpretation Theory: Discourse and the Surplus of Meaning* (Fort Worth: Texas Christian University, 1976): 79.

Benedictinism, elements of spiritual experience such as discernment, interrelations of factors in particular situations such as the mutual relation of prayer and social commitment, concrete processes such as spiritual direction, etc. While making use of a plurality of specific methods, the discipline itself has no one method of its own.[66] Rather, methods function in the explanatory moment of the hermeneutical dialectic between explanation and understanding.

The methodological style of spirituality as a discipline must be described as participative. It is certainly the case that most, if not all, students in the field come to the discipline out of and because of their personal involvement with its subject matter. And virtually all intend not only to do research and teach in the field when they graduate but to "practice" in the field in some pastoral sense of the word.[67] But the question of the relation of praxis to the discipline is most complicated in regard to the actual "doing" of spirituality.

Like psychology, spirituality deals with material that often cannot be understood except through analogy with personal experience. Spirituality deals with spiritual experience as such, not merely with ideas about or principles governing such experience (although these certainly have a role in the research). Just as one cannot understand anxiety unless one has experienced it, or the therapeutic process unless one has participated in it, it is difficult to imagine that one could understand mysticism, discernment, or spiritual direction without some personal participation in a spiritual life in which these phenomena or their analogues were experienced. Furthermore, as students readily testify, research in the area of spirituality is self-implicating, often at a very deep level, and the transformation experienced through study reverberates in the ongoing research.

All of this raises serious questions about the appropriate objectivity of the discipline, and where there is a mistrust of spirituality in the academy it tends to center on this issue. Some scholars fear that personal spiritual practice will be substituted for research in arriving at conclusions; others

---

[66] Edward Kinerk, "Toward a Method for the Study of Spirituality," *Review for Religious* 40 (1981): 3-19, proposes that Lonergan's method can be adapted for the study of spirituality. The problem with his proposal is that he seems to reduce the subject matter of spirituality to historical studies of spiritualities (in the sense of schools or traditions), whereas the studies in the field are of extremely diverse subjects, e.g. discernment, social-justice involvement, spirituality movements, bodily ramifications of spiritual experience, prayer, mysticism, etc.

[67] I say this on the basis of personal experience with doctoral students and am indebted to the students in the doctoral program in Christian spirituality at the Graduate Theological Union for their help in reflecting on this aspect of the issue.

that critical judgment will be clouded by religious commitment; others that programs in spirituality will function as clandestine formation programs or evangelization agencies. While these fears are belied by the quality of research and publication of both doctoral students and mature scholars in the field, there is no question that this issue of the participant nature of the discipline requires further investigation and clarification.

Third, studies in spirituality tend to involve a three-dimensional approach which, while not a "method" in the strict sense, does give a recognizable and distinguishing shape to many studies in the field and might eventually permit the type of cumulation of research results that has so far not been possible. The first phase is essentially descriptive and intends to surface the data concerning the experience being investigated. In this phase historical, textual, and comparative studies are of primary importance. The second phase is essentially analytical and critical, leading to an explanation and evaluation of the subject. Here the theological, human, and social sciences are of particular importance. The third phase is synthetic and/or constructive, and leads to appropriation.[68] Hermeneutical theory governs this final phase. Not every study in the field of spirituality will involve all three dimensions nor will they always occur in this order. But experience suggests that this type of approach distinguishes serious studies in the field.

Fourth, spirituality as a discipline seems to have an irreducibly triple finality. While research in the field is aimed first of all at the production of cumulative knowledge, there is no denying that it is also intended by most students to assist them in their own spiritual lives and to enable them to foster the spiritual lives of others. While this triple finality contrasts with the traditional understanding of an academic discipline, it is actually not much different from the objective of the study of psychology or art. And increasingly even speculative theologians are realizing that good theology is not an exercise in abstract thought but reflection on the lived experience of the church community which should affect that life.

No attentive observer of the contemporary cultural scene can fail to recognize the breadth and power of the "spirituality phenomenon" in virtually every part of the world. In the West various theories have been adduced to explain it. Some see it as the natural and even necessary culmination of the psychoanalytic movement inaugurated by Freud. Others attribute it to the final disillusionment with the Enlightenment ideal of

---

[68] I am using the term "appropriation" as Ricoeur does in *Interpretation Theory*, 91-95, to refer to the transformational actualization of meaning.

progress generated by the wars of the 20th century. Others think it is a response to the meaninglessness of existence in mass society. And some believe it is the proper name for the wholesome breeze that entered through the windows opened by Vatican II. But whatever its cause(s), there is no denying its grip on the contemporary imagination.

Although the interest in spirituality sometimes produces superficial, unhealthy, bizarre, and even evil manifestations, it represents, on the whole, a profound and authentic desire of 20th-century humanity for wholeness in the midst of fragmentation, for community in the face of isolation and loneliness, for liberating transcendence, for meaning in life, for values that endure. Human beings are spirit in the world, and spirituality is the effort to understand and realize the potential of that extraordinary and paradoxical condition.[69]

It is not surprising that scholars have been drawn to study this phenomenon. But what is more than surprising is the speed with which the original interest in charting and even measuring the phenomenon and then in facilitating the spiritual development of laity and ministers has become a serious, critical engagement with the subject matter within the academy. In the space of a couple of decades a new discipline has emerged. Spirituality is by no means a full-grown participant in the academy. Neither its self-definition nor its relationship with other disciplines is clearly established. It has not arrived at a commonly accepted vocabulary nor developed a sufficiently articulated approach to its subject matter to allow for the steady cumulation of research results that marks a mature field of inquiry.

Nevertheless, a steadily increasing number of graduate students are choosing spirituality as an area of specialization. Courses in the discipline are multiplying at the undergraduate and graduate levels. The tools of research and the organs for the communication of research are being developed. Serious and ongoing discussion is being pursued in academic societies and institutions. And some scholars from the traditional mainline disciplines are discovering that their deepest interests can be discussed more freely in the precincts of spirituality and are bringing the expertise of their developed scholarship to the new discussion. Spirituality stands at the junction where the deepest concerns of humanity and the contemporary concern with interdisciplinarity, cross-cultural exchange, interreligious dialogue, feminist scholarship, the integration of theory and praxis, and the

---

[69] This is the very point which cultural anthropologist Ernest Becker made in his Pulitzer Prize-winning study of the human condition, *The Denial of Death* (New York: Macmillian, 1973). He says toward the end of the book: "The distinctive human problem from time immemorial has been the need to spiritualize human life. . ." (231).

hermeneutical turn come together.   If the present of spirituality as an academic discipline is somewhat confused, it is also very exciting.

2

What Is Christian Spirituality?

EWERT H. COUSINS

It is indeed a challenging task to define or to give a working description of Christian spirituality. One could study the term in its history, draw its meaning from a genre of writing, see it in relation to the disciplines of philosophy and theology, or do a phenomenological analysis of the experience involved in spirituality. In addressing my task, I will touch several of these approaches. But I would like to take my point of departure from the publishing project *World Spirituality: An Encyclopedic History of the Religious Quest*.[1]

Since this 25-volume series deals not merely with Christian spirituality, but with the spirituality of all the major religious traditions, I may seem to be compounding the problem. Why bring in Hindu spirituality when we have enough problems defining Christian spirituality? I believe that this global perspective can be helpful. It can point to common elements in various spiritualities, and highlight differences as well. It can give a broad panorama against which to see ourselves. It is a challenge for Christians to identify the essentials of their own spirituality to Hindus, Buddhists, Jews, and Muslims. Often in defining our spirituality to ourselves, we may omit the most important elements.

---

[1] Ewert Cousins, General Editor, *World Spirituality: An Encyclopedic History of the Religious Quest*, 25 vols. (New York: Crossroad Publishing Company, 1985-).

It has been my privilege to work in the planning and development of *World Spirituality* as its General Editor. I have also worked in the planning and development of the 60-volume series *The Classics of Western Spirituality*, which has published chiefly Christian works. In this latter case, we did not think it necessary to formulate a working definition of spirituality for the editors and translators. The term *spirituality* had emerged into wide usage in the mid-1970s, with some broadly accepted horizons of meaning. Since we were dealing with classics, it was possible to identify these works and let them reveal the meaning of the term.

This was not the case with *World Spirituality*. Here we were dealing with contemporary authors from the major religious traditions of the world who were commissioned to write essays on specialized topics within the broad history of their tradition. Since *World Spirituality* is global in scope, it was necessary to formulate a working description of the term that would be acceptable to all traditions and not merely to the Christian. This was all the more challenging since not all of the traditions have a term that corresponds to *spirituality*. The following is the formulation which was distributed to the editors at the beginning of the project to serve as a guideline for them and their contributors. Since certain traditions, like the Buddhist, do not speak of the divine, it seemed best to formulate the meaning in terms of the human person:

> The series focuses on that inner dimension of the person called by certain traditions "the spirit." This spiritual core is the deepest center of the person. It is here that the person is open to the transcendent dimension; it is here that the person experiences ultimate reality. The series explores the discovery of this core, the dynamics of its development, and its journey to the ultimate goal. It deals with prayer, spiritual direction, the various maps of the spiritual journey, and the methods of advancement in the spiritual ascent.[2]

Spirituality In The Various Religions

In addition to this general description, each of the editors was asked to formulate the meaning of spirituality for his or her tradition. This was first to be sent to the contributors as a guideline and then incorporated into the editor's introduction to the volume. For example, Bernard McGinn focused on the experiential aspect of spirituality in his introduction to the first Christian volume, "Throughout its long and complex history

---

[2] Ewert Cousins, "Preface to the Series," in *Christian Spirituality I: Origins to the Twelfth Century*, eds. Bernard McGinn and John Meyendorff (New York: Crossroad Publishing Company, 1985): xiii.

Christianity has always insisted upon the primacy of the inner meaning of Christian documents, rituals, and institutions—their spiritual depth." Noting that the editors of the Christian volumes did not want to impose a single definition of spirituality on their contributors, he cites the following as one understanding of the term which the contributors might use as a guideline:

> Christian spirituality is the lived experience of Christian belief in both its general and more specialized forms. . . . It is possible to distinguish spirituality from doctrine in that it concentrates not on faith itself, but on the reaction that faith arouses in religious consciousness and practice. It can likewise be distinguished from Christian ethics in that it treats not all human actions in their relation to God, but those acts in which the relation to God is immediate and explicit.[3]

McGinn refined his understanding further by the distinction between experience and reflection: "What is contained in this [volume] . . . is obviously not Christian spirituality in the first instance, the actual lived experience itself, but reflection upon the historical manifestations of this experience, that is Christian spirituality as a discipline."[4]

The issue of reflection was taken up again by A. H. Armstrong in his introduction to *Classical Mediterranean Spirituality: Egyptian, Greek, Roman*. He claimed that the kind of spirituality that emerged in Greece in the philosophical movements was precisely a reflective spirituality.[5] This was especially true of the Platonic and Neoplatonic traditions, which were later adopted as the chief forms of reflective spirituality in Judaism, Christianity, and Islam. It is important to observe two things here: These philosophical perspectives became the accepted way of reflecting on spiritual experience, but they also became a spiritual path in their own right: namely, the path of knowledge, which has its counterpart in Far Eastern religions.

In the first of the Jewish volumes the editor, Arthur Green, focused on living in the presence of God as the characteristic of Jewish spirituality, "Seeing the face of God, striving to live in His presence and to fashion the life of holiness appropriate to God's presence—these have ever been the core of that religious civilization known to the world as Judaism, the collective religious expression of the people of Israel." Moving towards a more specified formulation, he stated, "Life in the presence of God—or the

---

[3] Bernard McGinn, "Introduction," in *Christian Spirituality I*, xv-xvi.

[4] Ibid., xvi.

[5] A. Hilary Armstrong, "Introduction," in *Classical Mediterranean Spirituality: Egyptian, Greek, Roman* (New York: Crossroad Publishing Company, 1986): xiii.

cultivation of a life in the ordinary world bearing the holiness once associated with sacred space and time, with Temple and with holy days—is perhaps as close as some can come to a definition of 'spirituality' that is native to the Jewish tradition and indeed faithful to its Semitic roots." Green points out that to focus on the inwardness of spirituality would not receive universal acceptance in Judaism, "Defining spirituality as the cultivation and appreciation of the 'inward' religious life, we find both assent and demurral in the sources of Judaism."[6] The tension between the inner and the outer is a pervasive theme in the spiritualities of Semitic origin, as we will see in the case of Islam.

In his introduction to the first Islamic column, Seyyed Hossein Nasr cited the equivalent of the term *spirituality* in Arabic (*ruhaniyyah*) and in Persian (*ma'nawiyyat*). Both terms are of Arabic origin, the first being derived from the word *ruh* meaning spirit; the second from the word *ma 'na*, literally 'meaning,' which connotes inwardness, "real" as opposed to "apparent," and also "spirit" as this is traditionally understood to pertain to a higher level than the material and psychic, being directly related to God. Nasr summarizes the different meanings of these terms used for *spirituality* as follows, "that which is related to the world of the Spirit, is in Divine Proximity, possesses inwardness and interiority, and is identified with the real and therefore also, from the Islamic point of view, permanent and abiding rather than transient and passing aspects of beings." Echoing the issue raised above, Nasr states: "The spiritual cannot be simply equated with the esoteric as opposed to the exoteric." It is true that the spiritual is closer to the esoteric dimension of Islam than to any other aspect of the religion. But "it is also very much concerned with the exoteric acts and the divine Law as well as theology, philosophy, and the arts and sciences created by Islam and its civilization."[7]

As one would expect, in his introduction to the Hindu volumes Krishna Sivaraman highlights the essence of Hindu spirituality as the transformation of an inner attitude. Commenting on a text from the *Katha Upanishad* 2.1.1., he observes: "This oft-quoted text sums up the spirit of the 'turning around' that singularly dominates the early religious landscape of India: Hindu, Buddhist, and Jaina." From a theistic point of view, it is "a turning around from facing the world to face God." From a trans-theistic point of view, it is a turning around from the sphere of what presents itself,

---

[6] Arthur Green, "Introduction," in *Jewish Spirituality: From the Bible through the Middle Ages* (New York: Crossroad Publishing Company, 1986): xiii-xiv.

[7] Seyyed Hossein Nasr, "Introduction," in *Islamic Spirituality I: Foundations* (New York: Crossroad Publishing Company, 1987): xvi-xvii.

not simply as actual but as real, to reality itself, the 'really real.'"[8] He proceeds to describe this transformed attitude as "worldlessness" not in the sense of being unconcerned with the world, but of not being attached to it. From this viewpoint, he presents two fundamental strands of Hindu spirituality: that which proceeds through the world—the cosmos, the community, and states of life—and that which follows the way of radical renunciation.

These definitions of the term "spirituality," seen from the perspectives of several traditions, underscore the qualities cited at the outset: spirituality is concerned with the experiential, with the inner—but not apart from the outer—with the real, the transcendent, the divine. If we examine the articles within the volumes, we will see that traditional spirituality contains an enormous amount of wisdom, guiding one on a journey, through the pursuit of virtues and the exercise of prayer and meditation, towards the goal of spiritual realization.

Christian Spirituality

I would like to return now to the question of Christian spirituality. In his introduction to *Christian Spirituality 1*, Bernard McGinn did not attempt to formulate the essence of Christian spirituality, as the other editors did for the spirituality of their traditions. In the third, and final Christian volume, Don Saliers will attempt to do that by looking back over the complex history of Christianity. At this point I would like to make some observations of my own that might lead to a description of the core elements in Christian spirituality.

I will begin by recalling a basic decision reached at the meeting of the Christian editors to plan the contents of their volumes. They did not want to cast the whole of the first Christian volume in chronological order, but devoted the second half to themes: Christ, the Trinity, the human person as image of God, grace, and several other themes related to practice, such as liturgy, prayer, and spiritual direction. The doctrinal themes were to be treated by the contributors not on a mere doctrinal level but in relation to spirituality. I believe that Christian spirituality proceeds through an experience of Christ, the Trinity, and grace, within the life of the community of the Church.

One implication is that there is a primacy of love in Christian spirituality: love of God and neighbor, and God's love for the world. This

[8] Krishna Sivaraman, "Introduction," in *Hindu Spirituality I: Veda to Vedanta* (New York: Crossroad Publishing Company, in press).

does not mean that the way of knowledge does not feature prominently in Christianity, for example, in the Pseudo-Dionysius, or that Meister Eckhart's radical entrance into the desert of the Godhead is not Christian. What I mean is that whatever path one takes, or wherever one arrives, love cannot be absent. Nor can Christ be absent, even though he may not feature centrally in a certain technique, as in the method of *The Cloud of Unknowing*. This adds up to the fact that Christian spirituality is personal and interpersonal. The Christian path consists of the awakening of the personal center of the human being, by God's personal grace and Christ's compassionate, redemptive personal love, within the Christian community, in a journey that leads to personal union with the tri-personal God.

This description I have given raises a number of questions. Within the context of *World Spirituality*, it naturally brings up the issue: How is this personal spirituality related to that of Hinduism, Buddhism, and other traditions? I believe that it has much resonance and complementarity with other traditions, which are being explored now in interreligious dialogue.

There are also questions concerning spirituality as a discipline. Is it an academic discipline? How is it related to other disciplines: to theology, philosophy, history, psychology, sociology, and anthropology? Is it a new discipline? As an academic discipline, the study of spirituality has not yet found its place with a clear understanding of its own content and methodology and its relation to other disciplines, although it is moving apace. However the realm of spirituality as a body of wisdom has been highly developed through the centuries. The transmission of spiritual wisdom may be the oldest discipline in human history. Is it, then, in any way a new discipline? I believe it is in two senses: first, it must identify its content and methodology in a modern context as well as integrate the findings of modern disciplines into its own realm; secondly, it must extend its horizons into a global context. From now and into the future, Christian spirituality can not be true to its own identity unless it understands itself in relation to the other spiritual traditions of the world.

3

Spirituality as Spiritual Theology

BRADLEY C. HANSON

In spite of the fact that *spirituality* is currently a very popular word, it is very difficult to say what is meant by it. What I propose is that the study of spirituality is best understood as spiritual theology or something analogous to it.

A field of study can be distinguished on the basis of two factors: a distinct subject matter and a distinct approach to that subject matter. Most fields of study are distinguished through a combination of these two factors. For instance, on the one hand, New Testament Studies focuses on the New Testament rather than some other piece of literature or subject matter, although it uses methods identical to those employed in Old Testament Studies, other sacred writings, and certain forms of secular literature. Within the study of religion itself, this specific subject matter marks New Testament studies off from other fields. On the other hand, while a New Testament scholar shares careful attention to the New Testament with the Christian preacher, their approaches to the document are different. What distinguishes the field of New Testament Studies from other fields of inquiry is a combination of subject matter and approach. The same two factors also distinguish music history as a field of study. Among all the many disciplines that employ historical methods, music history has a peculiar subject matter. Among the various disciplines in music such as performance, conducting, and theory, music history alone focuses upon the historical approach.

What about spirituality? Can it be distinguished on the basis of its subject matter and approach? We'll begin by examining its subject matter. Since there is no widespread agreement on the meaning of *spirituality*, the best we can do is to consider several proposals for what this subject matter is. One proposal concentrates on the human being as spirit in the sense of self-transcending. Joann Wolski Conn articulates this understanding of spirituality, "From the perspective of the actualization of the human capacity to be spiritual, to be self-transcending—that is, relational and freely committed spirituality encompasses all of life."[1] This is a broad philosophical meaning of the term. "Philosophers speak of our human spirituality as our capacity for self-transcendence, a capacity demonstrated in our ability to know the truth, to relate to others lovingly, and to commit ourselves freely to persons and ideals."[2]

A second proposal for the meaning of spirituality is stated by Ewert Cousins in his preface to the Crossroad series on World Spirituality: "The series focuses on that inner dimension of the person called by certain traditions 'the spirit.' This spiritual core is the deepest center of the person. It is here that the person is open to the transcendent dimension; it is here that the person experiences ultimate reality."[3] What is added to self-transcendence is terminology that points toward the supernatural—"transcendent dimension", "ultimate reality." In other words, the meaning of spirituality in this second proposal is really the same as "religion." Of course, there is also no universal agreement on the meaning of religion, but Cousins' use of the term spirituality is very close to what the history of religions scholar Robert S. Ellwood, Jr. says about religion: "Our basic idea will be that religious thought and activity represents one's acting out, or actualizing, who one thinks he is or she really is deep within. It simultaneously includes the corresponding relationship to our ultimate environment, infinite reality itself."[4] For Ellwood religion includes both a quest for the real self and a relationship to a reality that transcends the material. The fact that for Ewert Cousins spirituality is really another word for religion is borne out by the subtitle of the Crossroad series of which he

---

[1] Joann Wolski Conn, *Women's Spirituality: Resources For Christian Development* (New York: Paulist, 1986): 9.

[2] Ibid., 3.

[3] Ewert Cousins, "Preface to the Series," in *Christian Spirituality I: Origins to the Twelfth Century*, eds. Bernard McGinn and John Meyendorff, vol. 16 of *World Spirituality: An Encyclopedic History of the Religious Quest* (New York: Crossroad, 1985): xiii.

[4] Robert S. Ellwood, Jr., *Introducing Religion: From Inside and Outside* (Englewood Cliffs: Prentice-Hall, 1978): 1-2.

is general editor: *World Spirituality: An Encyclopedic History of the Religious Quest.* Even the title of the projected twenty-second volume on secular forms is consistent with this: *Spirituality and the Secular Quest;* the title suggests that the secular quest is parallel or analogous to spirituality, not a clear instance of it, similar to the way in which many have spoken of communism as a religion.

A third proposal for the meaning of spirituality is represented in "Theology and Spirituality: Strangers, Rivals, or Partners?" by Sandra Schneiders who says, "[V]irtually everyone talking about spirituality today is talking about self-transcendence which gives integrity and meaning to the whole of life and to life in its wholeness by situating and orienting the person within the horizon of ultimacy in some ongoing and transforming way."[5] This definition further specifies the nature of self-transcendence by adding the feature of ultimacy, yet without the suggestion that the ultimate is supernatural. This idea is familiar to anyone acquainted with the thought of Paul Tillich, for he talked about faith and even religion in a very broad sense as one's ultimate concern. Not just conventionally religious people have faith, but anyone whose life has a master commitment. As Schneiders points out, this faith or master commitment influences all aspects of a person's life, and also serves to unify a person's life by setting up the priorities of one's existence. It might be clearer to say that spirituality in this third sense is faith, and spirituality as a discipline would be faith studies.

A fourth point about the meaning of spirituality does not so much constitute another definition of it as it adds a nuance that could be combined with any of the above definitions. Sandra Schneiders expresses this nuance by emphasizing that spirituality refers to experience. This is echoed in Bernard McGinn's statements that "Christian spirituality is the lived experience of Christian belief" rather than doctrine, and that "Christianity has always insisted upon the primacy of the inner meaning of Christian documents, rituals, and institutions—their spiritual depth. This volume and the two that will follow it in *World Spirituality: An Encyclopedic History of the Religious Quest* are an attempt to present the inner message of Christian belief and practice."[6] Another way of putting this is that spirituality as a study does not focus on the outward forms of religion or faith but on the lived reality. This does not mean that a spirituality can

[5] Sandra M. Schneiders, I.H.M., "Theology and Spirituality: Strangers, Rivals, or Partners?" Horizons, 13/2 (1986): 266.
[6] Bernard McGinn, "Introduction," in *Christian Spirituality I*, xv.

exist without outward forms, but that the outward forms are important as means of inculcating and expressing the inward reality.

Using these four suggestions for the meaning of spirituality, can we discern a subject matter distinct from others in the academic world? In my judgment, the first proposal (the subject matter of spirituality is the human spirit in its multifaceted self-transcending) is too diffuse to be helpful. Conn says spirit is shown in the human ability to know the truth, to give of ourselves to others, and to make free commitments. In his discussion of the human spirit in volume three of his *Systematic Theology*, Paul Tillich sees the free, self-transcending character of the spirit expressed in three broad areas: the area of morality (the centering movement that constitutes the personal self), the area of culture (self-creativity that moves out to produce language, technology, "theoretical" acts of cognition and aesthetics, and human community and persons), and in the area of religion (the self's vertical movement beyond the finite). In short, there is very little that is human in which the human spirit may not be expressed. This makes it very difficult to have a reasonably clear subject matter called spirituality. While I agree that the human capacity of self-transcendence is an essential ingredient in anything called spirituality, I do not think this very broad meaning of the term is circumscribed enough to be the subject matter of a field of study. This seems analogous to freedom which is also an important human ability and concept, yet while it is worthwhile to clarify the concept, we do not have a distinct field of freedomology; this is probably because freedom has such pervasive influence in human life.

The second suggestion—represented by Ewert Cousins in his Crossroad series preface—also does not mark off a distinct subject matter, for in this case spirituality appears to be just another term for religion.

The third proposal, in which Sandra Schneiders seems to understand a person's spirituality as his or her faith, gains some in distinctness from religion by being more inclusive—in most cases spirituality would coincide with religion but in others it would be a non-religious faith.

Does this and her additional point about spirituality focusing on experience distinguish spirituality as a discipline with its own subject matter? I don't think so. Established disciplines such as religious history, history of religions, and systematic theology already examine faith and often include non-religious forms of faith. Moreover, what one might consider exemplary studies in spirituality do not appear to dwell much on experience. Schneiders' own chapter on "Scripture and Spirituality" in the first Volume of the Crossroad trilogy on Christian spirituality devotes only a few paragraphs to direct discussion of the religious experience of

Christians; most of the chapter discusses principles of exegesis until the Middle Ages with special attention to what I would call an existential relation of the interpreter to the Scriptures. This attention to an existential relation to the text points us toward the second major factor in distinguishing an academic discipline—the approach to the subject matter. It does not appear that spirituality can qualify as a discipline just on the basis of its subject matter, for the subject matter is not distinct enough from religion generally or from other fields within religious studies.

Now we must ask whether spirituality as a study has an approach to its subject matter that would help distinguish it from other academic disciplines. Sandra Schneiders says that the methods and approaches of spirituality are:

> irreducibly pluralistic and thoroughly interdisciplinary. Most research projects in spirituality will involve biblical, historical, theological, social, psychological, aesthetic, and comparative approaches. The use of these disciplines will be governed by the methods appropriate to these disciplines themselves but the underlying and guiding philosophical presuppositions for their use are usually hermeneutical since the fundamental problem in spirituality is always that of interpretation of particulars in order to understand the experience which comes to expression therein.[7]

I have difficulty seeing how this distinguishes spirituality from much else that is done in religious studies. A thorough historical study of the life of Martin Luther such as Roland Bainton's classic *Here I Stand* employs biblical, historical, theological, social, psychological, aesthetic approaches in order to understand Luther's experience and faith. The same thing would be true of much that is done in biblical studies; here too the approach is thoroughly interdisciplinary and hermeneutical. It seems that what is done in history of religions could be described in the same terms.

The element of its approach that I think does make spirituality distinctive is what Schneiders calls "the objectives" of the discipline of spirituality and what I would call the investigator's relation to the subject matter. She points out that the objectives of a study in spirituality are always simultaneously theoretical and practical, and I agree. What I mean is that a spirituality study combines, on the one hand, a rigor of reflection that requires a certain distance of the subject from the object very like that which distinguishes theology from praying and worshipping, and on the other hand, a strongly existential relation to the subject matter in which the subject is seeking in some way either to grow in his or her faith or to help

---

[7] Schneiders, "Theology and Spirituality," 272-273.

others grow in their faith through this reflection. This combination of serious reflection and strongly existential orientation distinguishes spirituality from all the disciplines in the natural sciences, social sciences, and religious studies that intend to be value neutral and objective, and it also distinguishes spirituality from devotional and homiletical undertakings that aim at growth in a particular faith but do not involve hard reflection. Perhaps this is what Schneiders means by concentrating on experience and what McGinn means by the inner meaning, but I think it is more accurate to speak of an existential relation to the subject matter; it is entirely possible to have a neutral or skeptical attitude toward the experience or inner meaning of another's faith. In fact, many a good study in the history of religions attempts to give an objective description of the inward meaning of a group's religious faith as well as pay attention to its outward forms.

I may sum up my view by saying that I think spirituality is that study whose subject matter is faith and which involves a stance of the subject toward the subject matter that combines hard reflection with a strong existential concern to grow in faith. If this is true, then spirituality will not qualify as a "scientific" discipline among the pantheon of disciplines in religious studies; it belongs to what we in the West have called theology in the broad sense. And even within theology spirituality does not have a clearly demarcated subject matter such as one can see in biblical studies, religious history, ethics, etc., for its topic might be biblical or historical, ethical or doctrinal; what distinguishes it is its reflective, existential approach that seeks to enhance the faith of the scholar or of those the scholar addresses.

I think an appropriate name for this discipline is spiritual theology, although I recognize that this term may have old, unsatisfactory associations. For instance, as a Lutheran I disagree with an older understanding of spiritual theology as the science of perfection. However, the name is rather unimportant. What matters is the stance or orientation that spiritual theology or spirituality represents, a stance that ought to infuse much that is done in biblical studies, systematic theology, and ethics. It may not be a good thing to establish spirituality as a separate discipline within the academy, for the effort to justify spirituality as an academic discipline is likely to be done on terms acceptable to the descriptive, scientific disciplines. The questions Carlos Eire raises come from that Enlightenment perspective. As a short term strategy it is probably necessary to identify certain courses as spirituality, but in the long run spirituality will be a much stronger undertaking if its existential stance pervades much that is done in religious studies.

Given my understanding of spirituality as spiritual theology, I doubt that much of what is labeled "spirituality" today qualifies, since most of it is done from a much more objective stance. For example, in *Christian Spirituality I: Origins to the Twelfth Century* chapters by Jean Leclerq on Western Christian monasticism and asceticism, Thomas Hopko on the trinity in the Cappodocians, Leonid Oupensky on icon and art, and Kallistos Ware on Eastern ways of prayer and contemplation (a random selection) could all just as well fit into an encyclopedia on religion, for while they all do very well in describing a certain expression of Christian faith, there is no hint (except in Ware's final paragraph) of inviting the reader to participate in this expression of faith. Good chapters in an encyclopedic history of religions would do the same.

Ewert Cousins says, "The transmission of spiritual wisdom may be the oldest discipline in human history. Yet this ancient discipline needs to be accorded its own place in academic studies."[8] The "transmission of spiritual wisdom" is a discipline that requires the student's desire to *live* that wisdom and the teacher's intention to help the student in that endeavor. The problem, as I see it, is that in the modern academy this kind of relationship to the subject matter is considered appropriate to the seminary but not to the university class room and its descriptive stance. My hunch is that books labeled "spirituality" often sell well to the public, because people are looking for a spiritual wisdom that they can live and for teachers who will help them live it. I grant that they can find it in the descriptive studies if they have the maturity and insight to dig it out, but I suspect that they are also looking in the text for some spiritual encouragement and direction, and those are generally lacking.

---

[8] Cousins, "Preface," *Christian Spirituality I*, xiii.

4

Major Problems in the Definition of Spirituality as an Academic Discipline

CARLOS M. N. EIRE

Centuries ago a frustrated Augustine scholar who found it difficult to keep up with his bibliography was driven to say, "Anyone who claims to have read everything written by St. Augustine must be a liar." In our own day and age, those who study that nebulous phenomenon known as spirituality are often driven to worse states of despondency by the seemingly inexhaustible torrent of books and articles generated by that subject. At least St. Augustine wrote a finite number of works. Those who have tried to keep up with the literature on spirituality know very well what the writer of Ecclesiastes meant when he said "of making many books there is no end, and much study is a weariness to the flesh" (Eccl. 12:12).

During the past decade, the term *spirituality* has rapidly achieved a special prominence, and so has the study of the subject that this term attempts to describe. Though interest in this field is certainly not new, there seems to have been a marked increase in the attention paid to it, as evidenced not only by how much has been published, but also by the growth in academic programs dedicated to its study.

What makes the study of spirituality especially different, however, is not so much the quantity of literature churned out by presses all over the

Another version of this essay appeared in *Religious Studies Review* 14 (January, 1988). Used by permission of the Council of Societies for the Study of Religion.

53

globe, but rather the fact that the subject seems to have no boundaries. As Sandra Schneiders has pointed out, the spirituality boom is somewhat baffling, "because of the widespread confusion about the very meaning of the term, not to mention the more complicated question of its relationship to other activities and fields of study."[1] At best one can get the impression that spirituality is very much like the proverbial infinite sphere of the philosophers, with its center everywhere and its circumference nowhere. At worst, one can see it as a fuzzy Gordian knot of sorts, a tangled and disorderly ball, woven of leftover threads from other reputable disciplines. If the study of spirituality had any serious detractors, they might be led to say: it is a riddle that defies solution even by the keenest of intellects precisely because it is not reasonably structured, a puzzle that should not be unravelled, but rather ignored or destroyed. The most serious obstacle faced by those who are trying to incorporate spirituality into the academic curriculum is precisely this problem of definition. If as Sandra Schneiders has said, "spirituality is . . . a phenomenon which has not yet been defined, analyzed or categorized to anyone's satisfaction,"[2] how can it ever hope to gain credibility or attract its share of attention in universities and seminaries? If the study of spirituality is to continue elbowing its way into the curriculum, and remain there, on a par with other subjects, it must become a discipline. The problem is that in order to develop a discipline, it is essential to clearly define one's subject, and no subject seems more difficult to define than spirituality.   What David Knowles said about mysticism several years ago is no less true about spirituality today:

> Everyone in our day who proposes to speak or to write of mysticism must begin by deploring both the ambiguity of the word itself and the difficulty of defining it in any of its meanings. Yet without some sort of definition and some kind of understanding between writer and reader as to what is being discussed no progress of any kind can be hoped for.[3]

The change from *mysticism* to *spirituality* has not only failed to clear up the waters, but apparently made them even murkier. To date, precise definitions remain elusive: the harder that scholars try to outline the boundaries, the fuzzier the picture becomes.   Take, for example, the solution offered by Raymundo Panikkar, in which spirituality is defined as

[1] Sandra M. Schneiders, I.H.M., "Theology and Spirituality: Strangers, Rivals, or Partners?" *Horizons* 13/2 (1986): 253-74.

[2] Ibid., 253.

[3] David Knowles, "What is Mysticism?" in *Understanding Mysticism*, ed. Richard Woods (New York: Image, 1980): 521.

"one typical way of handling the human condition."[4] Does this really help us distinguish spirituality from any other type of human behavior? Under such a definition, every human attempt to cope with life could be considered as spirituality; acupuncture, primal scream therapy, and the mystical ecstasies of St. Teresa of Avila would fall into the same category. The same is true of the definition provided by Richard Hardy:

> spirituality is that attitude, that frame of mind which breaks the human person out of the isolating self. As it does that, it directs him or her to another in relationship to whom one's growth takes root and sustenance.[5]

Here, the definition is vague and subjective enough to include almost anything. As an "attitude" or "frame of mind" directed towards growth in "relationship" with others, spirituality would have to include all kinds of human interaction, from the child who plays with an imaginary friend to the apprentice who learns how to unclog drains from a master plumber.

If we turn to *The Westminster Dictionary of Spirituality*, the one source in the English language which would seem to offer the greatest possibility of helping us, this is what we find under spirituality: "a word [used] . . . to describe those attitudes, beliefs, practices which animate people's lives and help them to reach out towards super-sensible realities."[6]

Here, the subject is narrowed considerably by limiting the focus strictly to forms of human behavior aimed towards an invisible dimension. But how is this definition of spirituality any different from a definition of religion in general, or from a description of every type of religious behavior? According to this definition, then, the boundaries of spirituality are coextensive with those of religion itself.

Those who try to be more specific sometimes find themselves trapped in a house of mirrors, laboring to escape from a labyrinth in which ultimate meaning is endlessly reflected in words that need further definition. One such example can be found in Ewert Cousins's introduction to the World Spirituality series:

> The series focuses on that *inner dimension* of the person called by certain traditions "the spirit." This *spiritual core* is the *deepest center* of the person.

---

[4] Raymundo Panikkar, *The Trinity and the Religious Experience of Man: Icon-Person-Mystery* (Maryknoll, NY: Orbis, 1973): 9.

[5] Richard P. Hardy, "Christian Spirituality Today: Notes on its Meaning," *Spiritual Life* 28 (1982): 154.

[6] Gordon Wakefield, "Spirituality," *Westminster Dictionary of Christian Spirituality*, ed. G. Wakefield (Philadelphia/London: Westminster, 1983): 361.

> It is here that the person is open to the *transcendent dimension*, it is here
> that the person experiences *ultimate reality*. (Italics mine.)[7]

Because it assumes that many of its metaphysical claims are self-evident truths, this definition raises more questions than it answers, and is desperately in need of further clarification. How, for instance, is one to understand what is meant by an "inner dimension," or a "spiritual core," or a "deepest center of the person"?   Further, what is a "transcendent dimension," and how does it differ from an "inner dimension"?   One could even ask the toughest question of all: what is "ultimate reality"?

Bernard McGinn, editor of one volume in this same series, defines the subject more carefully, in functional terms. This is the definition he used to describe the focus of this project to those who wrote its essays:

> Christian spirituality is the lived experience of Christian belief. .... It is
> possible to distinguish spirituality from doctrine in that it concentrates not
> on faith itself, but on the reaction that faith arouses in religious
> consciousness and practice. It can likewise be distinguished from Christian
> ethics in that it treats not all human actions in their relation to God, but
> those acts in which the relation to God is immediate and explicit.[8]

The boundaries of the subject are more clearly delineated here, but in a negative fashion. This definition only obliquely describes spirituality by saying that it is neither doctrine nor ethics.   The subject under consideration remains somewhat amorphous. McGinn provides another functional definition within the text of one of his essays, in which spirituality is explained as "the effort to appropriate Christ's saving work in our lives."[9] This formulation is very general, and, in fact, difficult to distinguish from a definition of ethics or moral theology. All of this leaves one wondering what spirituality really means.

In her perceptive article "Theology and Spirituality: Strangers, Rivals, or Partners?", Sandra Schneiders focuses attention on the vagueness of past definitions, and valiantly tries to forge ahead, suggesting a clearer set of boundaries.   All previous definitions, she argues, have "something to do with the unification of life by reference to something beyond the individual person." To avoid confusing spirituality with religion in general, she then proposes the following: "spirituality refers to the experience of consciously striving to integrate one's life in terms not of

---

[7] Ewert Cousins, "Preface to the Series," in *Christian Spirituality I: Origins to the Twelfth Century*, ed. Bernard McGinn and John Meyendorff, vol. 16 of *World Spirituality: An Encyclopedic History of the Religious Quest* (New York: Crossroad, 1985): xiii.

[8] Bernard McGinn, "Introduction," in *Christian Spirituality I*, xv.

[9] Bernard McGinn, "Christ as Savior in the West," in *Christian Spirituality I*, 254.

isolation and self-absorption but of self-transcendence toward the ultimate value one perceives."[10]

Since she does not want to exclude non-religious experiences from this definition, it remains intentionally broad, and could easily encompass the study of such disparate acts as a reverent Marxist's visit to Lenin's tomb and a cloistered nun's conversations with the child Jesus. To prevent the boundaries from becoming fuzzy, Schneiders established some more precise limits at the end of this same article, where spirituality, and more specifically, Christian spirituality, is defined as "that field-encompassing field which studies Christian religious experience as such."[11]

Here we have, at last, a definition with lucid boundaries: it is much easier to determine the subject under consideration when one is limited to experiences rather than attitudes or relationships. This definition also implicitly rejects the notion that spirituality can ever hope to develop a single, unifying methodology. Schneiders is careful to point out that, as a "field-encompassing field," spirituality commands the attention of many established disciplines, from theology and philosophy to history and anthropology.

But how is such a polyglot field to be developed? At this point there are more questions than answers. Can spirituality become an entirely new discipline, or will it always remain a multi-disciplinary field known as religious studies? How should the process of formation be divided among the historians, philosophers, theologians, psychologists, and anthropologists who are currently working on the subject? What should be its tools, methods and skills? These are not easy questions to answer. One thing is clear, however: before the study of spirituality can gain further integrity as an academic discipline, or sub-discipline, three basic questions need to be taken into account.

The first two questions are reflected in the words of St. Francis, which he was heard repeating over and over at one time "My God! My God! What are you? and what am I?" These questions relate to all approaches to spirituality, but should predominantly concern theologians and philosophers.

First, the central metaphysical assumptions behind the term spirituality itself need to be systematically analyzed. If the focus of spirituality is that of *experiences*, we will need a clearer sense of boundaries, and an unequivocal description of the kind of experiences that may be

---

[10] Schneiders, "Theology and Spirituality," 266-67.
[11] Ibid., 274.

termed spiritual. In order to arrive at such a description, the concept of spirit needs to be defined. This, of course, would entail a rigorous investigation of the metaphysical superstructure in which the concept of spirit is given meaning. From an ontological perspective, one would need to consider numerous questions regarding the nature of reality itself. From a phenomenological perspective, one would need to develop a framework for categories of human expression which interpret existence in terms of dialectical opposites such as spirit and matter, inner and outer, eternal and temporal, natural and supernatural or sacred and profane. From an empirical perspective, one would then need to carefully delimit those precise experiences that could be called "spiritual."

In other words, since the *experiences* studied by spirituality are principally those in which individuals claim to transcend the world in which they live, it is imperative that all future studies in spirituality, whether descriptive or analytical, examine closely the concept of reality which informs any given experience. Precisely what kind of experiences are to be considered worthy of attention? What is it exactly that is experienced in these instances? How does Christian spirituality define God and creation, or the relation between the infinite deity and the finite creature? How are these experiences related to the development of Christian doctrine? How much does accepted belief determine any given experience, or, conversely, how does any experience affect belief?

Second, detailed guidelines must be developed for ways of analyzing the cognitive structure of spiritual experiences. In order to analyze such experiences one also needs to wrestle with epistemological questions. If, as Cousins and many others assert, there is an ultimate reality to be experienced, how do human beings perceive and describe this reality? Since the term *spirituality* refers to some sort of cognitive experience in which the individual comes to know or understand the truth of existence, anyone who grapples with this problem needs to identify the epistemological assumptions which are at the foundations of truth claims. One would also need to address the intractable question of the truth claim itself. After all, a complete skeptic sees no *other* in religious experience, but only the human individual projecting some sense of order on the material universe.

Eventually, the skeptic's viewpoint could prove useful to non-skeptics as well. The study of spirituality reveals much more about the believer than about any other reality described in the believer's claims. Stripped of its truth claims, viewed strictly from an empirical, materialist perspective, the experiences that make up the study of spirituality are *human* experiences.

The study of spirituality needs to focus more attention on the claims made for human nature and its possibilities. What does it mean, for instance, when Gregory Palamas speaks about human beings who become divinized? What are we to make of his distinction between the energy of God that is eternally beyond their capacities? How should we dissect the meaning of Bernard of Clairvaux's statement, "Intelligence is love of itself"? Or, how should we interpret the claim made in *The Cloud of Unknowing* that it is through the affections rather than the intellect that humans can come to experience God? How have these insights been appropriated in the past? How are they to be appropriated now and in days to come?

Moving out of the more abstract world of pure thought to that of empirical observations, a third question emerges, one that should concern all approaches to spirituality, but which naturally falls into the domain of historians and other social scientists. How are the experiences to be related to their immediate setting? Since the individual religious experiences analyzed in the study of spirituality are also a universal human phenomenon, subject to the contingencies of time and place, one should also take the social dimensions of the experience into account. What Jure Kristo has observed about mysticism is also true about spirituality:

> Mystical experience is part of a story, and it should be considered as such if one wants to get to the bottom of the nature of mystical experience. . . . It cannot be sufficiently emphasized that the mystical journey is a response to a definite, specific horizon.[12]

But how, exactly, should the individual experience be related to its setting? Guidelines need to be established for the analysis of individual spiritual experiences as part of a larger whole. Setting experiences into their social context can be problematic, especially in cases where comparisons need to be drawn. It will never be easy to maintain a balance between the personal and social spheres when studying spirituality. Future research in this field should also retain an awareness of the uniqueness of each tradition, of the fact that there are different experiences, not one common experience shared by all, and that at any time, in any place, one person's spirituality could be another's superstition. Anyone writing about spirituality, then, will need to be careful not to impose preconceived categories on varying traditions, or on different personal experiences.

---

[12] Jure Kristo, "The Interpretation of Religious Experience: What do Mystics Intend When They Talk About Their Experiences?" *Journal of Religion* 62 (1982): 21-38, esp. 30, 37.

Those who engage in cross-cultural studies will have to be even more cautious.

This last point refers to the most difficult challenge posed by the study of spirituality: how does one define its general characteristics broadly enough to encompass different religious traditions and allow for comparative study, without at the same time detracting from the very specific, unique characteristics of the different experiences? Within each specific tradition, the development of the social structures that make such experiences possible and give them definition should be careful to avoid confusing the experience with its setting. It is not an easy task to separate the medium from the message. For example, many traditional histories of Christian spirituality have linked social structure to experiences so closely that the resulting narrative is little more than the story of the different monastic orders.

Conclusion

If claiming to have read all that is written about spirituality makes one a braggart and a liar, then claiming to know how to define the subject must make one a fool. This paper has so far raised many questions and offered few answers. Ultimately, it is doubtful that all who study spirituality will some day agree on the exact boundaries of their field. Such a luxury is denied even to the older, well-established disciplines. Without some general agreement or common sense of purpose, however, little progress can ever be made towards commanding the respect that spirituality deserves in the curriculum. Although no one can deny that spirituality is a popular subject nowadays, some of us would not be willing to wager on its durability. In academics, as in the world at large, there are trends and fashions. Some prevail and endure while others peak and fizzle. Those trends that endure and substantially contribute to the advancement of learning are generally those with well-defined limits and a clear sense of purpose.

In many ways, the current state of scholarly research in spirituality resembles a sprawling shantytown on the outskirts of a city. Inside the town limits, that is, inside the academy, it is possible to find a sense of community, history, order, and balance. At the fringe and beyond, however, on a community without boundaries, those same values become rare commodities, and a sense of permanence the rarest of all. Hastily erected structures dot the landscape helter-skelter. Although there may be a sense of community, it is constricted by liminality, tainted by a measure of suspicion.

It is not surprising to find mistrust festering on both sides of the boundary, as the inhabitants of these two different realms face each other. These misgivings are engendered by differences in self-definition. To those inside the city, the suburban realm is an inferior creation, and its residents second class citizens. Unlike some shantytown in a third world metropolis, the suburban realm in this case is not necessarily poor, and has not appeared from necessity. On the contrary, its dwellers are comfortable, and have come there by choice. These suburbanites revel in their freedom from constraint, view their community as *the* city set upon a hill, and sometimes even enjoy returning the contempt levelled at them by the urban elitists who inhabit the inner regions of the perimeter.

This paper is not some kind of master plan, or even a blueprint for future construction. It is simply a plea for order in the suburbs, no more, no less. At the very least, its meager suggestions point to those areas that could be most easily linked to the existing networks of the city, and single out those structures that could best benefit from remodeling.

This is not to say that the study of spirituality need become the exclusive domain of academics, that the older city should engulf its newer neighbor and deprive it of its independence. The study of spirituality will always remain somewhat liminal due to its subject matter. Many who love the field and dedicate their lives to it would no more want to lose their sense of independence than the desert hermits would have wanted to move to Alexandria.

Because the study of spirituality is focused on experiences, particularly as described in a literary corpus produced in a liminal realm, it continually needs to be refreshed by contact with that environment. Praxis and analysis will always depend on each other in the study of spirituality, even though they will each be at their best when detached from one another. To return to our previous metaphor, the city and one of its newest suburbs will best serve each other's interests when their roads flow one into the other and the citizens of one realm do not feel as aliens in the other. In other words, established academic disciplines and the study of spirituality will best coexist and promote each other's well being when their investigations share a common sense of order and direction. Without this coexistence, the study of spirituality runs the risk of becoming the victim of its own impermanent structures, and of some day joining all the other fads that briefly encamped near the academy, but failed to endure on the map.

PART TWO:

STUDIES IN MODERN CHRISTIAN SPIRITUALITY

5

The Christian Pilgrimage in George Herbert's
The Temple

DIOGENES ALLEN

This symposium is on spirituality, so I begin with an indication of what I mean by the term. We are not born fully formed, so our very nature puts a question to us, What am I to be or to become? The education we receive, both formally and informally in our society helps form us into some kind of person or other. Morality also puts a question to us, What sort or kind of person *ought* I to be or become? Finally our religion puts a question to us, perhaps in the form of a model, such as Christ's life, about the kind of person we ought to become. Our nature, morality, and religion all three have a contribution to make to our formation and are interrelated. The distinctiveness of approaching the question of what we are to become from the point of view of spiritual formation is that our potential is only partially determined by what is inherent in human beings. Our limits are transcended and our horizons extended by what God bestows.

Since human beings are in the process of being formed, spiritual formation or spirituality is often looked upon as a journey or a pilgrimage. In this paper I shall examine the spiritual pilgrimage presented in George Herbert's *The Temple*, describing the course we follow, with its conflicts and reversals, on the way to the goal of being fully formed.

Reprinted by permission from the *Anglican Theological Review* (October, 1985).

Biographical Information

Let me begin with some biographical information about Herbert. He was born in 1593 and died one month short of his fortieth birthday. He was ordained a priest of the Church of England in 1630 and served the parish of Bemerton, Wiltshire until his death three years later probably of tuberculosis. Because of Izaak Walton's biography in 1670 there is a misleading picture of a dear, saintly, innocent, simple man, living in a peaceful corner of the world. In fact, Herbert was born into a family which for two centuries was one of the most powerful and well connected noble families of the kingdom. He was a highly polished courtier, with the extensive learning of a Renaissance gentleman, the Public Orator for Cambridge University, twice a member of Parliament, living in a turbulent time. He was a friend of Francis Bacon, the great proponent of the physical sciences, and the authorized translator of Bacon's *The Advancement of Learning* into Latin. He was indeed a priest of the Church of England, but it is an anachronism to see him as an Anglo-Catholic, Broad Churchman, or Low Churchman, as these division are after his time, and he has been claimed not only by exponents of each of them, but also admired by Richard Baxter, the great Puritan, as well as by John Wesley, who set some of Herbert's poems to music. He certainly was a follower of *a* middle way, that is between Rome and Puritanism, but it was not any prepared path that he followed. He held to the Protestant doctrine of salvation by grace alone, predestination, and advocated the Reformation view of vocation. On the other hand, ritual, the institutional Church, and his love of music marked him off sharply from many of the Puritans in the Church of England. His three years in his parish were extremely busy and active ones. Not only was he conscientious in performing every kind of parish duty, instead of simply drawing the living and hiring someone else to do the work, but he rebuilt the church and rectory, wrote more than half of *The Temple*, took part in musical performances, and also took the responsibility of rearing two orphaned nieces. Still it was a life far different from that which his connections and early life had led him to expect. There was every reason before 1619 for him to expect preferment at the Court and in the Church, and Herbert, for most of his life, saw no clash between high office and service to God. But for many reasons he was passed over and from 1619 to 1630 he had no offer of employment of any sort. Bitter disappointment was put to good use, as it became a source of his understanding of the Christian pilgrimage as a resolution of the conflict between our desires and the ways of God.

The Christian Pilgrimage

The Temple consists of 164 individual poems. Each poem has a self-contained meaning and can be read apart from the others, so much so that Simone Weil in reciting the last poem in the series, Love III, had a mystical experience of Christ coming to possess her soul, as she put it. It is also the reason some of the poems can appear in anthologies isolated from the rest and still make sense. Nonetheless, the individual poems are arranged in an order that traces the Christian pilgrimage from "imputed righteousness" (justification) to holiness (sanctification), which is achieved only after this life.

The pilgrimage he traces is very different from that of John Bunyan in *Pilgrim's Progress*. Bunyan's Christian begins his journey to the Celestial City because he is afraid of the Wrath to Come. Herbert is very much concerned with the fact that we are dust and so we shall perish, and he mentions the "second death," but the focus of his attention and the parameters of the pilgrimage he describes are that of a stone heart, which he calls the altar, and God's love which is refused, and which results in the sacrifice of Christ. The movement of the pilgrimage is the transformation of stony hearts into hearts that yield to God's love. This contrast between Bunyan and Herbert can be illustrated briefly by these lines from the poem "Discipline."

> Then let wrath remove;
> Love will do the deed:
>   For with love
> Stony hearts will bleed. (17-20)[1]

The movement to be traced, then, is one that begins not from the perception of God's wrath, but from the perception of God's love, which can move a stony heart to weep for the grief it has caused. The problem of the Christian life for Herbert is what we can render to God in the face of his sacrifice for us in the person of Christ.

This can be seen most easily by a consideration of the title of the collection of poems and by their arrangement. *The Temple* refers in the first instance to the Hebraic Temple in which sacrifices are offered. It also refers to the Christian Church, the new Israel, in which the death of Christ is celebrated. But it also refers to us; for God does not dwell in temples made by hands, as Paul points out (I Cor. 6:19-20). The old self must be

---

[1] All quotations from Herbert's poems are taken from John N. Well, Jr., ed., *George Herbert, Classics of Western Spirituality* (NY: Paulist Press, 1981).

destroyed and we must become a new temple unto God in which he shall dwell. Our hearts form the altar of that temple, and it is in us that the sacrifice of Christ must be received. Finally, the temple refers to the eschatological temple in the heavenly Jerusalem.

Unlike the pilgrimage traced in *Pilgrim's Progress*, Herbert gives a central place to the Church in the process of the transformation of our hearts. The temple, as an objective, tangible institution is the place where the sacrifice of God is celebrated, where services are held, where the Bible is taught. It provides the discipline that forms us into temples where God is to dwell. The temple thus refers to what is outer, an institution with public worship, and refers to what is inner, our hearts which must be disciplined to receive the sacrifice, and also refers to the goal, the heavenly Jerusalem where we shall finally achieve our end, which is to be conformed fully to the love of God.

The arrangement of the poems conveys this same message. The two main divisions of *The Temple* are "The Church Porch" and "The Church." "The Church Porch" concerns our preparation for entering the Church. That series of poems is highly didactic; the poet instructs us on how we must conduct our life and discipline our desires, if we are to be free of the blindness which prevents us from perceiving the things of God. The next division, "The Church," begins immediately after with a poem entitled "The Altar" and is followed by the longest poem in the entire book, a poem of 63 stanzas, entitled "The Sacrifice." Each stanza ends with the question "Was ever grief like mine?" (except the stanza which contains Christ's cry of abandonment on the Cross, and the last stanza of the poem; they end with "Never was grief like mine"). Christ himself is the speaker in the entire poem, as he describes the love which seeks us, and the grief our response or lack of response causes him. This poem is followed by a poem entitled "Thanksgiving" and it seeks for a proper or fitting response to such a love which we have grieved. So it is not a "fleeing from a wrath to come" nor even a desire for "the celestial city" that puts us into motion in Herbert, but the grief we have caused God. Once freed of the blindness caused by our many desires, whose purgation or diminution is counseled in the poems that comprise "The Church Porch," those whose hearts form a "broken altar" perceive God's sacrifice, and their most pressing concern is, What can we render that is adequate or proper to such a love? In "Thanksgiving" the poet gives up wealth, honor, and the like, but no matter what is offered, nothing is adequate. For God in his love has always anticipated our gift with his own, greater gift. Thus before the passion of Christ, the pilgrim is utterly undone. "Then for thy passion—I will do for that— / Alas, my God, I know not what."

There is a hint given in the next poem, "The Reprisal" (meaning a second thanksgiving). The second line repeats the pilgrim's difficulty, "There is no dealing with thy mighty passion." The poem ends with a vow, which is a partial resolution. "I will overcome/ The man, who once against thee fought." We do not learn until the last poem of the entire series of poems which form *The Temple* and indeed not until the last line of that poem what a proper and appropriate response to the sacrifice of Christ is. But it is the perception of the grief we have caused and the desire to respond adequately to it which gives the goal of the pilgrimage and the motivation for it. It is to have a stony heart changed into one which is a fit altar, to be transformed into a temple or dwelling place of divine love.

> O let thy blessed SACRIFICE be mine,
> And sanctify this ALTAR to be thine.
> "The Altar," 1. 15-16.

There is one feature of the sacrifice—God's way of winning our hearts—which deserves special attention. The spectacle that the crucifixion presents is that of God, who is almighty, once again allowing creatures to use their power to resist the good he would bestow.

> The Princes of my people make a head
> Against their Maker: they do wish me dead,
> Who cannot wish, except I give them bread:
>   Was ever grief like mine?
>
> Without me each one, who doth now me brave,
> Had to this day an Egyptian slave.
> They use that power against me, which I gave:
>   Was ever grief like mine?
> "The Sacrifice," 1. 5-12.

God's response to our resistance in this instance is to endure it. He hopes to win us by our perception of his grief.

> I answer nothing, but with patience prove
> If stony hearts will melt with gentle love.
> But who does hawk at eagles with a dove?
>   Was ever grief like mine?
> "The Sacrifice," 1. 89-92.

Herbert's point in "The Sacrifice" is that we cannot defeat his love and design; for our very hateful refusal is turned into a sacrifice by his patient endurance and becomes our food. The means of our salvation becomes his painful endurance of our rejection. That grief is to melt our hearts. So God is always available to bless us; we cannot destroy the ever-enduring love, as it endures our rejection and returns even from the dead to claim us; that is, returns from our attempt to annihilate it. "I, who am Truth, turn into truth their deeds (*The Sacrifice*, 1. 179). This paradox is kept from being a clever and cheap paradox by being immediately followed by the ever-present refrain, "Was ever grief like mine?" And the problem of the Christian life or pilgrimage becomes what possible response can ever be adequate to such a grief.

> There is no dealing with thy mighty passion:
> For though I die for thee, I am behind;
> "The Reprisal," 1. 2-3

Herbert summarizes the core of Christian truth in so far as it relates to the Christian pilgrimage in the poem, "The Agony."

> Philosophers have measur'd mountains,
> Fathom'd the depths of seas, of states, and kings,
> Walk'd with a staff to heav'n, and traced fountains:
>   But there are two vast, spacious things,
> The which to measure it doth more behove:
> Yet few there are that sound them; Sin and Love.
>
>   Who would know Sin, let him repair
> Unto Mount Olivet; there shall he see
> A man so wrung with pains, that all his hair,
>   His skin, his garments bloody be.
> Sin is that press and vice, which forceth pain
> To hunt his cruel food through ev'ry vein.
>
>   Who knows not Love, let him assay
> And taste that juice, which on the cross a pike
> Did set abroach; then let him say
>   If ever he did taste the like.
> Love is that liquour sweet and most divine,
> Which my God feels as blood; but I, as wine.

Providence

Even though this much is clear to us concerning the ways of God, the course of our pilgrimage, that is, how we are to be conformed to the truth, remains unclear and unmapped to us even after the revelation of God's salvation in Christ. The course of the Christian pilgrimage is explained to us and actually made visible to us by the very shape of the printed words of the poem "Colossians 3:3," which quotes as part of the title the text. "Our life is hid with Christ in God."

> *My* words and thoughts both express this notion,
> That *Life* hath with the sun a double motion.
> The first *Is* straight, and our diurnal friend,
> The other   *Hid*, and doth obliquely bend.
> One life is wrapt   *in* flesh, and tends to earth.
> The other winds towards *Him*, whose happy birth
> Taught me to live here so,   *That* still one eye
> Should aim and shoot at that which *Is* on high:
> Quitting with   daily   labor   all   *My* pleasure,
> To   gain   at   harvest   an   eternal   *Treasure*.

There is a double motion in the Christian pilgrimage. Our daily life goes along a horizontal course, like the printed words of the poem, and like them has a meaning. But more is taking place in our lives; for as we move through our daily tasks, our hearts are being shaped so that our desire is for Christ, our treasure. This is shown by the diagonal line which connects a word from each horizontal line. This means that the Christian pilgrimage whereby we are formed into creatures well-pleasing unto God does not follow a *direct* course. Directly we go to Church, hear sermons, take part in the liturgy and music, pray and receive the Eucharist. As part of our vocation we engage in our work as labor undertaken for God's glory—in Herbert's own case it is to be both a priest and a poet. Our own inner moods of peace, anxiety, hope and fear, elation and distress come and go in no clearly predictable pattern nor in any very logical order. The most stable order in our lives which are marked by violent mood swings is the order provided by regular Church services and the Christian year, and indeed by our daily labor. In all of this we are being formed to find in Christ our treasure. The Christian life or pilgrimage even when explained by Herbert still remains full of the unknown for each of us. For we tread the horizontal, and do not see until near the end how the course of our life has another shape, another meaning, and how various things in our life have contributed to that meaning. But it is only by moving along the horizontal as best we can, obeying God by making use of the benefits of his church and the discipline of our work and offering to him in both our praise, the building blocks will be provided for the construction of that life which is hid with Christ in God. It means that we often trust that what we are doing makes a contribution rather than being able to see that it does. Every moment of dismay, dryness, as well as times of elation make a contribution to that life which is being formed but which is not visible to us, especially when we are in states of distress. The structure of the poem also indicates that some of God's work is open to view: Church services, the Bible, and the like. But some of his work is hidden from view. It does not take place apart from the visible, but from what is visible we cannot know all that is taking place. This interpretation of "Col. 3:3," and thus also of the course of the Christian pilgrimage, receives support from a direct statement in one of the last poems in the series, "A Wreath."

> A wreathed garland of deserved praise,
> Of praise deserved, unto thee I give,
> I give to thee, who knowest all my ways,
> My crooked winding ways, wherein I live,
> Wherein I die, not live: for life is straight,
> Straight as a line, and ever tends to thee,
>   (1. 1-6)

The poem "Time" is also important in explaining the nature of the Christian pilgrimage. A pilgrimage or our formation takes time, and so the transformation of time by Christ's coming for the pilgrim. Formerly time was an enemy; for if this life is all there is, then the passage of time is a fearful thing. But with Christ's coming, time is no longer a scythe cutting us as crudely as a dull hatchet, but is now a pruning-knife. "Christ's coming hath made man thy debtor, / Since by thy cutting he grows better" ("Time," 1. 11-12). This makes sense in light of "Col. 3:3" with the increments added to the diagonal line by the passing of our daily life. Time has been transformed from an executioner into a gard'ner, as our movement to greater and greater dependence on Christ's love with the passage of time is growth into that never failing life. Christ is the Lord of time because now our passing life is leading us to our end or goal.

Experts have speculated on the unity of the 164 poems which make up *The Temple*. This is of interest to us because arrangement of the poems indicates the pattern of the Christian pilgrimage. Everyone agrees that the very title image "temple" is an important element in the unity and accounts for some of the arrangement of the 164 poems, as we have noted with the multiple meanings of "temple," and also with the arrangement of a series of poems under the heading of "The Church Porch" which form a passage into "The Church," the next series of poems. Once inside "The Church" the first things we encounter are the poems "The Altar" and "The Sacrifice." Nonetheless the arrangement of the succeeding poems is considerably looser, and the swings in mood from poem to poem so violent that commentators have been puzzled over the significance of the sequence of the poems in many instances. If we take as our guide, however, the pattern of the poem "Col. 3:3," then a looser connection between the poems and a connection that is not obvious is precisely what is wanted to convey the fact that the *daily* course of life of a Christian's formation is not a straight-line, nor does it consist of a tight pattern which unfolds logically. The Christian's mortal life (the one that is visible and moves along the horizontal, so to speak) is not a straight-forward movement toward our goal. This is reflected in the arrangement of poems, with some structure given by the daily services of the Church and the Church year, but with many violent swings in the subjective life and the objective behavior of the pilgrim. Both objective and subjective aspects of our mortal life are enclosed in that hidden life which moves diagonally, but directly toward its end. The unity of the poems' arrangement as well as of our lives is thus theological. It is the hidden work of God, a work not possible without the visible objective and subjective courses of life, but also not identical with them. As we shall see, the unity of *The Temple* as well as the unity of our lives is our becoming so shaped or formed that we may receive Christ's sacrifice properly. To anticipate the final poem and resolution of the problem of the Christian pilgrimage, all that is visible contributes to our learning to rely on God's love alone.

No one has ever suggested that Herbert lacked the ingenuity to arrange the 164 poems into a tight and visible unity. The simplicity of his diction, including the absence of allusions to Greek and Roman figures, which was common in the poetry of his day, should not suggest to the casual reader that his poems are simple or that he was of limited poetic talent and so could not arrange his poems into a tighter and visible unity. This becomes evident from a study of the form of his individual poems. We have just seen that the visual form of the poem "Col. 3:3" is integral to the meaning of the poem. In all of Herbert's poems the form is integral to the meaning, occasionally in obvious ways, as in "Col. 3:3." But quite often it is hidden, and he never repeats a form. There is one poem that is an anagram, one echo poem, one based on a syllabic pun, and so on. Rhyme and metre are carefully selected to enhance and become integral to the meaning. All this while relying on the simplest of diction and remaining focused on the object, Christian truth, which was to be faithfully rendered. This is why no one has suggested that the lack of a tighter sequence to the poems reflects limited talent. These remarks lead us to consider Herbert's view of the role of his poetry, which was his work, in the Christian pilgrimage, and so too some understanding of work in every Christian's pilgrimage.

A Sacramental Universe

It was common-place in Herbert's day, and indeed right back to the earliest of the Greek Church Fathers, that divine truth could be discerned from a study of the created order. Of the "Two Books of God" nature was highly inferior to the Bible. But nature did supply theologians and poets with symbols of divine truth. A poet sometimes took some feature of nature and drew out the truths symbolically present in the natural object. Herbert uses natural things as figures, such as the double motion of the sun, as it rises and sets each day and also simultaneously moves along the ellipse, giving us our four seasons. But Herbert does not try to read divine truths from nature. The Bible is his source of knowledge, and he uses natural truths as figures to crystalize the meaning of his poems, as he does the sun's double motion as a figure for the double motion in the Christian's pilgrimage to God. He went one step further than other poets who used nature either to discern or teach divine truths. He constructed his poems in such a way that the poem itself mirrored the structural relation between the natural symbol taken from nature and the Christian life. He did this because he believed that God gives order or form. The Holy Spirit created the cosmos out of chaos, and does so now. Literary form is but a reflection of that form caused by God everywhere, indeed the source of Herbert's creative inspiration. The function of poetry was to exhibit the constructive, creative activity of God, which is often hidden, so that we may fulfill our function: to see the work of God and render praise. Herbert must craft his poems with utter devotion. If they are to be worthy instruments of praise, then they themselves should mirror the structural likeness between the works of God in nature and in the redemption of humankind. His poems thus seek to symbolize in their elaborate forms the beauty and variety of the divine creation.

Herbert, because he has poetic talent, has the vocation to offer praise through poetry, and to instruct others in divine truth through them, and thus enable them in the joy poetry gives, to join in praise. This employment, along with the vocation to be a priest, is what he is called upon to render unto God. But a person, such as Herbert, has to thread a course between two extremes. On the one hand, not to think that one's identity is in what one's work has created. On the other hand, because one's true life is not identical with the work one does, to resist the temptation to reject one's work as irrelevant to one's true life. Work is the horizontal, mortal life we lead. If we identify ourselves fully with what we there create, our true life is lost. But such work must be done with all our heart, mind, soul, and strength as our praise of God. Then it is part of that hidden life which winds its way to God. The Christian pilgrimage thus does not imply that one is to become a hater of this world because one's eternal home or end is not this world. It also is a firm rejection of quietism. God works as creator and redeemer, making of us a temple wherein to dwell, and that work requires that we engage in employment as our praise of God for his creation and for his gift of an eternal life. All of these matters can be seen in his poem, "The Elixir," which represents Herbert's penultimate resolution of what we can render unto God for all his benefits, especially his sacrifice.

> Teach me, my God and King,
> In all things thee to see,
> And what I do in anything.
> To do it as for thee:
>
> Not rudely, as a beast,
> To run into an action;
> But still to make thee prepossest,
> And give it his perfection.
>
> A man that looks on glass,
> On it may stay his eye;
> Or if he pleaseth, through it pass,
> and then the heav'n espy.
>
> All may of thee partake:
> Nothing can be so mean,
> Which with his tincture (for thy sake)
> Will not grow bright and clean.
>
> A servant with this clause
> Makes drudgery divine:
> Who sweeps a room, as for thy laws,
> Makes that and th' action fine.
>
> This is the famous stone
> That turneth all to gold:
> For that which God doth touch and own
> Cannot for less be told.

Let us now examine Herbert's ultimate resolution of the question, What shall we render that is an adequate response to Christ's sacrifice? "Then for thy passion—I will do that— / Alas, my God, I know not what" ("The Thanksgiving," 1. 49-50).

As we have pointed out, work done in honor of God is part of our response to the sacrifice. For Herbert this is to write poems. They are works of praise for what God has done, and hopefully will help others to praise God.   Also there is a sacramental quality to labor ("I am with thee..." "The Quiddity," 1. 11). Work is an appropriate response to the passion of Christ, because God is a builder. He is not only the maker of the heavens and earth and gives all things their proper employment in the functioning of an orderly cosmos, but he is also building us into a temple in which to dwell. Joseph H. Summers points out that although the sequence of the poems is that of a journey or pilgrimage, the content and language within the individual poems is often that of building or construction.[2] Since God is a builder, our proper response to him as his servants is likewise to be engaged in building or in work, work that renders him praise, work that contributes to his creation, work that contributes to our being made into a temple fit for him to dwell. This is why there are several poems in which there is a lament that others have work, but the poet does not. These may reflect the long period in which Herbert was without any employment either in civil or church life. (See "Employment II" and "Business.") But even when the poet has employment (both as a poet and priest), he complains that people are often unfaithful in their labor, and he frequently finds himself running dry as a poet. (See "Affliction IV.") But work, even when done faithfully, or sacramentally, is inadequate.   We are forever debtors, as we depend utterly on God for all our powers.

> I threat'ned to observe the strict decree
>   Of my dear God with all my power and might.
>   But I was told by one, it could not be;
> Yet I might trust in God to be my light.
>
> Then will I trust, said I, in him alone.
>   Nay, ev'n to trust in him, was also his:
>   We may confess, that nothing is our own.
> Then I confess that he my succor is:
>
> But to have nought is ours, not to confess
>   That we have nought, I stood amaz'd at this,
>   Much trouble, till I heard a friend express,
> That all things were more ours by being his.
>   What Adam had, and forfeited for all,
>   Christ keepeth now, who cannot fail or fall.

The progression of thought in the poem is from seeking with all one's own strength to be obedient, to reliance on trust, to a realization that even trust is not within our own power and that even a confession of this is not enough. We are not to *confess* that we have nought, but we *are to have nought*. This paradox is resolved when we see that God seeks to be our

---

[2] *George Herbert: His Religion and His Art* (London: Chatto and Windus, 1954): 89.

benefactor, and that our task is to receive. But we can receive from him on whom we utterly depend only to the extent to which we are in a condition in which we not only see that we are dependent on him but actually do become dependent on him. *The entire Christian pilgrimage is a process in which we are being so shaped and formed by him that we indeed not only confess that we are dependent on him, but actually become dependent on him.* Thus the various poems on such themes as guilt, repentance, thanksgiving, dryness, temptation, rebellion, peace, affliction, praise, as well as poems on the Church services and the Church year, such as Matins and Easter, are the movements of the Christian as he or she is being formed or shaped to fully receive God's benefits.   This is explicit in the last poem of the collection "Love III," which contains the final resolution concerning what we shall render to Christ's passion.

> Love bade me welcome: yet my soul drew back,
>   Guilty of dust and sin.
> But quick-ey'd Love, observing me grow slack
>   From my first entrance in,
> Drew nearer to me, sweetly questioning,
>   If I lack'd anything.
>
> A guest, I answer'd worthy to be here:
>   Love said, You shall be he.
>
> I the unkind, ungrateful? Ah my dear,
>   I cannot look on thee.
> Love took my hand, and smiling did reply,
>   Who made the eyes but I?
>
> Truth Lord, but I have marr'd them: let my shame
>   Go where it doth deserve.
> And know you not, says Love, who bore the blame?
>   My dear, then I will serve.
> You must sit down, says Love, and taste my meat:
>   So I did sit and eat.

Although now caught in the power of death (the natural end of that which is made from dust) and damnation (the just end of sin) neither is our end. Love suffers to relieve us of both. What can we do or render for such a sacrifice? We cannot even serve him of ourselves. Instead all we can do is to receive his sacrifice, and we can receive it properly only in being utterly dependent on that sacrifice. The pilgrimage forms us into utter dependence on his sacrifice; it so shapes us that we are "nought." And being "nought" we can receive him and be filled by him. Finally the only thing we can do is to obey the command, "You must sit down, says Love, and taste my meat." The words "sit down" suggest the cessation of work or

labor or striving. It is to stop. It is indeed "to be still and know that I am
God" (Ps. 46:10). There is also a certain robust, rustic, simplicity in the
obedience. After the intensity of all the previous lines, the guest in effect
says, All right, you say to sit down and eat, so I will do as I am told. There
is even the tone of lightheartedness; and indeed there should be, as the
poem is an allusion to the final banquet in heaven as found in Luke 12:37 in
which there is much rejoicing. So the final resolution to what we shall
render for his passion is simply to receive it: to receive it as ones who have
nought to render to God and indeed as ones now utterly won by the
sacrificial love of God. We are to live our lives attentive to his sacrifice, as
utterly dependent on it for our earthly lives and for our destiny.

   This concern for an appropriate response to Christ's passion leads to
a consideration of the relation of the emotions to their object in *The
Temple*. Most of Herbert's poems are highly charged. The reader is jolted
in passing from the series of poems grouped under "The Church Porch" and
the first poem, "The Altar," which opens the main series of poems grouped
under "The Church." The reader has been led to consider what must be
done as a preparation for entering the Church. The tone is instructive; and
the poet in control of the situation. Then "The Church" is entered and the
person of "The Altar" pours forth a poem from a passionately broken heart.
The rest of "The Church" contains poems which rise to great heights of
elation and sink to depths of agony, with violent alterations and abrupt
mood swings, but none matches the abruptness of change in mood as we
find in the transition from "The Church Porch" to "The Church."

   The poems of *The Temple* are not poems of self-expression. It is not
that Herbert himself did not feel many or even all of these emotions. But
the range of emotions felt and the order in which they are felt are not
controlled by the course of Herbert's own life. The pilgrimage of *The
Temple* is not, in other words, autobiographical. The reduction of the self
to "nought" provides us with the key to understand the relation of the
emotions to its object. That we are "nought" and that the Christian
pilgrimage is our reduction to it, in order that we might receive all that God
has to give to us, is alien to an age such as ours which is so concerned with
the expression of personality. But for Herbert there is a reality larger than
the personal, and my personal experience is not authoritative. Christian
doctrine and Church life provide the means of giving order and universal
significance to personal emotive experience. We find ourselves in the
essential, not in the accidental. Christianity reveals to us what is essential,
and it is identical for every person: the image of God. Christ is that image,
and we are to become like him, not in imitation of his sacrifice, which is

beyond us, (there is nothing which we can render him in which he has not already preceded us) but we are to become like him by receiving him. It is to receive that sacrifice properly, which in this life involves receiving his body and blood in the Eucharist. The ways in which human beings differ from each other, compared to their essential likeness, are accidental features of their personalities. Such features and the expression of those features, however interesting and remarkable, are from this point of view not authoritative and certainly not our end. Our fulfillment is not the expression of our personalities, or the realization of the potentials of our personalities. To become free of the illusion that the accidental is the essential is one way of describing the nature and goal of the Christian pilgrimage which Herbert has traced in *The Temple*. Our distinctive personalities find ample scope for expression by their employment in praise to God, as did Herbert's distinctive talent in the composition of the poems of *The Temple*.

The proper expression of ourselves is by a proper relation to the object. For Herbert that object is God, in particular in the passion of Christ. Christ's redemption has taught him how to measure his days ("Redemption measures all my time," "Holy Baptism" I, 1.10). That redemption is to be used to examine ourselves in our pilgrimage until we are so shaped that our emotions before the Christ who is sacrificed for us are wholly evoked by Him. Our emotions or sentiments are thus not expressions of our self, but proper responses to him. The emotions expressed in the poems of *The Temple* are thus wholly evoked by the object, wholly contained by the object, and wholly explained by the object. Thus what we have in *The Temple* is a Christian pilgrimage, or the Christian's sanctification, not Herbert's autobiographical pilgrimage, however much it depends on his own life-experiences.

T. S. Eliot pointed out in his essay "Lancelot Andrewes" that John Donne's poetry was a means of self-expression and that "he is constantly finding an object which shall be adequate to his feelings."[3] This is in marked contrast to Herbert for whom the object is above all Christ's passion, and the shaping of our person, including our sensibility, to conform to it. This is a highly instructive contrast for us today. Many people believe that they have an idea of the kinds of feelings which, did they but experience them, would fulfill their personality. For them the goal of life is to find that object or objects or activity which is adequate to produce those experiences. It is as if we have in mind an idea of the emotions we want

---

[3] *Selected Essays* (Faber & Faber, 1932): 341.

ahead of time and that all we need to do is to find the object able to evoke them for us to find our lives fulfilled, and as far as Christianity is concerned it is considered solely in terms of whether it is able to evoke those experiences.   This seems to be involved in some of the interest in spirituality today. The desire is not to conform ourselves to the truths of God or to the reality of God, but a search for the blessed state described by spiritual writers and people. It is the ecstasy of the mystic which some seek. That is what is sought and deity or some other reality is sought as an object able to evoke it. Neither emotions or experience nor the expression of personality are what guide Herbert. It is the Christian vision of truth and in particular the passion of Christ, as discerned by the mind, to which we are to be conformed.   Christian doctrine and the discipline provided by the Church's services guide the sensibilities of the Christian pilgrim.

The Relevance of Spirituality to Theology

Now that we have examined Herbert's presentation of the Christian pilgrimage, I want to consider the significance of spirituality to doctrinal theology and theological inquiry. Generally spirituality is treated as the *personal appropriation* of theological doctrines and recently as not necessary for the conduct of theological inquiry. I wish to point out some of the ways it is relevant to theology and in particular to resist the treatment of spirituality and spiritual theology as a hole-in-the corner enterprise.

That God is hidden and even when he reveals himself he remains hidden is an assumption with which I work, and I shall explain what I mean indirectly in what follows. A constant and consistent theme in the body of literature on spirituality and indeed on Jesus' lips is blindness. "Let those who have eyes to see, see." God is hidden to us and the truths he reveals in scripture remain inaccessible to us unless we have undergone some preliminary formation. In Herbert's case we find this preliminary formation in the series of poems he arranges under the division "The Church Porch." Among the passions or desires which must be controlled so that we may be re-shaped sufficiently to be able to perceive any significance at all in what is presented in "The Church" (here referring both to the poems collected under this heading and literally the witness of the Christian Church) are: lust, drink, vain talk about God, lying, idleness and gambling. It is always of interest to compare the various desires and activities which different writers select as blocking our access to perception of spiritual realities and truths. Herbert's are selected by reference to the immediate audience he had in mind, mostly the small educated class of courtiers and clerics, or would be courtiers and clerics. Hence he presents his account in verse, which would act as bait to a class of people who prize wit and language. But if we consider the three temptations Christ faced in the wilderness as the temptation of material goods, security, and prestige, and also consider them to be passions we must come to terms with if we are to overcome our blindness to the gospel, then Herbert emphasizes the first and last of the three, wealth and ambition, among the many he treats. However that may be, spiritual writers make it clear that without some preformation, spiritual matters are utterly incomprehensible to the fleshly person. Herbert stresses that without a preformation, including reverent Church attendance, the sacrifice of Christ is of no significance and his grief does not touch one. Thus Herbert begins his longest poem "The Sacrifice" with this stanza:

> Oh, all ye who pass by, whose eyes and mind
> To worldly things are sharp, but to me blind
> To me, who took eyes that I might find you:
>   Was ever grief like mine?

But there is another kind of blindness which Herbert does not treat, an intellectual blindness caused by a mistaken approach. Pascal treats it extensively in the *Pensées* with his distinction between three orders: the order of the body or the flesh (which as we have seen Herbert does treat), the order of the mind or intellect, and the order of the heart. Spiritual truth lies above, not below the order of the mind, but it is frequently misunderstood when reduced to the order or level of the intellect. A considerable amount of the *Pensées* is devoted to correcting this mistake which prevent one from having access to spiritual truths and access to the Holy Spirit.

Austin Farrer in a short essay draws a distinction between four kinds of blindness to spiritual realities which arise from a failure to note the different ways the mind has access to truths. They may be briefly characterized as follows:

1.   "Science of all sorts obtains precision by artificially limiting its subject-matter. Modern physics began to get under way when it began resolutely to refuse to consider anything but the *measurability* of physical processes . . . The same artificial limitations have been brought into the study of human affairs. The economist may concentrate on man in so far as he is an economic agent, but if the economist concludes that *because* it is possible to get sound results this way, man is nothing but an economic

agent and all the rest of his apparent action is economic activity under a disguise, then the economist is a fool."[4]

2.   "As soon as a man stops asking tidy questions about a single aspect of things and asks the very untidy question, 'What *whole* reality is confronting me here?', science stops . . . I may consider very scientifically a man's economic relationships, and the probable psychology of his instinctive urges, but the answers I shall get will do no more than point to what I am up against in dealing with this man. I have just got to know him through interacting with him. That is personal understanding."[5]

3.   The facts arrived at in both these ways take no account of moral evaluations. "It does not matter whether the facts are such as to be approved or deplored, whether the persons are acting a lie or living sincerely. . . . We open up a completely new dimension of questions when we ask what is that true essence of man which the insincere betrays and the fool misses and the callous ignores and the perverse distorts. This time we are up against an object which is quite differently related to us from the objects of science or personal understanding. . . . We may think about it abstractly, and that is ethical philosophy: we may think about it whole and in the round, and that is religion." The ethical philosopher like the scientists of human nature—economists, psychologists, and the like—limits the issue and picks out tidy questions. So he talks about "the limited fact of moral thinking—the recognition of obligation, the attempt to make moral rules consistent, the problems of particular duty."[6]

4.   "The ethical philosopher remains the master of his subject-matter by limiting his question."[7] But you cannot undergo the impact of the whole fact or reality before you by limiting questions. Just as you cannot be aware of the personal reality of another person by approaching him or her with physical questions, or economic questions, or psychological questions, or moral questions, so too with your own awareness of yourself. Religion puts before us realities which begin to make us aware of our own being and destiny and the demands placed on us by those realities and by one's own being. This is how the New Testament presents Christ: a reality which puts us as an entire being into question.

It is, of course, possible to refuse admittance to the realities a religion puts before us. Since they are not realities treated by our sciences and our ethical philosophies, we may refuse to attend to those realities to which a

---

[4] "On Credulity," in *Interpretation and Belief*, ed. Charles Conti (S.P.C.K., 1972): 3-4.
[5] Ibid., 4.
[6] Ibid., 4-5.
[7] Ibid., 5.

religion points. But if we do attend because we realize that such realities are not reducible to the facts other disciplines treat, then we have overcome an intellectual barrier to spiritual matters caused by a misunderstanding of how we have access to spiritual truths.

Herbert, after treating the blindness caused by our desires and passions (which as a matter of fact are the more serious barrier to gaining access to spiritual matters), boldly focuses our attention on the passion of Christ. It is the grief we cause God and the never failing Love that is God's nature to which we are to attend. We come to understand that it is by such love that we are formed into a temple in which it is to dwell.

In Herbert's way, or in some other way favored by a spiritual writer, we are put into touch with those realities which judge, illumine, and work in our lives to transform them.

Now we can point out how spirituality is relevant to doctrinal theology and theological inquiry. What give credibility to doctrines and to the intellectual constructions of theology are those realities which spiritual theology puts before us and directs us to attend to. By continual attention to them we gain nourishment, increased understanding, and undergo formation. Without that kind of activity, doctrinal teachings become arid and indeed increasingly unintelligible and arbitrary. Intellectual constructions become merely that, intellectual constructions lacking credibility and increasingly looking like options in a sea of possible intellectual options. By a lack of attentiveness to spiritual realities, we increasingly find it hard to credit claims in theology about the presence and work of God in nature, history, and personal lives.

Theology cannot and does not get its credibility from finding its basis in data which support inquiry in the first of the three domains specified by Austin Farrer. It must be rooted in the Fourth, which is the domain of spiritual theology and spiritual reflection. With such a rootage, the other domains can make a contribution to theological inquiry and doctrine. But today in many centers of theological inquiry, we act as though spiritual theology and reflection is not necessary. That a theologian should pray, for example, or submit to the discipline of public worship is considered a personal matter only. Because of this it is not surprising that theological claims often lack credibility among the practitioners of theology.

In addition to the relevance of spirituality to the theological enterprise in general, the work of Herbert and any other great spiritual writer is relevant to the present day preoccupation with theology, politics, and the social order. Spiritual writings should open our eyes to the tenacity and power of evil in us all and make us more dependent on God to remove

our evil. It took Herbert many years to realize that even though holding
high political or church office is not alien to the gospel, his ambition to do
so was. Jesus' teaching about the log in our own eye is highly relevant and
it is such spiritual self-examination which seems to be missing in the swirl of
talk and writings that abound today. Recognition of the depths and
tenacity of evil ought also to curb the utopianism in so much of our political
and social theologies. Such a witness should enable us to recognize the
shallowness of so much of the talk about social and political issues in
religious and theological circles.

Herbert's spirituality can make one aware, moreover, that our end is
not an earthly kingdom. Herbert is not "other worldly," as he condemned
indolence as the greatest vice of the privileged class of his day. In his own
life his greatest trial was his years of unemployment and his illness which
restricted his activities. Herbert's life and thought did not seek either the
easy way of reducing our consummation to an earthly end, however noble
or however much endorsed by God, nor to make our end an otherworldly
end. He held to that much more difficult middle way: of living and
working responsibly, realizing that our life "hath a double motion." It is by
responsible action in this world that our life is being created and formed, a
life that is hid with Christ in God.

6

Loss and Hope in Reformed Spirituality: The Example of Anne Bradstreet

CHARLES E. HAMBRICK-STOWE

Protestant and modern Catholic spirituality were born in the European devotional revival of the sixteenth and seventeenth centuries. While Roman Catholics by nature cultivate tradition, Protestants are not so careful and forget they once meditated and prayed according to methods they now think of as Catholic. The study and teaching of spirituality as a theological discipline has re-emerged as a fresh departure for Protestants, as new as Roman Catholic appreciation of Protestant spirituality. Both have begun to flower in the last decade, although the roots of the new scholarship can be traced a bit earlier. This essay first identifies some of these roots. Second, it poses the question of how seventeenth-century Reformed spirituality compares with Catholic spirituality. Third, it explores the spirituality of a representative New England Puritan, Anne Bradstreet, as an example of how the faithful experienced and expressed this Reformed spirituality.

1

Current interest in Reformed spirituality stems from developments

Reprinted from *Early New England Meditative Poetry*, edited by Charles E. Hambrick-Stowe. (c)1988 by Charles E. Hambrick-Stowe. Used by permission of Paulist Press.

over the twentieth century in the fields of Catholic and Protestant scholarship and in the secular study of history and literature.

The Catholic reappraisal of Reformed piety associated with Vatican II actually predates the Council by a few years. Vatican II's recognition of Protestants as "separated brethren" made official a new scholarly view. The shift is apparent in a comparison of Pierre Pourrat's classic four-volume *Christian Spirituality* 1922-1955, and the three-volume work by Louis Bouyer and others, *A History of Christian Spirituality* (1960-1965; Eng. ed. 1963-1969). Pourrat had nothing to say about Protestant spirituality; the notion was a contradiction in terms. Luther and Calvin, "Manichaean Quietists," negated the need to pray. Protestantism was "egoistic and altogether anthropocentric. The whole plan of redemption is brought down to man's salvation. Do not ask this kind of mysticism for acts of pure love. It is incapable of them. To pay to Jesus the homage of praise and love, to which he is entitled by his divine perfection, is far from its practice." Of the English Reformation Pourrat wrote, "There was no spiritual writing in England at this time."[1] By contrast, Bouyer devoted most of an entire volume to a positive assessment of Protestant spirituality. While not uncritical of Reformation theology, he found much that was traditional—and hence true—in its spiritual thought and practice. His loftiest evaluation, astonishingly, was of "the great spiritual writers of Puritanism" who carried Calvin's key doctrine of sanctification to its warmest experiential conclusion "with an evangelism still very much tinged with a late medieval love of Christ—evocative of Gerson and the *Imitation*." With "vehement mystical feeling for Christ," Puritans "were closer to many aspects of the Jesuits and Visitandines of the period than were the traditional Anglicans." Boyer even suggests the Puritan origin of the French Catholic cult of the Sacred Heart. Thomas Goodwin's *The Heart of Christ in Heaven towards Sinners on Earth* (1652) presented "a synthesis of the devotion to the Sacred Heart which irresistibly reminds us of Paray-le-Monial . . . but a good half-century before Margaret-Mary Alacoque." Just as English Puritans read Catholic spiritual works, evidence exists that French clergy knew some Anglican writings. Were they "incapable of also reading the Puritans? It is not self-evident. . . . Agreements of this kind in spiritual works of roughly the same period are at least a sign of the community of religious thought and culture that went much further than

---

[1] Pierre Pourrat, *Christian Spirituality*, vol. 3 (New York, 1927): 64-66, 70; vol. 4 (Westminster, MD: Newman, 1955): 436.

people have hitherto realized."[2]   Re-publication of Bouyer's volumes by Seabury Press in 1977 and cross-fertilization of Catholic and Protestant thought at seminaries and retreat centers has furthered Catholic interest in the history of Protestant devotion and opened the field of spirituality to Protestants in a new way.

Protestants have not written books like Pourrat's because no Protestant academic discipline existed to call them forth. Catholic theology consisted of three or four branches: dogmatic, moral, and spiritual theology. The study of spirituality was divided between ascetic and mystical theology, either as separate disciplines or parts of a single discipline. Ascetic theology was the study of the ordinary believer's purposeful and regular practice of meditation and prayer. Mystical theology studied the extraordinary, God-inspired spiritual states of saints like St. John of the Cross and St. Teresa of Avila. The three "Ways" of ascetic theology to be practiced   by   all   Christians—the   Purgative,   Illuminative,   and Unitive—shaded into mystical theology, often clouding the boundary between the two. If Louis Cognet paid little explicit attention to these distinctions, using instead the new term" spiritual ideas," his explanation was traditional.   "'Spiritual ideas' . . . are not, strictly speaking, the speculations of theologians, yet ideas which seem to be purely theological often have profound effects on the most practical aspects of Christian life." His concern for "the thought and conduct of the Christian, in so far as they form part of his devotion, his personal relations with God, his interior life" was the work of a well-established academic discipline.   But when Protestants outlined the theological curriculum they abandoned this discipline of spirituality.   Protestant seminaries, established in the nineteenth century, replaced ascetic and mystical theology with practical theology, encompassing liturgics, homiletics, the care of souls, and so on.[3]

Protestants had developed a new vocabulary of "religious experience" and sanctification to describe the work of the soul, instead of the Catholic concept of spirituality. Early Reformed theologians analyzed the scheme of salvation in intricate detail. Scripture suggested a doctrine of sanctification between justification through God's sheer grace and glorification with

---

[2] Louis Bouyer, *Orthodox Spirituality and Protestant and Anglican Spirituality* (New York: Seabury, 1969): 134-142.

[3] F. L. Cross, ed., *The Oxford Dictionary of the Christian Church*, s. v. "Ascetical Theology." Louis Bouyer, *The Spirituality of the New Testament and the Fathers* (New York: Seabury, 1963): vii-ix. Louis Cognet, *Post-Reformation Spirituality* (New York: Hawthorn, 1959): 7-8. Washington Gladden discusses the Protestant practical theology curriculum in *The Christian Pastor and the Working Church* (New York: Scribner's, 1898): 1-22.

Christ in heaven. Sanctification made possible the grace-filled life of the Christian while still on earth.   A saint—a believer undergoing sanctification—practiced the spiritual disciplines of reading (especially of the Bible), meditation, and prayer and was graced with various religious experiences, sometimes ecstasy of a high order.   In Puritan theology sanctification was a dynamic process of spiritual growth; saints expected to progress toward perfection and be prepared for glory at the hour of death. Numerous Puritan devotional manuals (such as John Downame's *A Guide to Godlynesse*, 1622), journals and meditative poetry (such as that of Edward Taylor), and spiritual biography and autobiography (exemplified by Jonathan Edwards' *An Account of the Life of the late Reverend Mr. David Brainerd*, 1749) expressed this spirituality of progressive sanctification through spiritual discipline. Puritan writings are certainly within the field of spirituality.   Protestants were not without those qualities and practices which Catholics have so systematically studied. But Protestants rejected much of the language of Catholic spirituality even as they retained traditional exercises. "Mysticism" called to mind supposed corruptions of monastic life and a false elevation of solitary celibacy over communal responsibility and fellowship. "Spiritual exercises" evoked the superstition of candles and beads.   American revivalism and anti-Catholicism emphasized biblical study and only the first step of the Christian life, conversion, to the exclusion of anything that smacked of being Catholic. Boyer agreed that the neo-orthodox theologians deepened Protestant antipathy to spiritual theology by classifying mysticism as neo-paganism. Without an academic discipline devoted to it, study of Protestant spirituality languished.[4]

Protestant interest in the field of spirituality survived through the work, not of theologians, but of philosophers and psychologists in the late nineteenth and early twentieth centuries. Josiah Royce and William James are best known of the scholars who undertook a new scientific study of "religious feelings and religious impulses." James' *The Varieties of Religious Experience* (1902) exercised influence until our own time. Baron Friedrich von Hügel's massive work, *The Mystical Element of Religion as Studied in Saint Catherine of Genoa and Her Friends* (1908) focused the scientific study of spirituality on a single figure and (though the author was Catholic) introduced academic Protestants to classical Catholic mysticism. Evelyn Underhill approached the subject in a uniquely persuasive way, most comprehensively in her widely-read *Mysticism* (1911). An Anglican, she

---

[4] Bouyer, *Orthodox, Protestant, and Anglican Spirituality*, 57-58.

wrote as a spiritual practitioner and director, but related her subject to the fields of psychology and philosophy.

Few Protestant church historians recognized the centrality of religious experience and devotional practice. Geoffrey F. Nuttall's *The Holy Spirit in Puritan Faith and Practice* (1946) and Gordon S. Wakefield's *Puritan Devotion* (1956) were exceptions that proved the rule. The Quaker scholarship of Rufus Jones insisted on the primacy of experience over doctrine and delved into the medieval Catholic roots of Quaker inner light mysticism. Jones' books, such as *New Studies in Mystical Religion* (1927) and *The Flowering of Mysticism: The Friends of God in the Fourteenth Century* (1939), attracted the attention of some liberal Protestants. These works, influential as they were, did not lead Protestants to see spirituality as anything but a sidelight. They did not constitute an organized field of study. There was little effort to uncover the history of Protestant spirituality until post-Vatican II ecumenical cooperation began to bear fruit. The publication of *The Westminster Dictionary of Christian Spirituality* (1983) would not have been undertaken even ten years ago. But now, Wakefield writes, "'Spirituality' is a word very much in vogue among Christians of our time. French Catholic in origin, it is now common to evangelical Protestants also."[5]

Developments in the study of early American history and literature have also contributed to current flowering in the field of spirituality. Perry Miller, in his seminal work, *The New England Mind* (1939), devoted his first two chapters to the Augustinian tradition and the Puritan practice of piety. That initial nod in the direction of spirituality was offset by the remainder of the book which achieved his real purpose, the recovery of Puritan theology's intellectual grandeur. In the intervening years, in spite of Alan Simpson's gem-like *Puritanism in Old and New England* (1955), which saw religious experience as "the essence of Puritanism," Puritanism was usually studied as an intellectual or social movement. Recently, however, the concept of popular mentality, including religious ritual and experience, has bridged intellectual history and the new social history. New biographical studies of key figures sympathetically discuss their spiritual experiences. Edmund S. Morgan writes, "The level of scholarship dealing with [the Puritans] has reached a point where it can address the human condition

---

[5] Gordon S. Wakefield, ed., *The Westminster Dictionary of Christian Spirituality* (Philadelphia: Westminster, 1983): v.

itself. In recent years the focus has shifted from theology to experience, from doctrine to devotion, and the results have been rewarding."[6]

A similar development has taken place in the field of literature. Louis L. Martz opened the way with *The Poetry of Meditation* (1954, rev. 1962). Martz discovered the pervasive influence of Catholic methods of meditation, outlined in the Ignatian *Exercises* and other manuals, on Anglican poets like Donne and Herbert and on Puritan Richard Baxter. Martz extended his analysis to the American poetry of Edward Taylor in his "Forward" to the complete edition of Taylor's poems. Since Taylor's entirely secret poetry was discovered only in 1937, critical reaction is an index of the emerging literary interest in spirituality. Working from the 1939 partial edition of his poems, scholars felt Taylor to be sui generis, unorthodox, an Anglican sympathizer, maybe a crypto-Catholic. No Puritan could write as he did. Martz and others published their studies of meditative poetry prior to the 1960 complete edition, preparing the way for a mature reading of Taylor's poetry in the light of classical spirituality and Puritan covenant theology. Karl Keller interpreted the poems convincingly as the products of Taylor's spiritual exercises, even revelatory of Taylor "in the process" of meditation. Barbara Lewalski has shown that English Protestant meditative poetry need not be explained simply by tracing Continental Catholic roots. Poets from Donne to Taylor shared an English, Protestant, Pauline, biblical spirituality independent of direct Ignatian influence.[7]

Anne Bradstreet scholarship has been dominated by a debate over the relationship of her religion and her art. One side devalued her poetry on the grounds that Puritan theology was inimical to inspiration; the other

---

[6] Alan Simpson, *Puritanism in Old and New England* (Chicago: U. of Chicago, 1955): 2. Edmund S. Morgan, "Heaven Can't Wait," *New York Review of Books* (May 31, 1984): 33. See, for example, David Levin, *Cotton Mather: The Young Life of the Lord's Remembrancer, 1663-1703* (Cambridge: Harvard U., 1978); David D. Hall, "The World of Print and Collective Mentality in Seventeenth-Century New England," in John Higham and Paul K. Conkin, eds., *New Directions in American Intellectual History* (Baltimore: Johns Hopkins, 1979) and *The Mental World of Samuel Sewall* in David D. Hall, et al., eds., *Saints and Revolutionaries* (New York: Norton, 1984); Charles E. Hambrick-Stowe, *The Practice of Piety: Puritan Devotional Disciplines in Seventeenth-Century New England* (Chapel Hill: U. of North Carolina, 1982); Patricia Caldwell, *The Puritan Conversion Narrative* (Cambridge: Cambridge U., 1983); and Kenneth Silverman, *The Life and Times of Cotton Mather* (New York: Harper & Row, 1984).

[7] Thomas Johnson, ed., *Poetical Works of Edward Taylor* (New York: Rockland, 1939). Donald E. Stanford, ed., *The Poems of Edward Taylor* (New Haven: Yale, 1960). Karl Keller, *The Example of Edward Taylor* (Amherst: U. of Mass., 1975): 92. Barbara Kiefer Lewalski, *Protestant Poetics and the Seventeenth-Century Religious Lyric* (Princeton: Princeton U., 1979).

praised her poetry as artistic rebellion against orthodoxy. Robert Daly laid the dispute to rest by demonstrating "that Puritan orthodoxy was conducive to the production of poetry, and that Bradstreet's poetry is illuminated by an understanding of the theology which structured the experiences her poetry expressed." Her poems "were prayers, religious acts." Daly echoes Bouyer's dictum on the inextricable relation of dogmatic and spiritual theology: "Christian spirituality is distinguished from dogma by the fact that, instead of studying or describing the objects of belief as it were in the abstract, it studies the reactions which these objects arouse in the religious consciousness." Anne Bradstreet's poetry will serve as an example of Reformed spirituality, both in its kinship with Catholic traditions and in its distinctiveness.[8]

2

The enthusiasm of discovering an ecumenical classical spirituality could lead one to ignore the violent separation of seventeenth-century Protestants from Catholics. If Puritans and Visitandines engaged in similar devotional acts, then dogmatic differences should not have mattered so much to them. Perhaps, as cynics are wont to say, dogmatic theology is destructive of humanity's common spiritual bonds. The separation was undeniable. How, then, can we best compare the spiritual exercises and experiences of Reformed Protestants and Roman Catholics?

One approach takes that in Reformed spirituality which fits the Catholic rubric and evaluates it by Catholic tools of scholarship. The Puritan contemplative was graced in ways that comport with this model. If Teresa of Avila wrote, "In this state . . . I saw close to me toward my left side an angel in bodily form," New England's Cotton Mather also saw and received messages from angels. In 1693 Mather recorded in his diary (in Latin, to honor the experience and conceal it from unlearned eyes), "After outpourings of prayer, with the utmost fervor and fasting, there appeared an Angel, whose face shone like the noonday sun." In 1718-1719, during a period of personal turmoil, the visitations returned. Instead of the angel descending to him, now Mather felt his soul ascending: "The flights, which I thus took among the holy Angels. I find my Pen unable to write the Things, and the Terms, to which my Soul mounted up as with the Wings of

---

[8] Robert Daly, *God's Altar: The World and the Flesh in Puritan Poetry* (Berkeley and Los Angeles: U. of California, 1978): 82-88, 127. Bouyer, *Spirituality of the New Testament*, vii.

an Eagle."   Other ministers and some laypeople wrote of similar experiences.[9]

Parallels between Anne Bradstreet (1612?-1672) and Teresa of Avila (1515-1582), gifted women a century apart, are fascinatingly close. Bradstreet's too brief autobiographical sketch, "To my dear Children," describes an early pilgrimage of faith similar to that presented in Teresa's volume, *The Book of Her Life*. Teresa wrote at the request of her spiritual fathers, Bradstreet to instruct her offspring after her death, but their common purpose was to glorify God. Teresa began, "May this account render Him glory and praise. And from now on may my confessors knowing me better through this narration help me in my weakness to give the Lord something of the service I owe Him." Bradstreet wrote, "I have not studied in this you read to show my skill, but to declare the Truth—not to set forth myself but the Glory of God." The women thanked God for their families, praising their "virtuous and God-fearing parents" but bemoaning their early tendencies to sin. Bradstreet recalled, "In my young years, about 6 or 7 as I take it, I began to make conscience of my wayes, and what I knew was sinfull, as lying, disobedience to Parents, etc. . . . I could not be at rest 'till by prayer I had confest it unto God." Young Teresa: "O my Lord . . . since you have granted me as many favors as You have, don't You think it would be good (not for my gain but for Your honor) if the inn where You have so continually to dwell were not to get so dirty? It wearies me, Lord, even to say this, for I know that the whole fault was mine." As a teenager Teresa "began to dress in finery and to desire to please and look pretty"; Bradstreet confessed, "about 14 or 15 I found my heart more carnall, and sitting loose from God, vanity and the follyes of youth take hold of me." God shook the young women from their natural impulses through illness. Teresa wrote that God "sent me a serious illness" to "prepare me for the state that was better for me." Bradstreet recalled, at 16 "the Lord layd his hand sore upon me and smott mee with the small pox. When I was in affliction, I besought the Lord, and confessed my Pride and Vanity and he was entreated of me, and again restored me."[10]

Both women were literate and enjoyed the world of books. When Teresa turned to spiritual authors, she went so far as to say, "my fondness

---

[9] Kieran Kavanaugh, O. C. D. and Otilio Rodriguez, O. C. D., trans., *The Collected Works of St. Teresa of Avila* (Washington: Institute of Carmelite Studies, 1976), 1: 193. C. W. Ford, ed., *Diary of Cotton Mather*, quoted in Silverman, *Life and Times of Cotton Mather*, 127-28, 311-12.

[10] Kavanaugh and Rodriguez, *Works of St. Teresa*, 1: 32-39. Robert Hutchinson, ed., *Poems of Anne Bradstreet* (New York, 1969): 179-180.

for good books was my salvation." Bradstreet read the Protestant
devotional manuals that corresponded to the *Letters of St. Jerome*, Osuna's
The Third Spiritual Alphabet, and Augustine's *Confessions* which guided
Teresa. Teresa had to abandon the chivalric romances she enjoyed with
her mother, but young Anne Bradstreet seems not to have been interested
in the easily available English "penny merriments" which Puritan
households abhorred. She later saw no reason to give up the serious
writers she adored, Sir Philip Sidney, Sir Walter Raleigh, and Guillaume
Du Bartas as translated by Joshua Sylvester. Secular poetry by reliable
Protestants was not without its uses, the encouragement of virtue and the
reinforcement of an English Reformed worldview.[11]

Teresa and Bradstreet experienced dryness following their initial
periods of illness, with subsequent cycles of deeper renewal, even renewed
conversions. Teresa took the habit and entered the convent; Bradstreet
married and crossed the ocean to "a new world and new manners." Teresa
immediately experienced "great happiness at being in the religious state of
life," while Bradstreet balked at first in New England: "my heart rose." But
she "submitted to it and joined the church at Boston." Illness continued to
play a role in the women's spirituality. In the convent, Teresa wrote, "the
change in food and life-style did injury to my health. . . . My fainting spells
began to increase, and . . . heart pains." In New England, Bradstreet "fell
into a lingering sicknes like a consumption, together with a lamenesse."
Teresa prayed that God "would give me the illnesses by which He would be
served." Bradstreet rejoiced: "Among all my experiences of God's gratious
Dealings with me I have constantly observed this, that he hath never
suffered me long to sitt loose from him, but by one effliction or other hath
made me look home, and search what was amisse . . . and these Times
(thro' his great mercy) have been the times of my greatest Getting and
Advantage, yes I have found them the times when the Lord hath
manifested the most Love to me."[12]

As women of spiritual depth, both knew the frustration of not being
understood. The men who arranged for the publication of Anne
Bradstreet's poetry in London without her knowledge or final editing
expressed patronizing wonder at her ability: "The Auth'ress was a right Du
Bartas girl. . . . I muse whither at length these girls will go." Teresa
lamented that for "twenty years . . . I did not find a master, I mean a
confessor, who understood me, even though I looked for one." Further,

---

[11] Kavanaugh and Rodriguez, *Works of St. Teresa*, 1: 35, 40, 43.
[12] Kavanaugh and Rodriguez, *Works of St. Teresa*, 1: 41-42, 46. Hutchinson, *Poems of Bradstreet*, 180.

both knew the political risks of female endeavour. Teresa recorded: "His Majesty began to give me the prayer of quiet very habitually—and often, of union—which lasted a long while. Since at that time other women had fallen into serious illusions and deceptions caused by the devil, I began to be afraid." She was referring to *alumbrados* like the illuminist Francisca Hernandez whose antinomianism led to her arrest by the Inquisition. Bradstreet recalled how New England was beset with "Blasphemy, and Sectaries, and some who have been accounted sincere Christians have been carried away with them. . . . I have remembered the words of Christ that . . . the very elect should bee deceived." She alluded to New England's other public Anne, Anne Hutchinson, the Puritan illuminist banished as an antinomian by the ministers and magistrates. Teresa and Bradstreet, in spite of their orthodoxy, could not be sure they were immune from danger. Bradstreet wrote, "Upon this Rock Christ Jesus will I build my faith; and if I perish, I perish. . . . I know whom I have trusted, and whom I have believed." Bradstreet knew her experience was true because it was rooted in the Bible: "If ever this God hath revealed himself, it must bee in his word, and this must bee it or none. Have I not found that operation by it that no humane Invention can work upon the Soul?" Teresa, who seems not to have even had a Bible, knew the truth of her experiences intuitively and directly: "I know through experience that what I say is true and that what can be said is the least of what You do, Lord, for a soul You bring to such frontiers." She knew what she experienced was true because she experienced it.[13]

Bradstreet assessed her spirituality modestly. "I have often been perplexed that I have not found that constant Joy in my Pilgrimage and refreshing which I supposed most of the servants of God have; although he hath not left me altogether without the wittnes of his holy spirit, who hath oft given mee his word and sett to his Seal that it shall bee well with me." Still, she wrote, "I have sometimes tasted of that hidden Manna that the world knowes not . . . against such a promis, such tasts of sweetnes, the Gates of Hell shall never prevail." She used the imagery of love to describe her relationship with Christ. Surveying the ashes of her destroyed house, Bradstreet considered how she would no longer hear the "bridegroom's voice" while meditating there by candlelight. In a preparatory meditation on her own death, she recorded that voice. When she prayed, "Come deare bridgrome," she heard Christ say, "Come away." Bradstreet's experience of

---

[13] Kavanaugh and Rodriguez, *Works of St. Teresa*, 1: 43, 152, 177. Hutchinson, *Poems of Bradstreet*, 183. Jeannine Hensley, ed., *The Works of Anne Bradstreet*, rev. ed. (Cambridge: Harvard U., 1981): 4.

Christ as bridegroom was the product of numerous sermons and her own study of Scripture. Teresa, with an astonishingly tentative grasp of Scripture, wrote in the same tradition. When "the Lord in His goodness desired that I should see and showed Himself to me in a rapture," she likened the experience to that of "two persons here on earth who love each other deeply and understand each other well." In her divine vision she and Christ were like "two lovers [who] gaze directly at each other, as the Bridegroom says to the Bride in the *Song of Songs*—I think I heard that it is there."[14]

Bouyer's approach in *Protestant and Anglican Spirituality* was to analyze Protestant spirituality according to the Catholic rubric in this fashion. This is a productive avenue of study, as the discussion above shows. Bouyer, writing as a Catholic, perceived Puritan spirituality as a re-Catholicizing process. "We can find nothing in these works to contradict, or even to disagree with, Catholic faith. We must go further: whatever their individual doctrine on other points, when these Protestants were dealing with spirituality they expressed a faith whose substance had become Catholic again." By this evaluation, having discovered the existence of the Puritan contemplative we would be led to identify Anne Bradstreet and the clergy (married and in the world) as would-be tertiaries who retreated as best they could for periodic communion with God.[15]

Bradstreet and other Puritans would not fare so well if we pressed this line of comparison. For all the similarities, she was no St. Teresa. Her experience of Christ inviting her to "Come away" to heaven does not compare with Teresa's ecstatic transverbation. Mather flew with the angels in what can be described as a unitive state, but he did not feel the sweet agony, continuing in Teresa for days on end, of the angel's spear plunged into his heart. Most of Bradstreet's devotions, and almost all Puritan piety would fall within the first stage or two of traditional Catholic ascetic theology. The exercises as we have them in Puritan diaries and devotional manuals largely describe Teresa's hand-dipped bucket or hand-turned water-wheel. The unitive states in which Bradstreet, Mather, and others experienced Teresa's third stage of heavenly rain probably were, according to the Catholic system, the highest rung of ascetic, not mystical, theology. There was no mysticism, strictly defined, in Puritanism.

Mystical theology describes the spiritual states of persons whose meditations and prayers are removed from daily human life. God elevated

---

[14] Hutchinson, *Poems of Anne Bradstreet*, 55, 78. Kavanaugh and Rodriguez, *Works of St. Teresa*, 1: 177. Hambrick-Stowe, *Practice of Piety*, 13-19.

[15] Bouyer, *Orthodox, Protestant, and Anglican Spirituality*, 143.

Teresa to spiritual states "often without [her] being able to avoid it" in ways unknown to Puritans. Teresa distinguished herself from other spiritual writers by insisting that only the most advanced should completely "turn aside from corporeal things," and protested that many who seek union with God directly without means are "left floating in the air" helplessly. "It is an important thing that while we are living and are human we have human support." But what she meant by "human support"—meditation on the humanity of Jesus and reception of the Sacrament—is quite different from what the Puritans meant by means of grace. Puritan spirituality at every stage was rooted in the earth of church fellowship, civil society, family relations, and personal trials.[16]

Without resorting to the "novel insistence on [plural] Christian spiritualities" which Bouyer criticizes, and negating the commonality which is so plain, we must remember that dogma helps shape spirituality. Bouyer rejects the penchant of comparative religion scholars to dissolve the boundaries between Christian and non-Christian mysticism. It is "impossible . . . to set up a serious comparison between spiritualities without taking account of the dogmas presupposed by each. . . . Dogmatic theology, therefore, must always be presupposed as the basis of spiritual theology." It follows that dogmatic distinctions between Reformed Protestants and Roman Catholics were bound to produce differences in spirituality. Chief among the theological differences was the new shape of Protestant anthropology. While Catholic spiritual theology was based on the faithful's ability to stir up the uncorrupted spark of the soul to seek God, in Protestant thought no part of the person's being was unmarred by the Fall. God became human in order to save sinners whose faculties were totally incapable of reaching up to God. Protestants based spirituality on God's justification and sanctification of corrupted humanity, as opposed to the Catholic concept of lifting one's soul to God, albeit through the gift of grace, by the strength of one's still pure inner spark. Theological differences require that Puritan spirituality must also be considered apart from the traditional Catholic rubric.[17]

Reformed Protestants transformed classic spirituality by applying it to a new worldly setting, while retaining traditional language, methods, and manuals. Puritan contemplatives and ordinary faithful alike looked to the stuff of daily life as the starting point and catalyst of meditation and prayer. Theirs was a spirituality not of would-be monks and nuns but of

---

[16] Kavanaugh and Rodriguez, *Works of St. Teresa*, 1: 144-152.
[17] Bouyer, *Spirituality of the New Testament*, vii-viii.

householders—husbandmen and housewives. As householders, Puritans would not leave behind the people and things they loved, nor did they believe God wanted them to even if they could. There was no distinction here between clergy and laity; all were called to sainthood and all lived and moved and had their being in Christ and, sanctified, in the world. Ministers, therefore, were not spiritual elite. The exercises they practiced were the very ones they directed their flocks to undertake, although not surprisingly they did so with greater zeal than many laity. Puritanism was a popular lay spirituality.

Calvin's doctrine of sanctification, Bouyer pointed out, played a key role in the development of Puritan spirituality. While the Catholic saint was an extraordinarily gifted mystic separated from the world by the cloister, the Puritan saint was an ordinary believer sanctified by God living and praying in the world. The English theologian William Ames, whose work guided New England thought, defined sanctification as "the real change in man from the sordidness of sin to the purity of God's image." The term could indicate "separation from ordinary use or consecration to some special use," but the theological doctrine implied not separation from the world but the salvation of the world. "The term is rather to be understood as that change in a believer in which he has righteousness and indweling holiness imparted to him." Moreover, "it pertains to the whole man and not to any one part." God sanctified people for life in this world, for proper creaturely enjoyment and fulfillment. Through God's Spirit, things and relationships even became means of grace. Sanctification was the doctrinal vehicle enabling a spirituality of the householder in which devotion began with the consideration of physical reality.[18]

Yet this world, as any devout Puritan knew, was transitory and love of the creatures led to grief. Earthen vessels, created by God and sanctified for human use, were bound to crumble, to die and decay. Here is the crisis that underlay Puritan spirituality. Householders were subject to the grief of losing those persons and things with which God blessed their lives. Devotional acts sparked by grief became for Puritans the means of a deeper sanctification; they still did not abandon the things of this world but humbly offered them up to the transcendent God. Devotional guides cautioned the Puritan to travel this world as a stranger and a pilgrim, not to look for ultimate meaning in any created thing. Puritanism was thus a spirituality of weaned affections, rooted always in this world but reaching

---

[18] Bouyer, *Orthodox, Protestant, and Anglican Spirituality*, 85-89, 143. William Ames, *The Marrow of Theology*, John D. Eusden, trans. (Durham, NC: Labyrinth, 1983): 167-169.

toward the other world. This world's dynamic matrix of change and mortality was the setting for the Puritan life of prayer. Puritan spirituality is characterized by its effort to embrace the pain of loss and seek in faithful prayer God's eternal word of hope.

3

The Puritans are famous for scrutinizing the details of their lives in meditation. We now know that their intensely human spirituality did not leave devout Puritans stranded in grim anxiety. Above all, the manner in which they approached the fundamental experience of loss created a spirituality that did not crush but healed and uplifted the human spirit in communion with God.

An episode in the life of the quintessential Puritan contemplative Cotton Mather again illustrates this characteristic. With his wife on her deathbed Mather was "in deep Distress" emotionally and spiritually; he described the impending loss of his "lovely Consort" as a "Trial of my Faith." He prayed in an attitude of utter mortification. "I retired unto my Bed-Chamber, and spent good Part of the Night, prostrate on the Floor, (with so little of Garment on as to render my lying there painful to my tender Bones), crying to God for the Life of my poor Consort, but humbly committing her Case, and submitting my Will, to His glorious Providence." A voice in the form of "a strange Impression on my Mind" said, "'Go into your great Chamber and I will speak with you!'" There, "prostrate on the Floor before the Lord . . . I felt an inexpressible Afflatus come from Heaven upon my Mind, which dissolved me into a Flood of Tears" and stirred Mather to pray "full of assurance." His prayers, rooted in grief over the loss of a finite creature, lifted him into "intimate Communion with Heaven."[19] Such was Puritan spirituality: a spirituality that began with sanctified love for the transient things of this world, a spirituality of the householder struggling with loss, a spirituality which never abandoned but finally looked beyond this sanctified mortality to eternal glorification, a spirituality which released the beloved creature to God in the sure hope that in God she was not lost but lived forever.

The writings of Anne Bradstreet have long commanded critical literary attention, but only recently have some scholars recognized her as a religious poet. The collection published during her lifetime, *The Tenth Muse* (1650), contained only her public poetry, largely unimaginative

---

[19] Ford, *Diary of Cotton Mather*, 1: 430, 436-438, 449.

renderings of conventional themes: "The Four Elements," "The Four Humours," "The Four Ages of Man," "The Four Monarchies," and elegies on her heroes, Sidney, Du Bartas, and Queen Elizabeth. The second edition, published posthumously in 1678, contained new poems prefaced: "Several other Poems made by the Author upon Diverse Occasions, were found among her Papers after her Death, which she never meant should come to public view; amongst which, these following (at the desire of some friends that knew her well) are here inserted." Her extant papers contained other private poems and writings which were edited and published in the complete edition by John Harvard Ellis in 1867. Bradstreet's private poetry and her well-wrought thirty-three stanza "Contemplations" establish her reputation as a fine poet. Critics have described them as love poems (e.g., "To my Dear and loving Husband"), domestic poems (e.g., "In memory of my dear grand-child Elizabeth Bradstreet"), and classical dialogues (e.g., "The Flesh and the Spirit"), though some are undeniably religious meditations by any standard (e.g., "What God is like to him I serve" and "By night when others soundly slept"). The concept of Puritan spirituality as a lay spirituality of householders shaped by the doctrine of sanctification and sparked by the experience of loss, however, opens the way for a reading of all of Bradstreet's private poetry as the expression of her spiritual life.[20]

Anne Bradstreet's continual confrontation with the experience of loss is a theme underlying her private poems. We have already seen that, with St. Teresa, she identified her loss of health as a spiritual catalyst. God seemed to chastize Bradstreet with afflictions "upon my own person, in sicknesse, weaknes, paines, sometimes on my soul, in Doubts and feares of God's displeasure, and my sincerity towards him, sometimes he hath smott a child with sicknes, sometimes chasstened by losses in estate." These times of loss were "the Times when the Lord hath manifested the most Love to me."

Bradstreet wrote her earliest extant poem "Upon a Fit of Sickness" in 1632 on this crisis of finitude.

> Twice ten years old, not fully told
> Since nature gave me breath
> My race is run, my thread is spun,
> Lo here is fatal Death.

---

[20] Hensley, *Works of Bradstreet*, xxix. These categories are the framework of Hutchinson, *Poems of Bradstreet*. Robert Daly reviews the traditional approaches to Bradstreet's poetry and argues for a religious interpretation in *The World and the Flesh in Puritan Poetry*, chap. 3.

Her amateurish attempt at verse concludes with an equally conventional Christian affirmation which nevertheless expressed a faith that was stronger for her survival of smallpox.

> The race is run, the field is won,
> the victory's mine I see,
> For ever know, thou envious foe,
> the foyle belongs to thee.

As she matured as a poet, Bradstreet did not seek to avoid suffering by fixing on another world or religious formulas; she passionately engaged with her illness. "In my distresse I sought the Lord," she wrote. It was when "in sweat I seem'd to melt" that God appeared and said, "Live." After "sore fits" and "fits of fainting" she embraced her own weakness; the utter need of her "wasted flesh" yielded her praise to God.

> In anguish of my heart repleat with woes,
> And wasting pains, which best my body knows,
> In tossing slumbers on my wakeful bed,
> Bedrencht with tears that flow'd from mournful head,
> Till nature had exhausted all her store,
> Then eyes lay dry, disabled to weep more.

Only then was she able to "look . . . up unto his Throne on high, / Who sendeth help to those in misery." God "eas'd my Soul of woe, my flesh of pain." Loss of health was a sign of mortality, a *memento mori*. Bradstreet's last poem, "As weary pilgrim, now at rest," already commented upon, recorded her most advanced meditation on her illness and imminent death. She began by composing the image of the pilgrim arriving in heaven, reflected on her own sufferings—"By age and paines brought to decay"—and longingly cried, "Oh how I long to be at rest / and soare on high among the blest." Meditation on the tomb of Christ, her own tomb, and the promises of Scripture opened her ears to the welcoming voice of Christ to "Come away."[21]

Anne Bradstreet's loving relationship with her husband Simon was a source of spiritual joy. She felt in her husband the love of Christ and in her passion for him a foretaste of heaven. Her love also filled her with fear—fear of losing him. Her love poems outwardly expressed her prayers struggling with the finitude of their relationship. A poem "Before the Birth of one of her Children" came from a spiritual experience faced by most women, the dark side of anticipating a baby's birth; sober preparation to

---

[21] Hutchinson, *Poems of Bradstreet*, 180, 62-64, 56, 77-78.

die in childbirth. Her general recollection that "All things within this fading world hath end" became personal.

> How soon, my Dear, death may my steps attend,
> How soon't may be thy Lot to lose thy friend,
> We are both ignorant, yet love bids me
> These farewell lines to recommend to thee.

The farewell poem gave voice less to Bradstreet's fear of death or Simon's possible need to grieve than to her own anticipatory grief over losing him when she died. She was loath to face a time "when that knot's unty'd that made us one." Knowing that he would remarry, she grieved at the thought of losing him to another woman.

> Yet love thy dead, who long lay in thine arms:
> And when thy loss shall be repaid with gains
> Look to my little babes my dear remains.
> . . . .
> These O protect from step Dames injury.

Anne Bradstreet in effect lost her husband for long periods of time when he traveled on Massachusetts colonial business. Her love poems to him paralleled her prayers for his safe return. She mourned his absence as a "loss," however temporary. "As loving Hind that (Hartless) wants her Dear . . . So doth my anxious soul, which now doth miss, / A dearer Dear (far dearer Heart) than this." Describing his absence as "this dead time," she knew that their reunion would be temporary: "Let's still remain but one, till death divide."[22]

The love poems paralleled Bradstreet's prayers for her husband's safe return. She shifted to addressing her poems as prayers directly to God in a series written in 1661 when Simon was in England negotiating with the new royal government. Since Bradstreet wrote these poems in hymn or psalter form, it seems likely that she sang them to God in her secret devotions. Some of these "spiritual songs" were simple petitionary prayers.

> Into thy everlasting Armes
> Of mercy I commend
> Thy servant, Lord. Keep and preserve
> My husband, my dear friend.
> . . . .
> Lord, let my eyes see once Again
> Him whom thou gavest me,
> That wee together may sing Praise
> For ever unto Thee.

---

[22] Ibid., 45, 41-42, 44.

> And the Remainder of oure Dayes
> Shall consecrated bee,
> With an engaged heart to sing
> All Praises unto Thee.

Others expressed her grief during "Solitary houres" in more personal terms.

> O Lord, thou hear'st my dayly moan,
> And see'st my dropping teares:
> My Troubles All are Thee before,
> My Longings and my fares.

She communed in meditation during her husband's physical absence with the Bridegroom of her soul, Jesus Christ, who was always present.

> And thy Abode tho'st made with me;
> With Thee my Soul can talk
> In secrett places, Thee I find,
> Where I doe kneel or walk.

> Tho' husband dear bee from me gone,
> Whom I doe love so well:
> I have a more beloved one
> Whose comforts far excell.

She prayed that as God had blessed her by her son's earlier return from England, God would grant her husband's return. In other poems her husband was an emblem of Christ; now her son's return evoked the resurrection of God's Son from death.

> O shine upon me, blessed Lord,
> Ev'n for my Saviour's sake;
> In Thee Alone is more than All,
> And there content I'll take.

> O hear me, Lord, in this Request,
> As thou before ha'st done:
> Bring back my husband, I beseech,
> As thou didst once my Sonne.

Biblical faith combined with personal experience—God did "bring back" both His Son and "my Sonne"—to produce hope. Bradstreet completed the cycle with a prayer of thanksgiving in poetic form when her husband returned a year later. If Simon's return was a kind of resurrection, Bradstreet also saw their love as a means of grace. She concluded her beautiful poem, "To my Dear and loving Husband": "Then while we live, in love lets so persever, / That when we live no more, we may live ever."[23]

---

[23] Hutchinson, *Poems of Bradstreet*, 72-77, 41.

Bradstreet's spirituality was shaped by the loss of offspring. Unlike Catholic spiritual writers, she prayed and wrote as a housewife and mother. The devotion of Cotton Mather and Samuel Sewall was fired by grief at losing many children to death. Anne and Simon Bradstreet saw all their children survive to adulthood. Nevertheless, as all mothers do, she lost them to adulthood. Her "eight birds hatcht in one nest" grew up and flew off to make new families. Bradstreet was too wise to cling to them or to her own youth.

> My age I will not once lament,
> But sing, my time so near is spent.
> And from the top bough take my flight,
> Into a country beyond sight.

Content that she had done well by them, she bid, "Farewel my birds, farewel adieu," and dedicated more time to meditation.[24]

Far more difficult was the task of burying three grandchildren, including her namesake, who died in infancy. Bradstreet's inner turmoil at the death of the three year old Anne bespoke the sense of crisis that generated Puritan spirituality, rooted as it was in this world.

> With troubled heart and trembling hand I write,
> The Heavens have chang'd to sorrow my delight.
> How oft with disappointment have I met,
> When I on fading things my hopes have set?
> Experience might 'fore this have made me wise,
> To value things according to their price:
> Was ever stable joy yet found below,
> Or perfect bliss without mixture of woe?

Bradstreet was not saying her love for her grandchild was misplaced. Her love for her (like that for her husband) was an experience of "perfect bliss"—a "shadow," and hence a fleeting glimpse, of "stable joy" and eternal bliss "without mixture of woe." The child had been "lent" as an "impermanent" earthly blessing and so had to be released with a "Farewel dear child." She had been a blessing nonetheless, and her death pointed Bradstreet to the place where "Thou with thy Saviour art in endless bliss." Like King David (2 Samuel 12:23), Bradstreet wrote, "But yet a while, and I shall go to thee." In grief over another grandchild, she found comfort in the thought that Christ "will return, and make up all our losses."[25]

Anne Bradstreet recorded her meditations on transiency and mortality in three excellent poems, "The Flesh and the Spirit," "The Vanity

---

[24] Hutchinson, *Poems of Bradstreet*, 47-49.
[25] Ibid., 57-58.

of all worldly things," and "Contemplations." In the first, refuting Flesh's claim that meditation was "Notion without Reality," Spirit explained, "I have meat thou know'st not of. . . . Mine Eye doth pierce the heavens, and see / What is Invisible to thee." In "Vanity," she wrote, the way of the world is "labour, anxious care and pain." But "There is a path, no vultures eye hath seen. . . . It brings to honour, which shall ne're decay, / It stores with wealth which time can't wear away." "Contemplations" is a classic exercise of meditation in nature, but frustrated by spiritual inability.

> Silent alone, where none or saw, or heard,
> In pathless paths I lead my wandring feet,
> My humble Eyes to lofty skyes I rear'd
> To sing some Song, my mazed Muse thought meet.
> My great Creator I would magnifie,
> That nature had, thus decked liberally:
> But Ah, and Ah, again, my imbecility!

Why did human beings not sing to God as naturally as the trees and the birds? The answer lay in the biblical doctrine of sin. Shifting her meditation to the Genesis stories of the Fall and Cain's murder of Abel, Bradstreet stood by the riverside as one afflicted by the effects of sin. Without God's grace even the "losses, sickness, pain" of earthly life would not make people "deeply groan for that divine Translation." And the blessings God granted on earth in themselves were useless. The "fool . . . takes this earth ev'n for heav'ns bower." Time, "the fatal wrack of mortal things," brought all to naught. Bradstreet saw that she must look beyond both the blessings and losses of life here to the only abiding hope: "Only above is found all with security." The way "above," of course, was through Christ who would write the saint's name "in the white stone" of Revelation 2:17. Bradstreet knew that she would "last and shine when all of these are gone."[26]

Anne Bradstreet's Puritan spirituality trained her to live fully and lovingly in this world but with the eyes of her heart ready for the next world. The loss of beloved people and things, the impending loss of her own life, were the crises within which she sought the Lord in impassioned prayer and found spiritual resolution. The loss of her home, and the poem which she wrote on the occasion of its burning, conform to this devotional pattern. In the poem, Robert Daly correctly observes, Bradstreet "compares her love for her house and her pain at its passing to Christ's love for man and His suffering on the cross; this comparison is a terribly powerful argument for the ultimate triviality of the house. It enables the

---

[26] Ibid., 89-94, 81-87.

speaker to achieve the perspective she seeks. . . . She finds 'above the sky' the promise of heaven, figured appropriately as a house."

Every analysis of this poem, "Upon the burning of our house, July 10th, 1666," reads Bradstreet's loss as the physical things of her house and its furnishings. Critics find her tender domestic memories of the house particularly feminine. An understanding of the true nature of her loss will further illustrate the Puritan spirituality of the householder.[27]

4

When fire destroyed their Andover, Massachusetts home, Anne Bradstreet sought the release of her emotional trauma and the consolation of God through prayer and poetry. As with other works, her poem gave voice and structure to her approach to God. "Upon the burning of our house" is a remarkable work, Bradstreet at her literary best. But we seek to learn not so much about her art as about the spirituality her art expressed. The poem lays bare the tension between love for creatures and Creator which fueled her life of prayer. It describes the moment when the stairway which she built between the one and the other—that is, the manuscripts of her devotional poetry—went up in flames with the house. Poems expressing prayers were divinely inspired, had lifted Bradstreet's soul above the created world. But even they had to be released. Love for them was no more permanent than love for any other thing or creature. Bradstreet knew what it was to be *almost* a "Fond fool [who] takes this earth ev'n for heav'ns bower."[28] Her love for both the Creator and the creature (for things, indeed, co-created by God and her) led her once more into the crisis of human loss and, ultimately, her receipt of grace and hope.

The poem's title included the date of the event, "July 10th, 1666." The last three digits of the year were fearful to any biblically minded believer. The satanic beast of the last days described in Revelation 13 "maketh fire come down from heaven on the earth in the sight of men . . . and his number is Six hundred threescore and six." In contrast to the damned with the "mark . . . or the number of his name," Bradstreet had long felt assured that her name was "grav'd in the white stone," as she wrote in "Contemplations," and that her poetry was preparation to sing the "new

---

[27] Daly, *God's Altar*, 100-101. For comment on "Upon the burning of our house," see Josephine K. Piercy, *Anne Bradstreet* (New York: Twayne, 1965): 82; Ann Stanford, *Anne Bradstreet: The Worldly Puritan* (New York: B. Franklin, 1974): 107-109; Wendy Martin, *An American Triptych* (Chapel Hill: U. of N. Carolina, 1984): 74-75.

[28] Hutchinson, *Poems of Bradstreet*, 87.

song before the throne" of the Lamb. But in her poem on "The Four Elements" Bradstreet wrote that while fire was normally a domestic servant, it "by force, master, [its] masters can." Whole towns, the palaces of kings "in confused heaps, of ashes may you see." Fire humbled the proud. It also signified the coming Last Judgment from which none were exempt: "The world I shall consume / And all therein, at that great day of Doom." The numbers three (symbolic of divinity) and six (symbolic of sin, judgment, and damnation) juxtaposed in her mind and provided a meditative structure. The fire was both judgment and grace. Bradstreet wrote the poem in three parts, each composed of three stanzas of six lines. The date of the fire, then, was no casual detail. The fire pushed her to the edge of mortality and judgement (the number six) and eternity (the number three).

The first three stanzas are Bradstreet's vivid recollection of the fire itself, and represent her later meditations on the terrible event.

> In silent night when rest I took,
> For sorrow neer I did not look,
> I waken'd was with thundring nois
> And Piteous shreiks of dreadfull voice.
> That fearfull sound of fire and fire,
> Let no man know is my Desire.

Like the thief and the Son of Man which "cometh at an hour when ye think not" (Luke 12:39-40), the fire struck "in silent night." The "thundring nois" of the fire and the "Piteous shreiks" apparently of the maid awakened her, but her lack of mention of her husband suggests that he was away at the time. Bradstreet faced the fire and escaped from the house as she must face God after death, as an individual.

> I, starting up, the light did spye,
> And to my God my heart did cry
> To strengthen me in my Distresse
> And not to leave me succourlesse.
> Then coming out beheld a space,
> the flame consume my dwelling place.

Puritan spirituality originated in the events of daily life. Accordingly, Rosamund R. Rosenmeier has written, "This is by no means a spiritual, allegorical, or symbolic fire."   The adjectives "thundring," "Piteous," "dreadful," "fearfull" evoke the night's immediate physical terror. Her prayer ("to my God my Heart did cry") was no methodical exercise, but an elemental cry for divine help.   Once outside Bradstreet "beheld a space"—that is, watched for a while—as the fire "consume[d] my dwelling place."[29]

The third stanza concluded Bradstreet's reflections on the night of the fire.

> And, when I could no longer look,
> I blest his Name that gave and took,
> that layd my goods now in the dust:
> Yea so it was, and so 'twas just.
> It was his own: it was not mine:
> Far be it that I should repine.

Her formulaic blessing of God (Job 1:21) for such a terrible act was more a ritual act of resignation than spiritual resolution, as her unrequited sorrow in late return visits demonstrated. The theological affirmation, "so it was, and so 'twas just," was the best she could muster that night. Significantly, however, it was less the house's structure than her "goods" contained therein for which she grieved. What were these "goods"? Traditional scholarship comments on Anne Bradstreet's love for her "domestic comforts," her "treasured possessions . . . her last link with her happy life in the Old World." Her son, the Rev. Simon Bradstreet kept his library in the house; his major lament was the loss of over 800 books. Of even greater value than an intellectual's books, however, are the unpublished papers of an author. Only Bradstreet's manuscripts were irreplaceable. In fact, she reported the loss of her work on "The Roman Monarchy" for a revised edition of *The Tenth Muse*.

> To finish what's begun, was my intent
> . . . .
> But 'fore I could accomplish my desire,
> My papers fell a prey to th' raging fire.
> And thus my pains (with better things) I lost,
> Which none had cause to wail, nor I to boast.

Closer to her heart than the formal poetry of "The Four Monarchies" was the private poetry she wrote for God and to her husband and children. Her "better things" were unknown to the public, and so "none had cause to wail." She did not boast about its literary quality, but it expressed the relationships and experiences that mattered most to her.[30]

---

[29] Hutchinson, *Poems of Bradstreet*, 54-56 (subsequent quotation of "Upon the burning of our house" are from these pages), 124. Rev. 13:14, 17-18; 2:17; 14:1-3. Rosamund R. Rosenmeier, "'Divine Translation': A Contribution to the Study of Anne Bradstreet's Method in the Marriage Poems," *Early American Literature* (Fall 1977): 131.

[30] Martin, *An American Triptych*, 75. Piercy, *Anne Bradstreet*, 82. Hutchinson, *Poems of Bradstreet*, 7, 177-178.

Bradstreet in several places referred to her poetic work as "my goods" or home-made clothing. In her preface to *The Tenth Muse* she defended herself against anticipated criticism because of Du Bartas' influence. "I honour him, but dare not wear his wealth; / My goods are true (though poor), I love no stealth." And in "The Author to her Book" she modestly apologized for failing to improve her poems for the revised edition. "In better dress to trim thee was my mind, / But nought save home-spun Cloth, i'th' house I find." Bradstreet attributed the inspiration of her private poetry, more than her public works, to God. Her meditative poems, which issued from her devotional exercises, were the means by which she communed with God and anticipated heaven. After "Deliverance from a fitt of Fainting," for example, she prayed:

> Thy Name and praise to celebrate,
> O Lord! for aye is my request.
> O graunt I doe it in this state,
> And then with thee which is the best.

Her poems therefore belonged to God and not to her. Anne Bradstreet could more truly say this of her private poetry than of any piece of furniture, "It was his own: it was not mine."[31]

The second part of the poem is set in the days after the fire and reflects her solemn meditation on the ashes. She addressed the house itself, which no longer existed physically. But in memory and imagination, God "sufficient for us left." As in classic composition of place a scriptural scene became real in the meditator's mind, the house was again real for Bradstreet.

> He might of All justly bereft,
> But yet sufficient for us left.
> When by the Ruines oft I past,
> My sorrowing eyes aside did cast,
> And here and there the places spye
> Where oft I sate, and long did lye.
>
> Here stood that Trunk, and there that chest;
> There lay that store I counted best:
> My pleasant things in ashes lye,
> And them behold no more shall I.
> Under thy roof no guest shall sitt,
> Nor at thy Table eat a bitt.
>
> No pleasant tale shall 'ere be told,
> Nor things recounted done of old.

---

[31] Hutchinson, *Poems of Bradstreet*, 14, 40, 64.

No Candle 'ere shall shine in thee,
Nor bridegroom's voice ere heard shall bee.
In silence ever shalt thou lye;
Adeiu, Adeiu; All's vanity.

Bradstreet not only recollected the house, but her many occasions of devotional exercise in "the places . . . Where oft I sate, and long did lye." She recalled times such as those expressed in an earlier poem: "By night when others soundly slept . . . to lye I found it best. / I sought him whom my Soul did Love. . . . In vain I did not seek or cry." The chair, the bed, and the table were not so sacred to her memory as her meditative poems composed in those places. Of course she thought wistfully of guest and mealtime conversations. But Bradstreet often used everyday things and relationships as signs of spiritual realities. Moreover, "things recounted done of old" were the subject of several of her poems. In "Contemplations" she began her meditation on Cain and Abel:

When present times look back to Ages past,
And men in being fancy those are dead,
It makes things gone perpetually to last.

This was the work, and the candle was the symbol, of meditation. Now she considered that the pieces of paper upon which she had written were less sacred than the fact that she had meditated and written. This knowledge must be "sufficient for us."[32]

Scholars point to the trunk and chest as pieces of furniture, and no doubt Bradstreet loved her things. Yet both of these items are containers. Bradstreet identified the contents, not the containers themselves, as "that store I counted best." More than the trunk and chest themselves, the "store" kept therein were her "pleasant things" reduced to ashes. One who defined her life through her writing could be referring to nothing else than bundles of notebooks and papers which she could now no longer peruse, revise, meditate and pray over. Bradstreet used the word "store" elsewhere in ordinary references to clothing and material wealth, but also metaphorically in reference to human emotion and her husband's priceless affection. Most importantly, in her "Elegie upon . . . Sir Philip Sidney" she used the word to describe the writing of poetry. Bradstreet wrote of the muses that Sidney's first published work did not "exhaust your store;" he wrote many volumes of poetry before his death. She emulated Sidney in her poetry but confessed her inabilities. Poetic inspiration seemed to have dried up. "The Muses aid I crav'd . . . they said they gave no more, / Since

---

[32] Hutchinson, *Poems of Bradstreet*, 61, 81.

Sidney had exhausted all their store. / They took from me the scribling pen I had." Like Sydney, however, Bradstreet kept writing, and found her own muse. A woman whose spirituality expressed itself in poetry, one who thought of herself as a poet and not an amateur versifier, who confessed in several places that she wrote poetry continually, must have written more than the scant 39 poems and journal entries and the prose "Meditations Divine and Moral" which survived the fire in her published volume and two slender notebooks (only one of which is now extant). Anne Bradstreet's deepest sense of loss as she gazed at the ashes was for her entire oeuvre. This was "that store I counted best." She was forced to say even to her writings: "Adeiu, Adeiu; All's vanity."[33]

The concluding part of the poem expressed Bradstreet's meditation on biblical images of sacrifice and the resolution of her crisis of loss.

> Then streight I gin my heart to chide,
> And did thy wealth on earth abide?
> Didst fix thy hope on mouldring dust,
> The arm of flesh didst make thy trust?
> Raise up thy thoughts above the skye
> That dunghill mists away may flie.

Bradstreet's house, her very life, was a "house of clay, whose foundation is in the dust" (Job 4:19). Beyond the imagery of finitude, however, Bradstreet may also have recalled the story of Elijah when "the fire of the Lord fell, and consumed the burnt sacrifice, and the wood, and the stones, and the dust" and the people "fell on their faces: and they said, "The Lord is God" (1 Kings 18:38). She must not think of the work of her own "arm of flesh"—"Ye have kindled a fire in mine anger. . . . Cursed be the man that . . . maketh flesh his arm . . . Blessed is the man that trusteth in the Lord" (Jeremiah 17:4-7). She must "raise up [her] thoughts" to heaven with the ascent of the smoke. Ezra 6 commanded the people to "offer sacrifices of sweet savours unto the God of heaven," and anyone who refused to contribute animals and produce to the sacrifice would face execution "and let his house be made a dunghill" (6:9-11). Bradstreet's house was reduced to a "dunghill," but in her meditation the "mists" that rose from the house and its contents—and particularly her manuscripts—became a more complete sacrifice or act of worship than they had been in their first composition.

Bradstreet's meditation turned instinctively to one of Puritanism's favorite passages, 2 Corinthians 5:1.

---

[33] Hutchinson, *Poems of Bradstreet*, 90, 44, 56, 109-111, 49.

Thou hast an house on high erect
Fram'd by that mighty Architect,
With glory richly furnished,
Stands permanent tho' this bee fled.
It's purchased, and paid for too
By him who hath enough to doe.

If she had offered her sacrifice, it was not to purchase salvation but in full devotion to Christ whose sacrifice alone was "enough" to purchase permanent union with God in God's own house.   Christ's death on the cross sanctified Bradstreet's experience of mortification as she released her written meditative poems to the God who had first inspired them and whose they truly were.   Her aim all along had not been poetic fame but the experience of love, in her family and with God.   All sanctified earthly love reached toward heaven.   Implicit in her meditation was St. Paul's next verse, "in this we groan, earnestly desiring to be clothed upon with our house which is from heaven."

A Prise so vast as is unknown,
Yet, by his Gift, is made thine own.
Ther's wealth enough, I need no more:
Farewell my Pelf, farewell my Store.
The world no longer let me Love,
My hope and Treasure lyes Above.

Quite literally, Bradstreet could say her "store," her "treasure"—the house, its furnishings, and her lifetime of meditative and private poetry—now "lyes Above."   Meditation on Christ's sacrifice and her own, and knowledge that "where your treasure is, there will your heart be also" (Luke 12:34), lifted her soul above this world to God.

* * * * *

The example of Anne Bradstreet suggests how hopeful is the prospect of a comprehensive study of Protestant and Catholic spirituality. The Puritan contemplative meditated and prayed according to classic methodology and experienced the high spiritual states.   English Puritan and Continental Catholic spirituality flowered simultaneously, so the one is not derivative of the other except in the way, for example, St. Francis de Sales' writings derived from centuries of tradition.   There is a common, ecumenical history of Christian spirituality.   Puritans and Catholic belonged, as Bouyer said, to a "community of religious thought and culture" overarching their dogmatic differences.

At the same time, the temptation to collapse the two completely into a single system ignores the real theological differences which separated the great branches of Western Christendom. Protestant anthropology and the Reformed doctrine of sanctification led Puritans to embrace a lay spirituality, based on close study of the Bible, rooted in sanctified love for the people and things of this world, and generated by the crisis of their mortality. Puritanism was a spirituality of the householder, in a family and home blessed by God, yet facing the loss of everything in this earthly home. Anne Bradstreet exemplified Puritan spirituality as she watched her house, its furnishings, and "that store [she] counted best," her devotional poetry, rise to the heavens. Her hope and her treasure were above, where sanctified believers received glorification.

The transformation of dogma resulted in a transformed spirituality. Sympathetic study of Reformed spirituality, therefore, will not limit itself to the Catholic model by merely looking for survivals of tradition or for evidence of re-Catholicizing. A broader approach will bear fruit both for Catholics ready to learn from the "separated brethren" and for Protestants discovering their own history of spirituality.

7

Jane de Chantal's Guidance of Women:
The Community of the Visitation and Womanly Values

WENDY M. WRIGHT

> Believe me, an affectionate and motherly love along with a gentle and thoughtful firmness win over all hearts. Continue to make this spirit your own in just such ways and you and all the sisters will profit from it.[1]

With these few graceful words, Jane de Chantal (1572-1641), co-foundress of the Order of the Visitation of Holy Mary, expressed the way in which she sought to guide her spiritual daughters as well as the mode of direction that came to be instilled in the Visitandine community as a whole. It was a style of direction which sprang naturally from its roots in the Catholic Reformation, especially from the Salesian spirituality of which it is a part. This method of religious guidance also reflects its genesis in a community formed specifically for women. This community was, moreover, one in which the foundress herself embodied and sought to teach a personal and communal attitude that was at the time, and still might be,

---

[1] Ste. Jeanne Françoise Frémyot de Chantal, *Sa Vie et ses oeuvres*, Edition authentique publiée par les soins des Religieuses du Premier Monastère de la Visitation Sainte-Marie d'Annecy (Paris: Plon, 1874-79), Tome VIII, Lettres 5. Translations from this work are mine or those of Sister Peronne Marie Thibert, V.H.M. Hereafter this work is cited in the text as *Sa Vie*.

deemed "feminine" inasmuch as it consciously cultivated the relational and affective potential of the human person.[2]

Francis de Sales and the Spirituality of the Visitation

Any type of spiritual direction, whether it is a specific method or simply a "style" of guidance, cannot be apprehended outside of the larger socio-religious matrix in which it is embedded. The direction that Jane de Chantal espoused belongs to the world of French spirituality at the beginning of the seventeenth century and especially to the person of Francis de Sales (1561-1622). It was de Sales, the Bishop of Geneva, the "devout humanist," the "gentleman saint," the pastor who taught an expansive love of God to religious and lay persons alike, who was Jane's longtime director and friend.[3] Together they founded the Visitation of Holy Mary and together they forged its specific form of religious life.[4]

At the core of Frances de Sales' spirituality is the simple phrase, *Vive Jesus*, a phrase which came to serve as the motto for the Visitation. Used as a motto, it was a straightforward exhortation to become Christ, to be so surrendered to the will of God that one might rightly use the words of St. Paul, "I no longer live, but Christ lives in me." In its simplicity and optimism the phrase aptly proclaims de Sales' spirit.

The Genevan bishop's spirituality, at one and the same time, is decidedly humanistic and profoundly ascetic. It is humanistic in the sense that it begins with human experience in its quest for God. Likewise it takes that experience seriously by affirming and celebrating human capacity and creativity in the spiritual life. De Sales envisions a universe in which an infinitely merciful and loving God creates a humankind designed to love

---

[2] It is certainly possible to claim that the culture of seventeenth century France assigned to its female population traits, such as affectivity, that were perceived to be different from the traits normatively possessed by men. The early part of this article will suggest as much. As for the question whether traits deemed "feminine" by that culture may have anything to do with women's spirituality or women's concerns in the twentieth century is the exploratory subject of the last part of this article.

[3] The first phrase is Henri Bremond's. See his *Histoire littéraire du sentiment religieux en France depuis la fin des guerres de religion jusqu'à nos jours*, Tome I (Paris: Bloud et Gay, 1921). The term gentleman saint was coined by Ruth Murphy in *Saint François de Sales et la civilité chrétienne* (Paris: A.G. Nizet, 1964). For a study of their friendship, see my own *Bond of Perfection: Jeanne de Chantal and François de Sales* (Mahwah, NJ: Paulist, 1985).

[4] On the collaborative work of Jane de Chantal and Francis de Sales and their joint authoring of the Salesian tradition see *Francis de Sales, Jane de Chantal: Letters of Spiritual Direction*, selected and intro. Wendy M. Wright and Joseph F. Power, O.S.F.S., trans. Peronne Marie Thibert, V.H.M. (Mahwah, NJ: Paulist Press, 1988): 11-13 and 70-86.

and adore in return. All persons by nature tend to this love of God, and, despite the wounding of human nature incurred in the primal fall, all persons can, through their own efforts aided by grace, enter into the fullness of the loving relationship they are created to enjoy. In Francis de Sales' view, men and women are above all lovers of God.[5] The perfect lover surrenders utterly to the beloved in an act of self-abandonment. Thus the abandonment of detachment and dependence upon divine providence are central to his spirit and define his asceticism. The austerity of that asceticism is belied by its lack of exterior show. For while he preaches a radical interior self-denial, the Genevan prelate does not emphasize rigorous exterior mortification. His is rather an asceticism of the will, a compliance and abandonment to the divine will realized in the minute and hidden details of everyday life.

Also forming Francis' notion of the spiritual life is the Renaissance tradition of *l'honnête homme* (the upright person), the person who appears to others as gracious, well-spoken, cultured and possessed of reasoned good sense. He believed that to achieve full human potential one must live well, in all senses of the word. In his mind, this living well had at its center a strong and consciously cultivated love of God. The fabled *douceur* (gentleness or graciousness) for which de Sales is so often remembered emerges from the tradition of *l'honnête homme*. His gracious cordiality was not merely a veneer but an outward reflection of an inner reality made possible because at its core was a person in a state of utmost liberty and at peace in God.[6]

All this lies in the background of the Order of the Visitation of Holy Mary and informs its charism. Throughout its various institutional phases it had as its special characteristic its hidden life of abandonment, its loving,

---

[5] De Sales' vision of this loving God is most clearly expressed in his *Traité de l'Amour de Dieu* found in *Oeuvres de Saint François de Sales, Evêque de Genève et Docteur de l'Eglise, Edition Complète,* d'après les autographes et les éditions originales . . . publiée par les soins des Religieuses de la Visitation du Premier Monastère d'Annecy (Annecy: J. Nierat et al., 1892-1964), Tome 5. English translation, *Treatise on the Love of God,* 2 vols., trans. John K. Ryan (Rockford: TAN, 1974). Elsewhere I have analyzed this Salesian vision of the loving God in terms of the imagery of the heart: "'That Is What It Is Made For': The Image of the Heart in the Spirituality of Francis de Sales and Jane de Chantal," in *Spiritualities of the Heart,* ed. Annice Callahan, R.S.C.J. (Mahwah, NJ: Paulist, 1990): 143-58.

[6] For a thorough discussion of de Sales as humanist see E. J. LaJeunie, O.P., *Saint François de Sales: L'homme, la pensée, l'action,* 2 vols. (Paris: Editions, Guy Victor, 1964), English trans. by Rory O'Sullivan, O.S.F.S., *Saint Francis de Sales: The Man, The Thinker, His Influence,* 2 vols. (Banglagore, India: S.F.S., 1986-87): esp. 25-29, 42-60; and Bremond's *Histoire littéraire,* vol. 1, *L'Humanisme dévote.*

unobtrusive and interior surrender to the will of God.[7] The sisters were to live Jesus, to become daughters of prayer. But they were to do so without the heroic exercises of mortification that usually accompanied the contemplative life. They were called, rather, to do the asceticism of living in community, to great gentleness and sisterly devotion. The relational gesture, the patient response: these were to be their mortifications. Jane de Chantal wrote to one of her community to describe the life and to exhort her sister in religion to embody and pass on the Visitandine charism:

> Go simply about your duties, my dear daughter. Do not be embittered or chagrined by insignificant things that count for so little in eternity. Live in your house with perfect gentleness, affection and love, happy to be so fortunate as to prepare a retreat for souls who are forever praising His divine majesty. . . . Try to establish solidly the spirit of the Visitation which aims at a perfection as excellent as it is hidden. It is none other than the death of nature and of the "old man" in order to establish firmly the reign of grace. This is the perfection to which we aspire. You know well that the perfection of the Visitation is not founded on extraordinary things, but on the solid and true virtues: true humility, gentle charity, affectionate mutual support, prompt and simple obedience, artlessness and sincerity toward one's superior, frank admission of our faults, tranquil modesty, pleasant and devout conversation, and attentiveness to the holy presence of God (*Sa Vie* VIII, 5, 605-6).

In this hidden, gentle life of mutual charity the women bound by the rules of the order were to realize their deep love of God. Francis de Sales saw them as "March violets," small unobtrusive flowers hidden among the luxuriant garden comprised of the more visibly austere orders of the Church.

The way of the Visitation was deeply marked by de Sales. As such, it belonged to the wider world of Christian humanism, a tradition in which the bishop was trained and steeped. This is seen especially in the community's assumptions about the education and character development of women. In the tradition of *l'honnête homme*, the ideal qualities of women as well as men were delineated, if in a subordinate manner. The education of women in the Renaissance tradition was primarily an affair of moral shaping, not of intellectual pursuit for its own sake. While there are a number of accounts of the accomplishments of learned women that stand out in the historical annals of Renaissance Italy and France, the general picture that emerges from treatises circulating at the time indicates that women's education consisted in the inculcation of the moral qualities

---

[7] Dom Robert Lemoine succinctly charts the transition of the Visitation from congregation to Order in *Le Droit des réligieux du Concile de Trente aux instituts séculiers* (Paris: Desclee de Brouwer, 1956): 183-200.

considered necessary to female innocence: humility, simplicity, modesty, piety, patience, and obedience.[8]   These same qualities came to be incorporated into the Order of the Visitation as its own specific charism, the mode of piety and personal deportment that made the order distinctive. Francis and Jane referred to these characteristics as the "little" virtues. Looked at from this perspective, the charism of the Visitation was very "feminine." Its actualization involved the conscious cultivation of traits that were found among the list of Christian virtues. But it was to be a selective cultivation. Other virtues esteemed as preeminently Christian, but more typically (in the view of the era) "masculine"—such as courage, fortitude, or justice—while not absent from the articulated ideals of Salesian spirituality, were subordinated to their more feminine counterparts.

Indeed, seen in this light, Francis de Sales' entire vision of Christian perfection was thoroughly "feminine." The Genevan prelate did not limit his prescription of these virtues to women (although in his practice of spiritual direction he did mainly guide women), but made the little virtues a hallmark of his own spiritual posture, encouraging their development in all to whom he preached.[9]

Jane de Chantal and the Spirit of the Visitation

The actual direction practiced in the Visitation does then owe a great deal to the spirit of its founder, Francis de Sales. However, the specific forms it took do not derive solely from him. For it was the person of Jane de Chantal, with her particular personality and range of life experiences, who, within the shared framework of Salesian spirituality, brought the community to birth. She brought to vowed religious life 38 years of lived experience "in the world." Daughter, wife, mother of four, mistress of her

---

[8] Cf. Phyllis Stock, *Better Than Rubies: A History of Women's Education* (New York: G.P. Putnam's Sons, 1978): 29-40. The Renaissance and the Reformation were periods in Western culture that saw the development of women's education. There were a number of stated reasons for this: to instill moral character, to raise male children more conscientiously, to be suitable companions to learned men, to encourage authentic piety. While there were champions of women's intellectual equality, for the most part the motives underlying women's education were, by modern standards, questionable. See Paul Rousselot, *Histoire de l'éducation des femmes en France* (New York: Lenox Hills Publ. Burt Franklin, 1971. Orig. pub. 1883); Georges Snyders, *La Pédagogie en France aux XVIIe et XVIIIe siecles* (Paris: Presses Universitaires de France, 1965); and Gabriel Compayre, *Histoire critique des doctrines de l'éducation en France depuis le seizieme siècle* (Genève: Slatkine Reprints, 1970. Orig. pub. 1879).

[9] On the little virtues see Wright and Power, eds., *Letters of Spiritual Direction*, 62-69, and my "The Hidden Life of the Gentle Humble Jesus: The Visitation of Holy Mary as Ideal Women's Community," in *Vox Benedictina* (Spring, 1991).

husband's baronial estates, widow: she had been all of these before her entrance into religion.

In the first several years of the community's existence, it is true, Francis de Sales' influence was supreme. He, as Jane's own spiritual director and the father-founder of the institute, had much to do with shaping the direction the Visitation would take, especially through the writing of the Rules and Constitutions. Yet, in the day-to-day running of the house, and, as time went on, in the shared operation of the institute, it was Jane's voice that was most clearly heard. Hers was a voice modulated by her intimacy with the great Bishop, but one essentially her own. In its music one can distinctly hear her own personality: her ardent love of God, her passionate devotion to friends and family, her unswerving fidelity to the particular path on which she felt God was leading her. One also hears the resonance of her life's experience: the maternal attentiveness fashioned in the many years spent tending her own and others' children, and the sensitivity to diverse personalities that experience brought. Furthermore, after Francis' death in 1622 and as new foundations were made (there were over eighty by the time of her death in 1642), it was Jane de Chantal's vision and her direction of the daughters of the institute that became formative.[10]

Direction of the Daughters of the Visitation

It will be helpful to search Jane's letters for evidence about the way she approached the task of direction. Apparent at first is the fact that in her understanding, spiritual direction is not an isolated method aimed primarily at the "spiritual" or "inner" part of the person. Although the distinction between inner and outer is maintained, Jane de Chantal's direction is oriented toward the whole person. Because theirs was a monastic context, the Visitation sisters strove to reform their lives entirely, giving themselves—inner and outer, soul and body—to the perfection of life in Christ which they understood to be surrender to the will of God. Within this world, direction is a holistic undertaking. So Jane understood her task to be the transformation of her charges' lives.[11]

---

[10] See Wright and Power, eds., *Letters of Spiritual Direction*, 70-86 for a discussion of Jane's unique internalization of the Salesian charism. Consult as well my "The Martyrdom of Love," in *Salesian Living Heritage* (Spring 1990): 13-23; and "Two Faces of Christ: Jeanne de Chantal," in *Peaceweavers*, vol. 2 of *Medieval Religious Women*, ed. Lillian Thomas Shank and John A. Nichols (Kalamazoo: Cistercian, 1987): 335-64.

[11] Cf. Wright and Power, eds., *Letters of Spiritual Direction*, 13-17.

She accomplished this task one on one and also by addressing herself specifically to the superiors and novice mistresses of the burgeoning order, seeking to instill in them the particular spirit of the Visitation charism as well as the specific precepts that they were enjoined to follow in their Rule and Constitutions. From the superiors of the order she expected an attitude of motherly attentiveness, the kind of care and solicitude for each candidate that a mother might show her own child. To a superior at Belley she wrote:

> Well, God be eternally praised, my dearest daughter, for there you are now—mother! I beg his divine goodness to give you the spirit that is proper to spiritual mothers who, with a tender and cordial love, see to the advancement of souls, and who are never rushed, especially about temporal matters. The trust they place in the providence and love of their Spouse relieves them of all kinds of anxieties and makes them confident that He will see to all their needs, provided that they try to please Him by a perfect observance and by a trust in His goodness. That's the disposition I want for you, dearest; I can assure you that it will bring you many blessings (*Sa Vie* V, 2, 57-58).

In this attentive concern and abandonment to providence, one sees, in practice, the Salesian emphasis on charity as a prime virtue. In the injunction not to be anxious about temporal concerns are heard echoes of the detachment so central to the Genevan Bishop's spirituality. All of this is carried out with the foundress' own maternal tenderness. Very aware of the importance of a nurturing presence while raising children, she insists that her superiors also attend in person to the raising of their "children." To another superior she wrote:

> To this end, as I'm always telling you, dearest, you must keep yourself free of too many preoccupations so that, insofar as your obligations allow, you can be with your sisters whenever they are assembled together, in order to instruct them and encourage them in the performance of their duties, as much by your example as by precept (*Sa Vie* IV, 1, 55-56).

Being mother meant for Jane de Chantal not only solicitude in a general way, but an affectionate allowance for the shortcomings of those under her care:

> I exhort you, my dearest daughter, to encourage them [the novices] to advance in their love of their heavenly Spouse as much as you can, but do it with a spirit of gentleness, patience, and charity, which will in turn help you shoulder all their little weaknesses—their negligence, tardiness,and failings—without ever being surprised so that their perfect confidence in you might never be disturbed (*Sa Vie* IV, 1, 198).

And while it was required that faults be noted and that advancement in virtue be cultivated, the way in which this would be undertaken must never be so judgmental that those under tutelage would be discouraged or intimidated:

> Yes, it is not wise to reprimand the sisters for every little fault. The mind grows weary of that and gets so used to it that gradually it becomes insensitive to correction. When a correction must be made, it is better to put it off a little and to make it graciously in private (*Sa Vie* IV, 1, 180).

Sustaining all this maternal care was the very real belief that this most attractive of methods would best draw the sisters into a loving relationship with God. They were to be attracted to this vocation in a manner that had less to do with rational arguments than with affective response. Jane wrote in 1621:

> In the name of God, my dear daughter, wait for the improvement of these good sisters with great patience, and bear with them gently. Treat their hearts affectionately, making them see their own faults without undue emotion or strong feelings or harshness, but so that through your help they will be encouraged to overcome them and still remain enamored of your maternal sweetness. This is the matchless way to win souls, and it is characteristically ours (*Sa Vie* IV, 1, 555-56).

Liberty of Spirit and Asceticism

The lack of coercion or authoritarianism in these methods of direction proposed by the foundress of the Visitation aimed at focusing the soul toward God in a spirit of absolute liberty and conscious choice. From the Salesian point of view, this free and loving human response to the divine call was essential to an authentic spiritual orientation. For God was understood to address humankind in just this loving, non-coercive way, desiring human cooperation with grace, but not demanding it.

While the pervasive attitude of Visitation direction is one of gentleness and liberality, it is anything but a careless or undemanding form of spiritual discipline. Underneath the gentleness there lies a radical insistence on absolute surrender to the will of God realized in the ordinary facts of everyday life. With such an expectation at its core, self-indulgence and excessive leniency are unacceptable. Yet, most essential, in Jane's eyes, was the avoidance of extremes in a director's approach. Zealousness and excessive austerity were to be avoided. Both ran counter to the spirit of gentleness central to the Salesian enterprise. With remarkable insight into the dynamics of personality, Jane wrote to a sister in Paris:

> Your letter has made me see the state of your soul very clearly as well as
> the source of your trouble and what impedes you. This comes simply from
> your impatience to find the true good you so desire, and from your lack of
> patience and submission to the will of Him who alone can give it to you.
> Now if you really want to acquire the spirit of our vocation, you must
> correct your eagerness to find the true good you so desire, and with a
> gentle spirit do faithfully what is taught to bring you to the place you
> should be, suspending all desires and thoughts of your getting there except
> when it is God's will to allow you the grace to have them. It seems to me
> that you are not content to perform the actions required for your
> perfection, but that you want to have the feeling and knowledge that you
> have done them. It is these you must suppress and be content. . . (*Sa Vie*
> IV, 1, 433-34).

Like impatience, excessive austerity was, in the foundress' eyes,
counter to the spirit of the Visitation of Holy Mary. As a recurrent theme
among her letters one can find the assertion that superiors with too much
ascetic zeal end by destroying the Visitation charism as well as their own
and their sisters' health:

> In the name of our divine Savior, I beg you and urge you to govern
> according to His spirit and that of our vocation, which is a humble, gentle
> spirit, supportive and considerate of all. In order to govern in this manner,
> my dear, you must not act according to the strength of your natural spirit,
> nor according to your inclinations which lean in the direction of austerity.
> What we are asking of you, my daughter, and without further delay,
> please, is to be most gentle in thought, word, and action, and to treat your
> own body and those of your sisters in a more kindly manner than you are
> in the habit of doing.
>
> What good does it do to put bread on the table for someone who doesn't
> have teeth that can chew it or a stomach that can digest it? So, without
> stalling any longer, let me emphasize once again that we do not want to
> hear any more talk about your gruffness and severity with the sisters and
> yourself. Your minds and bodies will be wrecked if you absolutely refuse
> to accept humbly what we are saying (*Sa Vie* V, 2, 513-14).

Fidelity to the Rule

The Visitation spirit, Jane de Chantal was convinced, was embodied
in the Rule which had been written for the Institute by Francis de Sales.
She deemed it the one sure touchstone for a Visitandine novice who was to
be assimilated into the charism by an absolute fidelity to the Rule in all its
detail. To the novices of the Visitation in Bourges, she wrote in 1619:

> May the holy peace of Our Lord be among you, my dear daughters! This
> is the blessing I wish for you, by which all our spirits united in one single
> vocation will be perfected. Yes, my dear daughters, I wish you to have only
> one heart and one soul. You have only one task, to unite yourselves to

> God by your complete observance of the same Rule. You must have only
> one will and one judgment, which is the will and judgment of your
> superior, whom you must allow to direct you without any resistance. If you
> do this, you will be very happy (*Sa Vie* IV, 1, 168.)

Over and over again in her instructions to novices, one sees Jane's
insistence on absolute fidelity to the Rule. Within the context of any other
spiritual milieu this strict observance might approach legalistic rigidity.
However, within a Salesian world in which liberty of spirit is uppermost, a
happy balance between obedience and individual freedom is maintained.
Superiors are entrusted with the task of seeing that not only are the rules
diligently followed, but that they are being followed without any experience
of constraint or oppression:

> I beg you, my dear sister, govern your community with a great
> expansiveness of heart: give the sisters a holy liberty of spirit, and banish
> from your mind and theirs a servile spirit of constraint. If a sister seems to
> lack confidence in you, don't for that reason show her the least coldness,
> but gain her trust through love and kindness. . . . The more solicitous,
> open, and supportive you are with them, the more you will win their
> hearts.   This is the best way of helping them advance toward the
> perfection of their vocation (*Sa Vie* VIII, 5, 557).

The issue of this faithful observance should be a wide-reaching and
joyous faith, as Jane makes clear in a rapturous passage:

> O my dear daughter, if you read and practice our Rules faithfully, how
> happy you will be! They will heal us of everything. This is our path; we
> travel on it, never turning aside no matter what trouble might befall us. If
> we search this little book well, we will find every remedy in it. Go forward
> joyously and do not consider whether you have insight or knowledge or the
> like. Be content that Our Lord is rich in all gifts and grace. Love these in
> Him and do not desire any of them for yourself. Blessed are the poor in
> spirit! Oh! what great wealth to want nothing but God. Our happiness
> consists in this (*Sa Vie* VIII, 5, 602)!

Jane de Chantal's repeated insistence on utter conformity to the
Rule derives in part from her own personal attitude of unswerving loyalty
and fidelity.   In greater part, it derives from the wider atmosphere of
Catholic Reformation piety. One of the central directives of the Council of
Trent to men and women living the monastic life was to return to a faithful
observance of the primitive Rule they professed to follow.[12]   For many
older orders, by this time decadent in their practices, this meant a
thoroughgoing reform. For new communities, like the Visitation, punctual
and specific regular observance was likewise of paramount value. In the

---

[12] Decree on Regulars and Nuns, Council of Trent, Session 25.

Salesian context, this observance was given emphasis as a type of interior asceticism. The more visible contemplative orders —notably the Carmelites who were then enjoying a vogue in French society—relied greatly upon physical austerities to spur their members on to religious perfection. Since the Visitation shunned the use of many penitential techniques, it relied for its asceticism upon the ordinary means available in everyday life: a simple surrender of the will to the specifics of the circumstances in which one found oneself. For the nuns of the Visitation of Holy Mary, absolute observance of the Rule of the Institute became the means of their self-emptying and thus their perfection. To the community at Annecy, Jane wrote in 1619:

> Let us have in our hearts only the single desire for His holy love and in our actions only obedience and submission to His pleasure by an exact observance of the Rules, not only for their exterior value but more so for their interior good: this sweet cordiality among ourselves, the sacred recollection of our hearts into His divine Majesty's heart, the true humility and sincerity which makes us simple, supple, and pliant as little lambs and finally the loving union of all our hearts which produces peace (*Sa Vie* V, 2, 365).

So deep was this perfection through the Rule to reach that the superiors of the Order were to become "Living Rules." They were to incarnate the spirit found in the letter of the Rule and become for their spiritual daughters teachers by example:

> My very dear daughter . . . I pray God that He will take you under His holy protection and lavish upon you the perfect spirit of our Rules, so that by this work His divine majesty might be glorified and our neighbor edified. . . May all your daughters be Living Rules and may they carry in their hearts and on their faces only gentleness, modesty, and sweetness along with a holy joy which shows how freely they are cooperating in this holy work (*Sa Vie* IV, 294).

Difficult Souls

The hopeful foundress painted thus an ideal representation of a Visitation community: superiors, themselves surrendered to embody perfectly the spirit of the Institute as realized in its Rules, leading and guiding, with great sisterly affection and maternal attentiveness, a household of women likewise united in heart and mind in a spirit of abundant *douceur* (gentleness). In practice, the historical record often resembles more a canvas in progress than a finished work. Yet Jane de Chantal had a genius for spiritual direction which made that continuing work a viable and commendable one. Her genius is most evident in her letters of advice concerning "difficult souls" or personalities that did not easily conform themselves to the Visitation model of religious perfection. Here she shows herself adept in the art of dealing with many types of individuals, and here the fruits of her life's experience as mother and householder are plainly displayed.

Like her daughters in religion, not all of Jane's biological children conformed to the "March violet" image of personal demeanor. Her oldest and her youngest daughters (her second and fourth children) were in the Visitandine mold: sweet-tempered, pliant, inclined to piety. Her eldest offspring and only son, as well as her middle daughter, were of another ilk: impetuous, headstrong, and both inclined in their youth to "worldly" tastes.[13] These four different personalities gave Jane an opportunity to deal firsthand with a variety of temperaments and to learn to love and guide them each in his or her own way. In her letters is abundant evidence of her facility for perceiving the dynamics of varied personalities and for releasing the potential latent in each. She is especially maternal and lenient toward the youthful novices:

> Yes, it would be charitable to indulge our poor Sister N__ because she has a good, gentle heart. We must have great patience with the novices and do all that we can to set [their spirits] free. But we must never let them be nourished in their own self-centered will (*Sa Vie* IV, 1, 321).

She likewise inclines charitably toward beginners who are prone to specific emotional and temperamental difficulties:

> Goodness, my dear daughter, how touched I am when I see souls decline like that! They still are good at bottom, but they are so despondent that they are to be pitied. I know that your good heart never forgets to help revive them. The example of your affectionate maternal love will profit them greatly (*Sa Vie* VIII, 5, 193).

Another time she writes:

> What can we do, my dearest Sister, but support these sorts of [suspicious] personalities with great patience and gentleness, trying to uproot those suspicions from their hearts by our cordiality and sincere affection for them. Our blessed Father once told me that when submission and humility fail in these spirits, our charity must incline to their infirmity, giving them what they want. But this must be done dexterously so that they don't notice it and know that we are condescending to them, but only see that we are loving them. Then, when they have been healed by our

---

[13] The classic study of Jane's daughters is Ctesse. Alexandre de Menthon, *Les Deux Filles de Sainte Chantal* (Annecy: Monastère de la Visitation, 1913).

condescension and have been given the confidence that they are loved, one can deal with them as one would wish (*Sa Vie* VIII, 5, 567).

As abundant as her maternal solicitude was, Jane de Chantal nevertheless exercised shrewd discrimination when it came to discerning which types of personalities would do well in the Visitation and which would not:

> The effects of this good sister candidate's frivolousness are unpleasant and of consequence. Note that the Rule singles out this condition of frivolousness as a legitimate cause for turning an applicant away. So that if, given time, she does not change, I don't think it would be wise to keep her, especially if she is a girl who has reached the age of 20 or 22. There is then little chance she would lose this weakness (*Sa Vie* VI, 3, 227-28).

About an aspirant who had applied to the monastery at Montferrand, she advised:

> And so, you say, this widow has a strong will, shows great concern about her health, has a mind full of excuses, and a desire to know everything. Heavens, dear, she must be awfully busy! That's why, in my opinion, you should talk at length with her, all the while trying to bring about her healing by gradually pointing out her maladies without shocking her. . . . Tell her not to get discouraged. If, however, she is receptive to the light you are trying to bring her, . . . if she undertakes really to desire to serve God by a perfect observance of these words of Our Lord's—"gentle and humble of heart"—which permeate our Rules, she will some day be a great servant of His and promote His glory. But she must make a firm resolution and have a clear understanding of her faults; otherwise, she will be disturbed and will disturb the house (*Sa Vie* IV, 1, 598-99).

Advanced Souls

Jane's directions for novices reflected their youth and inexperience.[14] Through maternal attention she drew them into the atmosphere of a Christian love that was both attractive and demanding. As they progressed in virtue and the spirit of *douceur* (gentleness), the Visitandines were asked to conform more and more to the divine will. While gracious in their approach, her letters to those more advanced in their lives in religion challenged them to the heights of detachment and self-denial. One such

---

[14] Although the Visitation was designed for women in any age group and encouraged the entrance of widows, in practice most entrants were youthful. Cf. Roger Devos, *Vie religieuse féminine et societé: Les Visitandines d'Annecy aux XVIIe et XVIIIe siecles* (Annecy: Memoires et documents publiés par l'Académie Salésienne, Tome LXXXIV, 1973).

missive to an unknown superior who wished to humble herself by becoming a domestic sister shows as much:

> My dearest daughter, it would be out of the question for me to flatter you or treat you too delicately since you place so much trust in me and allow me to speak freely. I think that Our Lord has given you a spirit that can overcome its strong natural inclinations, worthy as these may seem to be. To move beyond them is the greatest sacrifice you can make to the Lord.
>
> As for that old hankering of yours to be a domestic sister, take my word for it, our blessed Father's advice to "ask for nothing and refuse nothing" is far superior to this desire of yours or any other self-chosen practice of humility. I admit that God surely wants you to be most humble, but in the way He chooses, and not according to your fancy. So make good use of the low self-esteem you feel, or the scorn or the false accusations of others. God, in His providence, permits these things to happen, and you may be certain that they are the means by which you will acquire the kind of solid humility that he wants you to have (*Sa Vie* VII, 5, 651-52).

The direction given by Jane de Chantal with its maternal tenderness, its *douceur* and its sensitivity to individual difference reflects her own experience as wife and mother as well as the influence of Renaissance humanist values that her mentor and friend, Francis de Sales, sought to establish in the community. But to see the uniqueness of the Visitation charism it might be useful to compare its practices with practices encouraged in other women's communities of the time.

Feminine Pedagogy

The Visitation and its foundress were very much at one with other Catholic Reformation women's communities in their vision of radical religious perfection and the singlemindedness with which this was pursued. This period is notable for its notable women: Madame Acarie was spearheading the effort to introduce the Teresian Carmel onto French soil; Angelique Arnauld was absorbed in the demanding task of reforming the Cistercian Abbey of Port Royal; and Louise de Marillac was giving her life over to the effort of founding, along with Vincent de Paul, the Daughters of Charity. These and other contemporary women worked with an enthusiasm that matched Madame de Chantal's.[15] Religious seriousness and heroism were in the air and are enfleshed in these women's stories.

---

[15] The number of foundations established for women in France during the seventeenth century is remarkable. Of congregations erected between 1600 and 1690 for the education of impoverished children alone, one can count upwards of twenty. Cf. Rousselot, *Histoire de l'éducation*, 300ff.

Yet each of these stories is different. To see in what ways Madame de Chantal's Visitation is distinctive and in what ways the spiritual direction practiced therein is in keeping with contemporary French women's communities, it may be helpful to glance at some of the educational perspectives held by several of these, particularly the Canonesses of St. Augustine, the Ursulines, and the religious of Port Royal. There are a number of reasons why it might be helpful to evaluate the direction of Visitandine women by comparisons with other pedagogical methods of the day. First, the education and shaping of the female population of Europe was traditionally the preserve of monasteries. Long past the time when their male counterparts had left monastic environs and were receiving instruction in Cathedral schools and universities, young girls continued to be taught by nuns.[16] In the broad period we are concerned with, this tradition was just beginning to break down. There are some Renaissance examples of noble women educated by tutors in the home with their brothers, and the rising middle class emulated this practice. Jane de Chantal herself appears to have received most of her educational instruction in her own father's house and in the household of her older sister and brother-in-law. Yet women's formal education still remained primarily the work of religious women, either in monastic settings or in teaching congregations. There is thus a strong correlation between the view of personal development held by women religious and the way the majority of Europe's educated women were brought up.

Second, the correlation between pedagogy and religious formation of women was affirmed by the era's assumption that the education of women was primarily a matter of moral instruction, not one of intellectual cultivation. This assumption underlies the depiction of the ideal woman reflected in the Renaissance tradition of the *l'honnête homme*.[17] However, the spirit of Renaissance humanism does seem to have infused itself into the practices surrounding the education of females. One breathes a more "humane" air in the educational methods practiced by many of the new women's congregations, especially in their emphasis on persuasion and example as means of direction. This trend parallels the trend in Renaissance education of men, exemplified especially in the Jesuit tradition.[18] While the questions raised by these assertions ideally would call

---

[16] Stock, *Better Than Rubies*, 24.

[17] Cf. note 8.

[18] On the evolution of European pedagogy, see Georges Snyders, *La Pédagogie en France*. On the Jesuit methods of education which forbade chastising of students,

for more detailed study, they can stand as background for a brief glance at some of the pedagogy found in women's communities contemporary with the Visitation.

The Canonesses of St. Augustine and the Ursulines were groups founded in the wake of the reform movements sweeping the Church. They were both established for the purpose of educating poor girls, and, like the Visitation in its original form, were simple congregations that functioned without cloister or formal vows.[19] Port Royal was a monastic community of medieval origins, Cistercian in affiliation and recently reformed under the auspices of Mere Angelique Arnauld.   Like the Visitation in its final incarnation, it was a strictly cloistered environment focused in both its intent and methods on the cultivation of the contemplative life.

All three groups occupied themselves with the education of young women between the ages of four and sixteen. The Canonesses and the Ursulines were concerned with the daughters of the poor, most of whom were preparing for life "in the world," who would adopt the traditional female roles of wife and mother. At Port Royal, poor girls as well as the daughters of the wealthy were boarded. Some of these would return to the world and a good many would remain in the cloister.[20]

One distinction between the modern congregations and the older monastic foundation must be drawn. The latter was firmly bound to the cloistered, contemplative life and its form of piety while the former were less bound, both in institutional structure and in educational purposes. They were also more imbued with the "humane" spirit evident in the educational theories of Christian humanists. Thus the differences that appear in the pedagogical styles employed.

These three examples include the range of contemporary feminine pedagogy, bounded as it was, on the one hand, by the traditional assessment of women as requiring a specific type of education appropriate to their "weak" nature and gender-defined roles and, on the other, by the period's pervasive enthusiasm for feminine education.

"mildness and charity," refrained from insults and encouraged emulation, see Pierre Janelle, *The Catholic Reformation* (Milwaukee: Bruce, 1963): 127-130.

[19] The Ursulines, like the Visitandines, eventually underwent an organizational mutation. The issue of claustration was central to their development. The group was enclosed by papal decree in 1612, but "primitive" Ursuline communities continued for some time afterwards. See Stock, *Better Than Rubies*, 74ff.

[20] Parents sending their daughters to Port Royal were required to submit to the condition that they remain indifferent to the vocational choice of their offspring. Education in the convent itself was strongly biased to dispose girls to choose religious life. Rousselot, *Histoire de l'éducation*, 335.

Specific Pedagogical Methods—The Canonesses of St. Augustine

The founder of the Canonesses of St. Augustine, Pierre Fourier, envisioned his instructresses as:

> healthy in body and spirit, of good humor, courage, good will and filled with a great zeal to bear the weariness incurred by this holy work. They should be perfectly humble, patient, modest, obedient, industrious, discreet, devout, and fervent. . . . Their ministry is that of a neighbor, or companion, and is joined to the ministration of the girls' guardian angels.[21]

Fourier exhorted his teachers to a style of guidance that was unusually mild and kindly for the era, judging from the educational approach against which he inveighed:

> The teachers should not show any sign of anger or impatience or disdain, not vexing or offending those girls who have trouble understanding. They should not call them asses, beasts, stupid or bad girls. They should not raise their voices around them nor beat or strike them, nor should they shove them or dismiss them rudely. They should instead use patience and gentleness, making allowances for them by encouraging them highly.[22]

To fit the young charges for their stations in life, they were taught those things that would help them live well: "the catechism, loving virtue, good works and Christian morals, courtesy and decorum, reading, writing, arithmetic, sewing and the arts deemed proper for girls."[23] In both the method and content of the pedagogy envisioned by Pierre Fourier, one sees a representative example of the spirit of religious humanism as applied to the female sex.

The Ursulines

Another contemporary community founded with the intention of educating the daughters of the poor, the Ursulines, exhibits the same humane spirit. Life in an Ursuline boarding school was formal but not rigorous. Classes were limited to thirty-five students and allowed for special instruction in smaller groups. Time was provided for recreation. The subjects taught included the rudiments of reading and writing as well as practical skills needed for managing a household. Discipline was moderate. In an age when beating children was common, the Ursulines reserved it for extreme cases. Ursuline nuns adopted a maternal attitude

---

[21] Quoted in Ibid., 325.
[22] Ibid.
[23] Ibid., 326.

toward their students and attempted to re-create the life of a family in their schools.[24]

Both Canonesses and Ursulines were markedly modern in spirit and attitudes toward the education and guidance of women. Similarly these communities were modern in their institutional structure. They were originally established as congregations, not as formal orders, a fact which allowed the members the flexibility of movement needed to devote themselves to their apostolic work.[25] One can clearly see from these examples that the Visitandines were not alone in their gentle motherly approach to feminine guidance. But with Jane de Chantal, this approach seems to have been raised to an art form. Under her watchful and experienced eye, what was a general disposition in these contemporary religious communities became a full-fledged spirituality articulated and worked out in monastic life.

The Cistercians at Port Royal

Port Royal, also contemporary with the Visitation, was a traditional monastic community that had been deeply influenced by the reforming spirit manifesting itself in France.[26] Yet there remains a contrast, as evidenced in the educational principles laid down in the *Constitutions*, between the spirit of feminine direction practiced at Port Royal and at the Visitation.

First, it should be noted that the approach used at Port Royal for the upbringing of girls must be distinguished from that employed for young men in the same institution. Port Royal had schools for boys, *les petites écoles*, that, in the eyes of one researcher, were infused with the spirit of the humanistic Renaissance through the reform of rigid educational practices and the introduction of new pedagogical principles as well as through a liberal attitude toward discipline.[27] The *petites écoles* were designed to prepare boys for a variety of vocations in the world.

The young women attached to Port Royal did not enjoy quite the same experience as their masculine counterparts. Females remained very much under the monastic aegis, with the pious atmosphere of an austere contemplative life permeating their day. Instruction was almost entirely religious in character. The regime of daily life at Port Royal was

---

[24] See Stock, *Better Than Rubies*, 76-77.

[25] Cf. note 16.

[26] On Port Royal see F. Ellen Weaver, *The Evolution of the Reform of Port Royal: From the Rule of Citeaux to Jansenism* (Paris: Beauchesne, 1978).

[27] Compayre, *Histoire critique*, 246ff.

demanding: prayer, recitation of the divine office, devotional reading, absolute silence, instruction in religious matters, seriousness of demeanor, discouragement of levity and playfulness, exactitude of observance. The atmosphere was that of the cloister that strips away all worldly pretensions and attachments in order to dispose the soul to a life of self-denial and interior prayer. As might be expected, discipline was more stringent than in the newer congregations.

Yet the vision of how the students should be guided was not unyielding in its severity. In the *Constitutions* written by Jacqueline Pascal, one detects a humane intent:

> They [the students] must be treated with civility and spoken to with respect and yielded to as much as possible. It is good to sometimes stoop to their level in things that in themselves are unimportant so that their hearts might be won.[28]

There is respect here and a modification of the severity often attributed to the Jansenist spirit that came to pervade Port Royal as the century progressed. At the same time there is a reserve in the *Constitutions* about expressions of familiarity and affection as well as about confidences between teacher and pupils. And while there is lightening of the austere physical regime for younger girls and flexibility in the administration of punishment for offenses of various kinds, still there is a quality of attentiveness and care in the professed educational spirit of Port Royal, as the following passage demonstrates:

> Our example is the greatest instruction that could be given to them. The devil gives them a memory of our least faults, and he deprives them of any memory of any little good we might have done. That is why we must pray to God to humble us greatly and be ever watchful of ourselves to perform our duty toward those children. . . . We must put all our confidence in God and by our pleas cause Him to grant that which we do not merit by ourselves. . . . We must always regard these little souls as sacred deposits that He has confided to us and for which we must render accounts. That is why we must speak less to them than to God for them.[29]

The Visitandines

Port Royal and the Visitation were alike in their contemplative orientation and in the earnestness with which they undertook to form young women for a life of Christian prayer. In both cases the approach was

---

[28] Quoted in Rousselot, *Histoire de l'éducation*, 339.
[29] Ibid., 347.

tailored for those destined for cloistered life.[30]   However, a contrast between the spirits of the two communities is discernible. Perhaps this spirit is not so clearly discovered in what is articulated about the guidance of women as in how that guidance is viewed. Both Jane de Chantal and Jacqueline Pascal argue for an approach that honors civility and a certain leniency as formative principles. Both women proceed from a profound sense of personal responsibility and high calling. But the anthropological assumptions behind these two mother superiors' words make for a striking difference.

In Jane's motherliness there is an optimism and a real appreciation of the value of human effort. It is in *community* that Visitandine *douceur* springs to life, and the love of God that the sisters profess is actualized in human relationships, not apart from them. The charism of the visitation of Holy Mary is truly a relational one, one in which the congregation's motto—"Live Jesus!"—is realized between persons in the sensitive gesture or the compassionate word.

At Port Royal, on the other hand, the theological currents flowing there provide a certain devaluation of human effort and relationships and encourage a single-minded focus on the divine, not the human, domain. There is a selfless giving in the direction envisioned by Jacqueline Pascal, but a shying away from the maternal involvement, sense of identity and unreserved affection that one feels in the writings of Jane de Chantal.

Direction in the Visitation

One can claim with reasonable certainty that, like her contemporaries among the Ursulines and the Canonesses, Jane de Chantal guided her charges in the spirit of humanism, forming them by her own example to a life of perfected Christian womanhood that was gracious, gentle, obedient, and full of charitable concern. Yet her own motherly experience rendered her capable of practicing the art of maternal direction with great sensitivity, taking her beyond her contemporaries in her practice of the art. Like her counterparts at Port Royal, she seriously pursued the goal of the contemplative life: transformation of her daughters' lives to conform to the divine will. But unlike her sisters at Port Royal, Jane did not eschew the intimate familiarity of motherhood and the attachments and attitude of identity that motherhood brings. She encouraged just such an intimacy

---

[30] However, in both cases this was not an exclusive orientation. At Port Royal some of the students would choose life in the world and at the Visitation the piety was seen, in principle if not in specifics, as applicable to people in the world.

among the members of the Visitation. While her "spiritual conversations" do warn against the misuse of familiarity when it disrupts community, forms factions, and impedes the harmonious functioning of the whole,[31] Jane consciously cultivated a maternal and relational style of direction.

Her own personal contribution to this style must not be underrated.[32] While it is nourished by Frances de Sales' spirit and forms a part of the wider atmosphere of Christian humanism, her direction of women demonstrates the influence of her personal experience. Deftly Jane de Chantal moved among her spiritual daughters, discerning their strengths and weaknesses, inclining to them not simply out of responsibility, but out of love that regarded each girl, each novice, each Visitandine in her uniqueness and encouraged each in her development. It is the specificity of her love for each sister, the sense of familial warmth that she exuded and which she urged on all her mother superiors that was Jane's gift. This gift was purchased at the price of biological motherhood, and earned in the long years of patient parenting that fell to her alone after her husband's death. It was the gift that she gave, as a method of direction, to the religious order that she founded.

A Contemporary Perspective

These assertions could be more fully explored. But it might also be profitable to shed some light on Jane's direction of women from a twentieth century perspective. From this vantage point, the question that emerges is whether the specific mode of direction practiced in the Visitation of Holy Mary was or is in any way uniquely suited to women and whether it encouraged (or encourages) their development. It has been shown that Visitandine direction both differed from and paralleled other styles practiced in contemporary French houses for women, and that it drew its nurturant spirit in part from current humanistic practice and in part from the maternal experience of its foundress. It should also be noted that the Visitation was unique among women's contemplative orders (although not among the more active congregations emerging in this period) in being established solely for women, as well as in not being dependent upon either the jurisdiction or visitation of a male monastic community. Each Visitandine house was directly under episcopal authority in its diocese and this hard-won privilege guaranteed the communities a

---

[31] For Jane's opinions on the dangers of friendship, consult *Sa Vie*, Tome 2, *Exhortations*, 195ff.

[32] See Sister Patricia Burns, "La Tendresse en Ste. Jeanne de Chantal," *Annales Salésiennes* 3 (1972): 10-11.

certain autonomy of spirit and life.[33] This autonomy effectively safeguarded the feminine character of Visitation monasteries. Thus they present themselves as suitable subjects for study of a specifically feminine spirituality.

The Psychology of Gender

Recent research in women's psychology suggests that there may be a unique woman's way of viewing the world that does not mirror the viewpoint held as normative by most of modern psychology. Studies undertaken by researchers like Carol Gilligan, Mary Belenky and her colleagues, and Jean Baker Miller and her associates at the Stone Center at Wellesley College suggest that women's moral development, epistemological perspectives and self-identity are formed and best described quite differently than they have been by dominant psychological theories (which have been developed by men and draw mainly upon male experience for confirmation). Not primarily concerning themselves with the question of whether such gender differences are created by innate or culturally imposed factors, these women psychologists have persuasively argued for a distinctive woman's voice and self-knowledge.[34]

Carol Gilligan's research on moral development suggests that men are generally more concerned with autonomy and achievement, while women are more oriented toward relationships of interdependence. From this she extracts an entire list of correlated phenomena: women may make moral judgments based less on abstract principles than upon evaluated priorities of care; they may be more likely to make decisions based upon individual circumstance than upon precedent; more than men, women tend to experience themselves as embedded in the networks of relationship that surround them and to evaluate data based upon the interactions in those relationships; they tend to choose games that are non-competitive and cooperative in nature rather than games that emphasize the attainment of skill and competitiveness. In the same vein, Belenky and her associates

---

[33] A complete account of Jane's struggle to resist the introduction of an apostolic visitor into the order can be found in Roger Devos's "Le testament spirituel de Sainte Jeanne-Françoise de Chantal et l'affaire du visiteur apostolique," *Revue d'histoire de la spiritualité* 48 (1972): 453-476; and 49 (1973): 199-226 and 341-366.

[34] Carol Gilligan, *In A Different Voice: Psychological Theory and Women's Development* (Cambridge: Harvard, 1982); Mary Field Belenky, Blythe McVicker Clenchy, Nancy Rule Goldberger, Jill Mattuck Tarule, *Women's Ways of Knowing: The Development of Self, Voice and Mind* (New York: Basic, 1986); Jean Baker Miller, *Toward a New Psychology of Women* (Boston: Beacon, 1987); the Stone Center Associates publish *Work in Progress*, available from Wellesley College, Wellesley MA, 02181.

envision a woman's "way of knowing" that emerges best through the empathetic and "connected" eliciting of women's unique sense of voice and the validation of women's experience. They contrast the process of knowing with the dominant "male" model of knowing held up in education, which proceeds through criticism, debate and "separate" knowing. Similarly, Stone Center researchers contend that the pervasive models of human development based on modern (male) psychological theory, depict the person as maturing most authentically when separation, autonomy, and individualization are achieved. The self is seen as developing essentially outside of and away from relationships. Women's experience, these scholars suggest, offers another vision of maturation in which the self is only forged and known *in* relationship. They base their work on the notion of the "self-in-relation" which grows to the extent that it enjoys and fosters relationships that are empathic and mutual. Thus the quality of relationships, not the capacity for separation, is seen as key to the healthy development of the individual.

Christian Monasticism and Masculine Values

Seen from this modern perspective, the Christian contemplative tradition is, in general, a tradition in which values which might be deemed masculine are paramount. While it is important to underscore that "masculine" values are not found only in men nor "feminine" values only in women, still the distinction does have implications when considering the spirituality of Christian monastic life. The tremendous emphasis in that tradition on the autonomous person (the very terms *monk* and *monastery* connote the solitary life), the stress on ascetic achievement, the pursuit of individual perfection, and the accent on detachment from relationship are decidedly in the masculine vein. The eremitic tradition most firmly enshrines the values of autonomy and detachment, but they are found strongly in the cenobitic tradition as well, although that tradition also stresses values that can be seen as essentially feminine, such as humility. Even in the Rule of St. Benedict the emphasis is not upon the life of the community, but upon the development of the individual within the context of that life.[35] Traditionally, women in monasticism have lived by the same values and sets of priorities as their masculine counterparts. And, with the

---

[35] Carolyn Walker Bynum points out in her *Jesus as Mother: Studies in the Spirituality of the High Middle Ages* (London: U. of California, 1982): 76-77, that in the Benedictine tradition a real spirituality of community life was not developed until the twelfth century Cistercian reform.

exception of a more strict claustration of women, they have tended to live like their male counterparts.[36]

Certainly the ascetic vision with its implied individualism and asceticism undergirds the foundation of the Visitation. The detachment from all created things that is encouraged, the emphasis on absolute surrender to the will of God, the pursuit of perfection, these shape the "masculine" monastic face of the Institute.

Relational Emphasis in the Visitation

But in the Visitation, the networks of relational life were also carefully laid. Sisterly gentleness is not mere formalism, but a conscious cultivation of the affective and relational aspect of each person. There is real love between the sisters, and it is expressly encouraged. Even the institutional bonds that hold them together are relational, not legal, in nature, for the organization of the Visitation allows for the autonomy of each house. The "Holy Source" at Annecy retains only the authority of respect and tradition. There is no legal structure provided for insuring the conformity of the individual houses. While there are custom books, constitutions, and other documents that are to be followed in order to maintain a unity of spirit, the binding force that ensures this unity is simple charity.

Similarly, the tremendous sensitivity to the particular person and a preference for the specific case over the principle embodied in statute marks this Visitation spirit as "feminine." The prime virtues practiced in the order are not the heroic ones which foster independence and achievement, but the little ones that encourage interdependence and mutual support. The moderation of asceticism, the exercise of gentleness, the avoidance of extremes—hallmarks of Jane's direction—likewise characterize the order as "feminine," especially in contrast to the strong emphasis on achievement in the zealous "masculine" ascetic impulse. It is not necessary to belabor the point or to be too slavish in describing certain aspects of Visitation spirituality as either "masculine" or "feminine." Yet given contemporary gender research, one is encouraged to look at this spiritual tradition of gentleness with new eyes.

At first glance it might appear that a spirituality and mode of direction which stresses so keenly the "March violet" image of womanhood

---

[36] Jane Tibbets Schulenberg, "Strict Active Enclosure and its Effects on the Female Monastic Experience (550-1100)," in *Medieval Religious Women*, vol. 1, *Distant Echoes*, (Kalamazoo: Cistercian, 1984): 51-86.

would be suspect. Much contemporary criticism of the way women have traditionally been regarded both by themselves and others notes the negative effects of passivity, non-assertiveness, and low self-esteem from which women have often suffered. Does the direction practiced in the Visitation not lead women down this well-worn path?

Yet, seen from another perspective, the "March violet" ideal of womanhood, with its attendant emphasis on the "little virtues" that one finds in Visitation literature, may have a distinctively positive and countercultural value for women when experienced in the context of the monastic tradition. Indeed, this tradition emphasizes autonomy in a number of ways. This emphasis was especially marked in the Greco-Roman world when current philosophical notions about the nature of the human person were assumed. Men were thought to be innately more "spiritual." If women (who were felt to be more intrinsically related to the body and thus not to the spirit), were to embark upon a life of religious dedication, they had to "become male." The giving up of female roles, affective ties, and procreative powers was felt to purify women and fit them for a life of spirit. The first centuries of Christianity very explicitly acted out this model.[37] Certainly throughout the history of monasticism, there have been periods such as the twelfth century in which spirituality was more "feminized" and the language of relationship, both between the individual and God and between individuals, was articulated.[38]

Nevertheless, on the whole, a woman seeking holiness and selfhood within the Christian monastic tradition finds herself in a world in which priorities of separation and achievement are expressly valued and cultivated, often to the exclusion of values that would foster relationships of interdependence and the types of interaction that these involve. That women's contemplative communities have been for the most part founded as offshoots of male monastic communities, or are under their jurisdiction and scrutiny, contributes to this reality. Might it be asked if there has been adequate opportunity in Christian monasticism for a distinctively feminine spirituality to emerge?

The Visitation seems to be an exception to this rule. Founded independently of any male order, it was designed for women alone. Its

---

[37] Elizabeth A. Clark stresses this point in her *Jerome, Chrysostom and Friends. Essays and Translations* (New York: Edwin Mellen, 1979). See also John Anson, "The Female Transvestite in Early Monasticism: The Origin and Development of a Motif," *Viator* 5 (1974): 1-32.

[38] On the feminization of religious language in the twelfth century, see Bynum, *Jesus as Mother*, 135ff.

father-founder's own spirituality was markedly "feminine" in flavor (indeed, as has been remarked, Francis de Sales "specialized" in the direction of women).[39] Moreover, the Renaissance humanist tradition from which he drew inspiration emphasized the cultivation of the little relational virtues for womankind. But perhaps most importantly, the community's mother-foundress was a woman deeply molded in the traditional female roles of wife and mother, and disposed, by temperament and training, to a spirituality that gave a large place to relational values.

The charism of the Visitation stressed community and taught that abandonment to the will of God is realized most clearly within a network of human relationships. High value was placed upon the gentleness and sensitivity with which one strove to love one's neighbor. One went to God through the God-directed cultivation of relationships. Further, the order was structured in such a manner that the institution itself continued to function with relational values uppermost in priority. Only by doing this could it maintain its distinctive character.

Given these facts, one is tempted to see in the Visitation a unique form of Christian contemplative experience. Within its communities, women were encouraged to cultivate the strongly "masculine" qualities of autonomy and detachment which were given direction and focus in the larger monastic tradition of which the sisters were a part. At the same time, they were encouraged to temper these characteristics with those relational and affective gifts which both their own era and our contemporary age suggest are intimately their own. Might it be possible to say that the Visitation provides an example of a Christian contemplative community in which distinctively women's ways of being serve as a healthy counterbalance to a spiritual tradition that too often ignores and undervalues interdependence and the capacity for mutual growth through relationships? Might it also be possible to say that such a foundation holds out to the entire Christian community an example of a way of loving one another that emerges from women's experience, a way and an experience rooted in the gospel, yet little in evidence in the annals of Christian history?

---

[39] Cf. Theódore Schueller, *La Femme et le saint: la femme et ses problèmes d'après François de Sales* (Paris: Les Editions Ouvrières, 1970).

8

The Problem of Religious Complacency in Seventeenth Century Lutheran Spirituality

ERIC LUND

During the seventeenth century, Lutheran writers who were devoted to nurturing the practice of piety began to produce a collection of devotional writings in Germany which surpassed the influence of almost all the edificatory literature published by their predecessors during the century of the Reformation. These books are notable for several reasons in addition to the extent of their circulation and the durability of their appeal. They presented a new vocabulary for speaking about the development of the Christian life and expressed new ideas about what should be the most significant concern of clergy and laity who were committed to the promotion of spiritual development on both the individual and communal levels. Unlike the theologians of this so-called Age of Orthodoxy, who were still primarily concerned with clarifying and defending the doctrinal consensus which had been established after much conflict in the first sixty years of the Lutheran movement, many of the authors of these devotional books turned their attention away from subtle disputes about doctrine and addressed the practical problems of daily Christian living with unprecedented intensity. Without repudiating the traditional Lutheran preoccupation with the doctrine of justification by faith, the new generation of popular religious writers added a strong emphasis on the process of sanctification. Under their influence, a form of Lutheran spirituality emerged in the seventeenth century which was indebted to the Reformation's reordering of religious life but also full of novel elements.

Many factors contributed to the emergence of this new devotional literature and the type of piety it encouraged. Frustration with the interminable disputes of political and theological parties in Germany stimulated a turn toward a more introspective, individualistic and practical religiosity. Non-Lutheran spiritual literature also had a strong influence on the major Lutheran authors who were pioneers in the development of the new style of devotional writing. The comparative study of sixteenth and seventeenth century books of edification reveals another major factor: a gradual shift in judgment about the major shortcomings of religious life in Germany. As the Lutheran movement approached the beginning of its second century, an increasing number of pastors and religious writers became concerned with the problem of religious complacency or false security. They became convinced that emphasizing the consoling message of the Gospel, the promise of God's gracious acceptance of the unworthy who live by faith, was not always having an edifying effect on the way people were living their lives. If we examine the four most widely read Lutheran devotional writers of the seventeenth century, Johann Arndt, Heinrich Müller, Christian Scriver and Philipp Jacob Spener, against the background of earlier Lutheran spirituality, we will notice a growing preoccupation with the problem of religious complacency and various ways in which this issue influenced how they portrayed the nature of the Christian life.

The Spirituality of Martin Luther

What Martin Luther wrote about the nature of the Christian life was, quite obviously, of great importance for seventeenth century Lutheran devotional writers, but it was also evident that the religious context which shaped his reflections on this topic was not identical with their own. Stated most simply, Luther's conception of the Christian life centered around the theme of "faith active in love" (Galatians 5:6). Luther elaborated on this theme most distinctively in his 1520 treatise *On the Freedom of a Christian*.[1] Here he described the Christian who is justified by faith as a free lord needing neither the law nor works to be reconciled with God. This means that Christians who trust in Christ should feel liberated from any self-

---

[1] Martin Luther, *Tractatus de libertate christiana in Luthers Werke*, (Weimar: Hermann Bohlaus Nachfolger, 1897): III: 20-38 (German edition), 42-73 (Latin edition). Henceforth, *Luthers Werke* cited as WA.

interested impulse to calculate the meritorious value of thoughts, words or deeds. Living by faith ought to produce a sense of freedom from anxiety about one's eternal destiny. This does not mean, however, that works have no place in the life of a Christian. According to Luther, "Good works do not make a good man, but a good man does good works."[2] Christians who have given up foolish presumptions about acquiring justification by works will still do good works "out of spontaneous love in obedience to God." Christians who truly appreciate the gift of salvation they have been given through Christ will joyfully act like Christ towards their neighbors. Thus they can be compared to both free lords and dutiful servants.[3] Their spiritual freedom becomes the foundation of a new purely-motivated sense of responsibility toward God and other people. Such faith made active in love benefits others who are in need; it also has the effect of helping Christians impose a suitable discipline on their own bodies to control the evil passions and desires which remain part of human nature even after the gift of grace has been received.

Luther's stress on active faith and Christian freedom grew out of his own personal religious experience. Having struggled during his years as a monk with the agony of spiritual despair, he was inclined to speak a word of consolation and relief to others who may have felt similarly oppressed. Luther continuously accented the difference between law and gospel because he feared the persistence of a theological tradition which contradicted the scriptures by a burdensome insistence on works-righteousness. Contrary to what he had been taught, Luther came to believe that the possibility of new life proclaimed in the teachings of Christ was not obtainable through frenetic religious or moral activity. Rather, it came to those who acknowledged their own impotence and passively received it as a gift from God.

The accent on human passivity before God is pervasive in Luther's theology, but he also acknowledged at times the danger of interpreting Christian freedom as a justification for idleness or wickedness. His treatise on Christian freedom ends with the advice that a Christian should steer a middle course between the errors of "ceremonialist" (*pertinaces, obdurati cerimoniistae*) who falsely view works as a means of justification, and the errors of "simple-minded, ignorant men" (*simplices, idiotae, ignari et infirmi in fide*) who confuse liberty with license. When Luther wrote these words in 1520, the former extreme seemed to be the greater danger. He believed

---

[2] Ibid., 61: "Bona opera non faciunt bonum virum, sed bonus vir facit bona opera."
[3] Ibid., 49.

that a tyrannical band of ceremonialists held the Catholic Church captive and aggressively sought to destroy souls by stubbornly condemning the proclamation of faith and freedom. In contrast, the party inclined toward the opposite extreme seemed to amount to little more than a collection of untrained youths who simply needed to receive more instruction about the meaning of the Gospel.[4] Later in his ministry, Luther corrected this quick dismissal of the problem of irresponsible behavior. The events of the Peasant's War and the evidence derived from his visits to Lutheran parishes in 1528-29 convinced Luther that the common people easily "mastered the fine art of abusing liberty."[5] Subsequently, he was more careful to condemn both works-righteousness and licentiousness with almost equal fervor.

Late Sixteenth Century Spirituality

Some of the doctrinal controversies which preoccupied Lutheran theologians in the first three decades after Luther's death can be viewed as disputes about which of these two problems constituted the greatest danger. The Lutheran Philippists who argued in the Majorist controversy that good works are necessary fruits of faith were concerned primarily with the threat of antinomianism. Their Gnesio-Lutheran opponents, who continued to see false reliance on good works as the most pervasive problem, were fearful of any claim that good works were essential for salvation. Some of them even asserted that good works were injurious to salvation. Similarly, some Philippists also argued that the human will cooperates with God in the process of salvation by not resisting the gift of grace. They were almost certainly inclined to this interpretation because they saw religious complacency as a real danger encouraged by the preaching of complete human passivity in the process of conversion. Their Gnesio-Lutheran opponents viewed any claim that the human will is a

---

[4] Ibid., 71.

[5] *Der kleine Katechismus*, WA 30:1, 266. "Und nu das Evangelion komen ist, dennoch fein gelernt haben aller freyheit meisterlich zu missebrauchen." This issue came up again during the years 1537-40 when a dispute developed between two of Luther's colleagues, Philipp Melanchthon and Johann Agricola. Melanchthon favored the continued preaching of law-oriented sermons as a way of combatting moral laxity. Agricola argued that this would drive people once again into a state of spiritual despair. Luther criticized Agricola's view that the law had been superseded by the gospel in his tract, *Against the Antinomians* (1539). In the *Third Disputation Against the Antinomians* Luther also stated, "But now our softly singing Antinomians paying no attention to change of the times make men secure who are of themselves already so secure that they fall away from grace." Quoted in *Luther's Works* 47 (Philadelphia: Fortress Press, 1971): 105.

factor in conversion as a return to the synergistic "errors" of the Catholic Church.

In 1577, most of these conflicts were resolved by the adoption of the Formula of Concord. This new confessional document condemned all of the most extreme theological statements by both the Philippist and Gnesio-Lutheran parties. Once again, the Lutheran movement affirmed that the Christian life is a middle course between the two styles of life which Luther criticized in his treatise *The Freedom of a Christian*.

The balanced emphasis on liberty and responsibility expressed in the Formula of Concord also became a standard theme in many of the most favorably received devotional books of the late sixteenth century. Representative of such works is the *Treasurechest of Holy, Divine Scripture*, a lengthy summary of correct doctrine and piety written by Matthaeus Vogel (1519-1591), a south German Lutheran pastor.[6] In the characteristic manner of old-style Orthodox Lutheran writers, Vogel combined both doctrinal polemics and edifying advice for the development of the Christian life. He stressed the sufficiency of faith and faulted the Jews, the Pelagians, and the Council of Trent for demanding a pharisaic righteousness as a condition for salvation. Vogel accepted the idea that love and other good works necessarily follow from faith but denied that such fruits bear in any way on justification. He was particularly concerned to distinguish between the act of justification and the process of spiritual renewal lest his readers forget that salvation is based on the imputed righteousness of Christ.[7] Such a strict separating of justification and sanctification was a common feature of Lutheran theology at the end of the sixteenth century. Vogel stressed this theme because he feared the persistence of perfectionist tendencies within Protestantism. The worst perpetrators of such "illusions" were the Anabaptists whom Vogel portrayed as subtle preachers of a "new monkery." In opposition to their belief that the Spirit of God effects an evident transformation in the character of a person who has become a Christian, Vogel warned his readers not to expect perfection in this life.[8] There should be signs that regeneration has begun, but the inner conflict between flesh and spirit never disappears until the Christian is received into eternal life.

---

[6] Matthaeus Vogel, *Schatzkammer heiliger göttlicher Schrifft/darinnen nicht allein alle Articul Christliche Religion gründtlich erklärt/ und die Irrthumb widerlegt: Sondern auch andere Lehr/ und Trostpuncten/ so irgen mögen fürfallen/ mit vielen Sprüchen/ und Exempeln H. Schrifft aussgeführet werden.* Lübeck: Martin Janov & Heinrich Schernwebet, 1639). The first edition appeared in 1587.

[7] Ibid., ch. 12: "Von der Rechtfertigung," 468-469.

[8] Ibid., Ch. 13: "Von Ernewerung und guten Wercken der Gerechtfertigen," 503.

Like Luther, Vogel sought to comfort and encourage believers who were surrounded by enemies of Christian freedom. On the other hand, he also acknowledged the possible abuse of freedom. As examples of this problem he cited the peasants who revolted against the German nobility in 1525, the individuals who took a liberal stand in the adiaphoristic controversy at the time of the Interim crisis in 1548, and the "coarse Epicureans" of his own era who lived in false security.[9] Since these complacent individuals were not an organized party warring against the church, Vogel devoted less attention to them than to the menace of the Catholics and Anabaptists. Nevertheless, he recalled Luther's description of the Christian life as a middle course between two extremes. In response to the Epicureans, Vogel noted that repentance and new obedience are also essential elements of the Christian life.

New Concerns about Complacency

While this balanced pattern of exhortation established by Luther and repeated by Vogel continued in the spiritual writings of some seventeenth century Lutherans, other authors began to treat the problem of false security or religious complacency as a matter deserving more extensive consideration. The beginning of this trend is already evident shortly after Luther's death in the publications of Andreas Musculus (1514-1581), an influential church leader in the territory of Brandenburg.[10] For several decades, he carried out an energetic campaign against the prevalent vices and offensive social customs of his day by writing tracts in which he portrayed each vice as the work of a specific devil. The first of these tracts was *The Trouser Devil*, an attack on the extravagant new fashions of his era. Subsequent devil-books called attention to the problems of blasphemous language, wife abuse, and excessive drinking. In other writings, Musculus commented more generally on the low level of moral and spiritual life in his beloved Germany. His *True Christian Warning Against the Dreadful and Damnable Security of the Whole World* (1559), showed how each social class lived in a state of corruption.[11] The peasants, he claimed, had so completely forgotten religion that they loved their beer mugs more than the church. They did not want to hear about the devil or hell, and they

---

[9] Ibid., Ch. 16: "Von der Christlichen Freyheit," 536. See also Ch. 18: "Von der Buss," 540.

[10] See Richard Grümmer, *Andreas Musculus* (Eisenach: Hofbuchdruckerei Eisenach, 1912).

[11] Andreas Musculus, *Christliche Trewe Warnung und Vermanung/wider der grewliche und verdamliche Sicherheit der gantzen Welt* (Erfurt, 1559).

regarded the Ten Commandments as nonsense. The towns people had turned from the promised land of the holy gospel back to the "fleshpots of Egypt." For the most part they lived like irrational animals, habitually belligerent and preoccupied with worldly pleasures. Similarly, the artisans or merchants lived like outlaws while keeping up the appearance of being Christians, and the nobles scorned both word and sacrament. Germany was a veritable Sodom and Gomorrah in the eyes of Musculus. False security and contempt for true religion were so widespread that he confidently predicted a fearsome punishment for the nation from God.

Many Lutherans in the late sixteenth century shared Musculus' sense of impending doom. Everything seemed to be going wrong in both the political and religious spheres of life. Soon after the doctrinal conflicts among Lutherans subsided, tensions mounted again between the Protestant and Catholic princes of Germany. Despite the establishment of the Peace of Augsburg in 1555, the survival of Lutheranism remained open to doubt. Pessimism about the future was enhanced by the widespread feeling that many people were still only superficially influenced by the Christian faith. At the end of the Reformation period, most Lutherans were affiliated with a territorial church by requirement, not always by choice. Inevitably this meant that some church members lacked a high level of commitment and sometimes even resented the clergy. Numerous pastors bemoaned the fact that after a half century of Lutheran preaching and institutional reform, many of the perennial weaknesses of moral and spiritual life in Germany persisted. The visitation reports which gathered data on the state of religious life in Lutheran parishes often seemed to confirm their impressions. The mood of gloom was so intense that extravagant predictions about the approaching end of the world became commonplace. Apocalyptically-minded Lutheran clergy interpreted the occurrence of natural disasters, such as severe weather and earthquakes, and the revival of the Turkish menace as early signs of the approaching divine judgment.[12]

Johann Arndt

Johann Arndt (1555-1621), the most influential Lutheran devotional writer of the seventeenth century, proclaimed these critical sentiments even more vigorously in the last two decades before the advent of the Thirty Years War. While serving as a pastor in several north German parishes

---

[12] See for example, Daniel Schaller, *Herolt- Aussgesandt in allen Landen offentlich zuverkündigen und auszuruffen. Das diese Weldt mit irem wesen bald vergehen werde/ und der Jüngste Gerichtstag gar nahe für der Thur sey* (Magdeburg: Johann Franken, 1595).

and later as general superintendent of the territorial church of Braunschweig-Lüneburg, Arndt focused his attention on the problem of religious complacency. Like Musculus, he lamented the presence of false security in all classes of society and warned of the approaching end of the world. There was, however, a new element in Arndt's attack on this problem. Unlike most earlier critics, Arndt did not blame only the devil and the lay people themselves for the deficiencies in their piety. He also suggested that Lutheran pastors and theologians contributed to the growth of complacency by the way they proclaimed the Christian message. According to Arndt, many of them treated theology as if it were mere learning instead of living experience and practice. They also devoted so much attention to doctrinal disputations that they failed to communicate the true meaning of repentance and faith to the parishioners they served.[13]

Arndt set his diagnosis forth in several books and tried to rectify the problem by showing that a correct understanding of Lutheran teaching should promote the development of continuous spiritual growth. Unlike other devotional writers such as Matthaeus Vogel, Arndt showed little interest in pointing out the theological errors of other religious traditions. He focused his attention on the internal problems of the Lutheran churches and tried to intensify the religious devotion of simple believers by showing the practical implications of certain key theological concepts. The result was the most comprehensive analysis of the nature and development of the Christian life yet to appear in the Lutheran tradition.

Arndt first addressed the problem of religious Complacency in a collection of sermons published as *A Book of the Ten Egyptian Plagues.*[14] In this work, Arndt presented an allegorical interpretation of the ten plagues described in Exodus and compared the sins of the German people with the wickedness of the ancient Egyptians. Like Musculus, Arndt perceived an absence of true repentance and sincere faith among all classes of society. He made no predictions about the date when the end of the world would come, but he urged his readers to change their conduct so that the avenging angel of God could be averted. Arndt provided a more constructive guide to spiritual growth in his popular but controversial book,

---

[13] Johann Arndt, *Sechs Bücher vom wahren Christenthum*. See Book I, ch. 39 and Book VI, *Erstes Bedencken über die deutsche Theologia*. The first four books of *Wahres Christenthum* were in print by 1609. The last two books are an assortment of short pieces collected around 1620. More than 141 different editions of this work were published between 1621 and 1721.

[14] The only surviving edition of this work is a version published in Frankfurt in 1657 under the title: *Zehen Schöne Lehr- und Geistreiche Predigten von den Zehen Grausamen und- Schrecklichen Egiptischen Plagen.*

True Christianity, first published in 1605 and expanded several times in subsequent years. In the preface of this work, Arndt clearly distinguished between a false Christianity which many church members comfortably embraced and the true Christianity practiced by those who understand the true meaning of faith. Christianity, he observed, involves more than believing certain doctrines and utilizing the sacraments. It should involve the transformation of a person's whole life. Renewed by the Word of God, the Christian should become a new creature who not only believes in Christ but also lives in Christ. "True Christianity consists in the exhibition of a true, living faith, active in genuine godliness and the fruits of righteousness."[15]

Like Vogel and the other Lutheran devotional writers of the Age of Orthodoxy, Arndt warned the reader not to confuse the righteousness of faith with the righteousness of the Christianity life. He never explicitly criticized the forensic view of justification or the idea that salvation is based on the imputed righteousness of Christ. Nevertheless, the way Arndt described the Christian life in *True Christianity* suggests that, in his mind, most of his fellow clergy had too limited a sense of the change which should take place after a person has been justified. Arndt stated that Christ was not simply offered as a payment for all our sins ("as imprudent, godless people truncate it and thereby badly jeopardize their salvation").[16] His death and resurrection are a fountain from which renewal and sanctification flow. In order to make clear that the true Christian becomes a new person, Arndt described the whole process of salvation as rebirth.[17] This metaphorical term, which several of Arndt's contemporaries also favored, became one of the distinctive emphases of Lutheran spirituality in the seventeenth century.

In addition to describing the features of true Christianity, Arndt also attempted in his writings to encourage spiritual growth. He accomplished this task not by offering detailed rules for the practice of piety but by stimulating certain attitudes and suggesting certain incentives which might foster personal renewal. In the early chapters of *True Christianity*, Arndt attempted to make his readers feel dissatisfied with themselves. He tried to destroy complacency or false security by contrasting the state of humanity before and after the Fall. Adam who was created in the image of God willfully sinned and became like Satan in his heart. As a result, the spiritual

---

[15] *Wahres Christenthum*, Preface to Book I.
[16] *Informatorium Biblicum* in *Johann Arnds Geistreicher Schrifften*, ed. by J. J. Rambach (Leipzig: Marcheschen Buchhandlung, 1736): 606.
[17] *Wahres Christenthum*, Book I, ch. 3.

image of God which was the original endowment of humanity became what Arndt called "an earthly, fleshly, and brutish image of Satan." He vividly described original sin as a poisonous snake-seed (*Schlangensaamen*) sown in humans by Satan. From this evil seed a poisonous tree grows which yields fruit such as false belief, rejection of God, and the sin against the Holy Spirit.[18]

After his forceful appeal for contrition, Arndt consoled his readers with the promises of the Gospel. This was standard practice in traditional Lutheran preaching, but Arndt also used his consoling remarks to enhance expectations for spiritual progress. He portrayed the saving work of Christ in such a way that his readers would anticipate an empirically observable and consciously experienced change in their lives under the influence of grace. More took place than the imputation of Christ's merits and the remission of the punishment for sin. Arndt often described Christ as a doctor or medicine through whom a work of healing begins in the life of a sinner. Christ eradicates the snake-seed or image of Satan and makes possible the restoration of the image of God. God "makes the divine blood of Christ our medicine and cleansing for sin, his unifying flesh our bread of life, his holy wounds, his holy death, the ridding of our temporal and eternal death."[19]

Arndt tried to make people dissatisfied with the current state of their lives and also stimulated hope for improvement. He assured his readers that they were totally reconciled with God when they were freed by Christ from the guilt of sin, but he also prepared them for a long and hard struggle against the power of sin. Arndt advised Christians to monitor their spiritual progress by developing the habit of examining themselves daily. They should also make self-denial a primary task of daily Christian living. By practicing daily contrition and renouncing personal pleasures, honors or gain, they allow their new spiritual natures to grow and win the battle against the powers of the flesh or their old sinful natures.[20]

In the second book of *True Christianity*, which Arndt subtitled "The Book of the Life of Christ," he presented Jesus as a model of love and other virtues whom Christians should try to imitate. Arndt developed this theme, so common to Catholic devotional literature, in a Lutheran way.

---

[18] Ibid. Arndt also used animal imagery to portray the sinful state of humanity. "Then see, is not your anger and ferocity lion-like? Is not your envy and unsatiable avarice like that of a dog or a wolf? Is not your impurity and immoderation sow-like? Yes, you will find in yourself an entire world of evil animals."
[19] Ibid., Book II, ch. 1.
[20] Ibid., Book I, ch. 11-18.

He never portrayed the emulation of Christ as a means of attaining salvation. His emphasis on the imitation of Christ supplemented rather than replaced his recognition of Christ as a savior. Arndt stated, "Faith grasps the person of Christ and his office; love follows him in his life."[21] This statement echoes Luther's affirmation that a Christian should follow him first by faith and then by heeding his example. Nevertheless, it is evident that Catholic sources inspired Arndt's emphasis on this theme. Extracts from a book by Angela de Foligno, a thirteenth century Franciscan tertiary, underlie a large part of the second book of *True Christianity*. Arndt also used the *Imitation of Christ* by Thomas à Kempis. He clearly respected some features of Catholic spirituality and passed them on to Lutherans as a way of combatting the problem of complacency.

Arndt completed his advice for the development of the Christian life by adding a contemplative dimension to the practice of Lutheran piety. He attempted to sustain the pursuit of spiritual growth by offering his readers the promise that they could ultimately experience a joyful union with Christ. In the third book of *True Christianity*, subtitled "The Book of Conscience," Arndt cited scriptural passages which suggest that Christians can become partakers of the divine nature (2 Peter 1:4) and can experience the indwelling of Christ (Galatians 2:20). Arndt concluded that these verses speak of a kind of mystical experience which comes when the soul has emptied itself of love for worldly things. To receive this foretaste of eternal life, Arndt advised his readers to leave the world at least once a day and turn within to the inner ground of the soul.[22] If all worldly cares and thoughts are put away and the Christian maintains a "still Sabbath of the soul," the soul is prepared to experience the inner working of God. The soul will thereby receive the heavenly food which can give it the strength to endure the sufferings and burdens of the Christian life.

The idea of turning within to the ground of the soul and holding a still Sabbath came primarily from the sermons of the German mystic, Johann Tauler. Once again, however, Arndt gave the Catholic ideas he borrowed a special Lutheran twist. Unlike the German mystics whom Luther criticized for positing an inner part of the soul (*Seelengrund*) untouched by the Fall which is capable of becoming the dwelling place of God, Arndt believed that the Fall devastated the image of God in human nature. In the process of salvation, God, by His grace, restores this image of God and creates a capacity for His indwelling which no person naturally

---

[21] Ibid., Book II, ch. 12.
[22] Ibid., Book III, ch. 2.

has. Arndt also altered the passages he appropriated from Tauler in order to make clear that the soul remains substantially distinct from God in the state of mystical union. He was optimistic about the possibilities of spiritual growth but stopped short of suggesting that the soul can be ultimately deified. God and the soul remain as two separate entities but are bound in a relationship of love which removes all opposition between them.[23]

Arndt's preoccupation with the problem of complacency, his different way of describing the process of sanctification, and his use of Catholic sources incited a hostile response from some Lutheran theologians. He was charged with reviving all the heresies Lutherans feared most, including synergism, perfectionism, and enthusiasm. Some thought Arndt exaggerated the impact of original sin on human nature. Others criticized his optimism about spiritual progress and called him a Catholic or an Anabaptist. The most damaging accusations focused on Arndt's mystical tendencies and his paraphrasing of passages from Tauler. Noting that radical protestant spiritualists such as Caspar Schwenckfeld and Valentin Weigel had a similar interest in Catholic mystical literature, Arndt's most hostile critic urged the rejection of Arndt's writings and recommended the devotional books of Matthaeus Vogel and others as a more orthodox substitute.[24]

However much Arndt disliked engaging in doctrinal disputations, he was forced to reply to these charges in order to prevent dismissal from his pastoral work. His self-defense, the *Repetitio Apologetica* helped salvage his reputation, and was quickly supplemented by the supportive writings of other authors who shared Arndt's fear of complacency.[25] Misgivings about Arndt's *True Christianity* never entirely disappeared, but the vast majority of Lutherans who wrote devotional literature in the seventeenth century expressed great respect for his understanding of the development of the Christian life. Arndt's contrasting of true and false Christianity, his emphasis on active faith and perpetual spiritual growth, his description of rebirth, and occasionally his interest in the experience of union with God appeared again and again in subsequent edificatory literature. Even

---

[23] For a full study of Arndt's use of Tauler see Edmund Weber, *Johann Arndts Vier Bücher vom wahren Christentum als Beitrag zur protestantischen Irenik des 17. Jahrhunderts* (Marburg: Elwert Verlag, 1960); Christian Braw, *Bücher im Staube: Die Theologie Johann Arndts in ihrem Verhältnis zur Mystik* (Leiden: E. J. Brill, 1986).

[24] Lucas Osiander, *Theologisches Bedencken welcher Gestalt Johann Arndes Wahres Christenthum zu achten sey* (Tübingen, 1623).

[25] For a fuller study of the controversial writings concerning *True Christianity* and the defense of Arndt by other writers, see Eric Lund, *Johann Arndt and the Development of a Lutheran Spiritual Tradition*, (Unpublished doctoral dissertation, Yale University, 1979).

Johann Gerhard, the most influential of the orthodox theologians of this era, repeated many of these themes in his devotional books, *Sacred Meditations* and *The School of Piety.*

Müller and Scriver

The last years of Arndt's life coincided with the first stage of the Thirty Years War (1618-1648). The carnage and confusion of this era only aggravated the religious deficiencies which Arndt had hoped to eradicate. Contemporary descriptions of social life suggest that the war made many people insensitive to moral or spiritual ideals. In response to this situation, the Lutheran devotional literature of the middle decades of the seventeenth century comforted despondent Christians with the promise of God's blessings but concentrated even more on awakening the insensitive out of their state of religious indifference. The two most influential writers of this era, Heinrich Müller and Christian Scriver, both considered themselves advocates of the kind of piety which Arndt had described.

The campaign against complacency intensified in the early decades after the Thirty Years War especially under the leadership of Heinrich Müller (1631-1675). This Lutheran professor at the University of Rostock repeated Arndt's critique of superficial, comfortable piety and added more detailed criteria for determining the presence of true Christianity.[26] In numerous widely-circulated devotional books, Müller warned the people of Germany that they were in great danger. "Theological rogues" more interested in earning a good salary than preaching true Christianity had supposedly lulled them into thinking that it was easy to be a Christian.[27] Müller called many of his fellow clergy wolves in sheep's clothing who consoled the people with dainty orations and thus allowed false security, "the devil's poison, the plague of the soul," to spread throughout the churches.[28] He argued that the clergy should first prick the consciences of their parishioners before they offered the sweet honey of the Gospel.

Müller seemed to suggest that many Lutherans simultaneously committed both of the misinterpretations of the Christian life of which Luther spoke in *The Freedom of a Christian.* Their complacency and abuse

---

[26] For a more detailed study of Müller in relation to later Pietist theology see Gary Sattler, *Nobler Than Angels, Lower Than a Worm: The Pietist View of the Individual in the Writings of Heinrich Müller and August Hermann Francke* (Lanham, MD: University Press of America, 1989).

[27] Heinrich Müller, *Geistliche Erquickstunden* (Hof: J. C. Leidenfrost, 1664): chs. 43, 177, 252, 277.

[28] Ibid., chs. 232, 234, 252. See also his *Creutz-Buss und Bet-Schule* (Frankfurt: Joachim Wilden & Johann Piener, 1687): 182.

of Christian liberty was based on a mistaken belief in the immediate efficacy of certain religious ceremonies. They did not consciously try to earn salvation by doing good works, but they had come to assume that their salvation was assured by partaking of the sacraments. In his *Spiritual Hours of Refreshment* (1664), Müller described the baptismal font, the pulpit, the confessional bench and the altar as four idols worshipped by complacent "mouth-Christians."[29] In *The Divine Flame of Love* (1676), he explained this charge in the following way: "They think it is a precious thing if they only go to church, hear preaching, confess, receive the sacrament, read, sing, pray with many words, (and) give alms." This form of piety, he noted, revived the Catholic concept of an *opus operatum*.[30]

Müller did not intend to belittle the significance of the sacraments, contrary to the claims of some of his critics. Rather, he sought to restore appreciation for the regenerative consequences of faith. He believed that the sacraments could be means of grace, but that more often than not observant Lutherans failed to reap the true benefits of them because religious activity was not accompanied by true repentance and faith. "How many have the appearance of godliness and still deny the power of the same, consider themselves pious but are rogues at heart, manifest the manner of Christ but have not the mind of Christ, approach God with their lips but are far from him in their hearts."[31] These themes recall Arndt's differentiation between true and false Christianity. The distinctive feature of Müller's spirituality, however, is his emphasis on the need for a change of heart. Certain religious feelings such as ardent love of God are as important defining elements of true piety for him as are the external signs of true godliness.[32]

Like Arndt, Müller devoted little attention to the description of specific devotional practices which might further spiritual growth. Most of all, he stressed the importance of diligently examining the conscience. Christians should pay attention to the inclinations of their hearts and scrutinize the motivations of all their actions. Like a wise merchant who always keeps his eye on an untrustworthy servant, they should watch for signs of back-sliding and should take immediate action to prevent spiritual decline. Müller considered such perpetual vigilance necessary because "the

---

[29] *Geistliche Erquickstunden*, ch. 152.

[30] *Göttliche Liebes-Flamme oder Auffmunterung zur Liebe Gottes durch Vorstellung dessen unendlichen Liebe gegen uns* (Frankfurt: Balthasar Christoph Wust, 1676): 655.

[31] *Thränen und Trost-Quelle bey Erklärung der Geschichte von der Grossen Sünderin Luc. 7* (Hanover: Nicolaus Forster, 1724): 14.

[32] See especially the theme of ardent love in *Göttliche Liebes-Flamme*.

new man is a small spark, a tender twig, a sick child, a dilapidated house (which) if you do not always blow on it, bind it up, repair and improve it, will burn out, break, die and fall apart before you realize it."[33]

Müller was so critical of the clergy and so concerned with the danger of misusing the word and sacraments that some Lutherans suspected him of encouraging an individualistic piety unrelated to communal religious life. Since he, like Arndt, was also influenced by Catholic ways of describing the experience of union with Christ, he was open to the charge that he had abandoned the confessional standards of Lutheranism.

One of his contemporaries managed to carry on the campaign against complacency without provoking so much controversy. Christian Scriver (1629-1693), a north German pastor wrote several devotional books which had an enduring popularity in all of the Lutheran countries of Europe.[34] Like Arndt and Müller, Scriver criticized all the classes of German society for living hypocritically, and warned against being seduced by the devil into a state of false security. He described the church as a field full of thorns and blamed the clergy for leading the people astray. Considering himself a disciple of Arndt, Scriver repeated the now familiar refrain that a Christian way of life involves an arduous, never-ending struggle against the influences of sin. He stressed the importance of repentance and rebirth, noting also that living faith and ardent love ought to produce evident signs of spiritual growth. Despite the similarities between Scriver and his predecessors, his orthodoxy was less subject to doubt because he made an explicit effort to show how these themes were consistent with the teachings of Luther. This is especially evident in his comprehensive guide to the Christian life entitled *The Treasure of the Soul* (1675). This work, which rivaled Arndt's *True Christianity* in its comprehensiveness, frequently quoted Luther and expressed Scriver's primary concerns within a larger survey of the fundamental articles of Lutheran theology. He was also respected for his stress on catechetical training and diligent use of the sacraments.

Scriver played a significant role in the development of Lutheran spirituality for several other reasons. First of all, he began to express concern about another factor which contributed to religious indifference in Germany. In *The Treasure of the Soul*, he lamented the influence of "bad books about natural religion."[35] New currents of liberal thought from other

---

[33] Ibid., 686.
[34] For further analysis of Scriver's major book see Martin Schmidt: "Christian Scrivers *Seelenschatz*—ein Beispiel vorpietistischer Predigtweise," *Wiedergeburt und neuer Mensch* (Witten: Luther Verlag, 1969).
[35] *Christliche Seelenschatz* (Stuttgart: C. F. Etzel, 1841): ch. 23, 1319.

countries were encouraging people to think that revealed doctrine was open to question. The result, he claimed, was that Germans were beginning to favor whatever religion gave the most freedom to their fleshly impulses. Along with these foreign ideas came new styles and customs which were incompatible with true Christianity. This trend toward religious scepticism would become a growing concern of Lutheran spiritual writers.

Secondly, although most of the themes of Scriver's books were not new, he was especially creative in developing new ways of communicating old ideas. One of his most imaginative books was *Gotthold's Occasional Meditations* (1663-69), a collection of stories and descriptions of natural phenomena which are interpreted to convey a spiritual lesson. Recognizing that young people especially learn more easily when they are given pictures and illustrations, he used this device to awaken people to the need for rebirth.   One example is sufficient to illustrate this type of devotional writing. Scriver pictures a dandy walking along so absent-mindedly that he trips on a herdboy's staff and falls into a pool of water. This illustrates the plight of many who proceed through life in great security oblivious to the dangers which threaten their souls.[36]

Emblematic literature of this sort was already popular in Germany but the immediate inspiration of Scriver's use of it was a book of meditations by Joseph Hall, an English bishop with Calvinist theological sympathies. This fact reveals a third interesting development of Lutheran devotional literature which Scriver helped to spread. Spiritual writers in Germany at the end of the seventeenth century began to recognize that they shared some concerns with English Puritans and thus began to draw on their writings with increasing frequency.

Philipp Jacob Spener

Scriver carried on the tradition of Arndtian piety to the point where the paths of Lutheran Orthodoxy and Lutheran Pietism divided. In the final decades of the seventeenth century it was especially the Pietists who concerned themselves with the problem of complacency. Some historians speak of Arndt, Müller and Scriver as early Pietists, but the development of Pietism as a movement with a specific program of reform centering around the use of conventicles began with Philipp Jacob Spener (1635-1705), the author of the famous reform tract *Pia Desideria*. This controversial Lutheran reformer who held prominent church positions in Frankfurt, Dresden, and Berlin produced the most extensive reflections on the

---

[36] *Gottholds zufällige Andachten* (Leipzig: Joh. & Friedrich Luderwald, 1686), 1:29, 43f.

characteristic themes of seventeenth century devotional literature and helped make this distinctive spirituality an enduring influence on the future development of Lutheranism. An extensive analysis of Spener's pastoral theology is beyond the scope of this paper, but a brief consideration of his handling of this problem of complacency can illustrate how interest in this issue was as intense at the end of the seventeenth century as it had been during the lifetime of Johann Arndt.

Spener originally published his *Pia Desideria* as a preface to a new edition of some sermons by Johann Arndt. Although seventy years had passed from the first publication of *True Christianity* to the appearance of this Pietist manifesto, Spener repeated Arndt's diagnosis of the state of religious life among the German people. Spener went on to suggest that the low standards of religious life in the church could be improved if preachers, writers and teachers would observe how Arndt simply and powerfully explained the rudiments of Christianity.[37]. In his positive description of true Christianity, expressed in great detail in numerous books, Spener followed his own advice. He elaborated on the conception of sanctification which Arndt and his followers had developed earlier in the century. Spener did not think of himself as an innovator, and the truth of this acknowledgement is borne out, at least with regard to his basic understanding of the Christian life, by study of his writings. There is a high degree of continuity in the theological perspectives of the most influential Lutheran devotional writers of the seventeenth century.

Spener's most systematic attack on the problem of complacency appeared in a book published in 1693 entitled *Words of Scripture Misused by the Worldly to Foster Security*.[38] Intended primarily for Christians who assumed that being saved by grace freed them from the need to strive diligently for spiritual growth, this book began with a consideration of problematic passages in Genesis and continued until Spener had reached the book of Revelation. A few examples will serve to show the lengths to which Spener felt compelled to go to combat the problem of complacency.

Spener devoted considerable attention to the book of Ecclesiastes because it contained numerous passages which might suggest the futility of attending wholeheartedly to spiritual development. One could read this

---

[37] Philipp Jacob Spener, *Pia Desideria*, ed. Kurt Aland (Berlin: Walter de Gruyter, 1955): 81-85.

[38] Philipp Jacob Spener, *Sprüche heiliger Schrifft/ welche von welt-leuten mehrmal zu hegung der sicherheit/ und wider die so nothwendigkeit als möglichkeit des wahren innerlichen und thätigen Christenthums/ missbraucht zu werden pflegen/ kürtzlich/ aber gründlich gerettet* (Frankfurt: J. D. Zunner, 1693).

book as an endorsement of an Epicurean attitude toward life since it claimed that "there is nothing better for a man than that he should eat and drink and find enjoyment in his toil" (2:24). Most shocking of all is the verse which reads, "Be not righteous overmuch" (7:16). Spener explained that in such passages Solomon was either confessing what his former philosophy had been or was repeating what other people thought. Read in its entirety, Spener argued, the book conveys a different message noted especially in its final recommendation that a person ought to fear God and keep his commandments (12:13).[39]

The writings of Paul, however, proclaim faith as the basis of salvation and state that Christ has freed humanity from bondage to the law. Spener feared that this theme might encourage complacency so he also carefully commented on Paul's letters to the Romans and the Galatians. He warned his readers not to forget that the writings of Paul deal with sanctification as well as justification. Paul is speaking of justification when he states that faith is reckoned as righteousness. Other passages, especially Romans 6, make clear that justification by faith does not free Christians from concern for the development of a holy life. Spener insisted that the articles of justification and sanctification be given equal consideration. If they are placed together in proper relationship to each other, Christians should recognize that true faith will produce continuous spiritual growth.[40]

Other passages in the Bible, however, suggest that human nature is so tainted by sin that perfection is an impossible goal. Especially in the New Testament there are verses which give a low estimate of the ability of humans to do what they might rightfully will (Matthew 26:41, Romans 7:18-19). In response to these passages, Spener argued that the grace of God gives a new power to the human will which allows the reborn to grow in holiness. In support of this claim he quoted 2 Peter 1:4, a verse which had long been an important focus of seventeenth century spirituality. Like Johann Arndt, Spener believed that Christians become partakers of the divine nature. They are granted divine power to do all things which pertain to godliness. The flesh has been put to death and they have been made "alive in the spirit" (1 Peter 3:18). Spener stopped short of suggesting that perfection is expected of Christians as a condition of salvation. He noted that true believers already lay claim to the perfection of Christ through faith. This imputed righteousness of Christ, however, is not the final gift of

[39] Ibid., 77f.
[40] Ibid., 231f.

God to fallen humanity. Christ also comes to dwell in the hearts of Christians and gradually transforms their lives.[41]

Conclusion

Arndt, Müller, Scriver and Spener all acknowledged, at least tacitly, that some of the criticisms which other confessional groups made of Lutheranism were to be taken seriously. Catholic reformers such as Erasmus and Ignatius Loyola feared that the Lutheran stress on faith alone would encourage indolence. The seventeenth century Lutheran spiritual writers could have accepted this judgment, although they would have noted that this result occurred only where the Lutheran message was improperly proclaimed or misunderstood. They continued to criticize Roman Catholicism and other forms of Protestantism in the rare moments in which they engaged in inter-confessional polemics, but they also revealed by their borrowings from representatives of these groups that they appreciated the sincere concern for spiritual growth which the other traditions exhibited. In this respect, their outlook was more ecumenical then the traditional orientation of many Lutherans.

Lutheran theologians and pastors in the Reformation era had certainly believed in the importance of sanctification, but the felt need to differentiate Lutheranism from Catholicism was so strong in those formative years that the relationship between justification and sanctification was not always explained in a way which ordinary lay people could comprehend. By concentrating on this specific deficiency, the devotional writers of the seventeenth century succeeded in making many simple believers see for the first time the far-reaching implications of the faith which they were taught to confess with their mouths.

A frontispiece engraving in one of Spener's books, *The Duties of Life*, vividly depicts the chief problems addressed by seventeenth century spirituality and neatly summarizes the view of the Christian life which Arndt, Müller, Scriver and Spener all shared. At the bottom of the frontispiece are small emblems picturing three kinds of imperfect Christians: the sleeping Christian who is alive but not active; the hypocritical Christian who is active but not living in true faith; and worst of all the lifeless Christian who is neither living nor active. In the center of the frontispiece stands a woman who displays the tablets of the law written on her heart and holds in her hand a crucifix and a mirror which confronts her with an image of her own face. This figure symbolizes the true Christian

---

[41] Ibid., 11f, 125f, 253f, 322f.

who is both living and active, whose heart and external mode of life have
been transformed by true faith.   In contrast to the complacent or
indifferent figures who are really false Christians, this person illustrates the
idea that grace effects a rebirth and changes the way a person acts and
thinks.[42]

These seventeenth century Lutherans were convinced that this
optimistic estimate of the possibility of spiritual growth was consistent with
the confessional articles of their tradition and the theology of Luther
himself. They often supported their view of sanctification by citing Luther's
comments about faith in his 1522 preface to the Epistle to the Romans.
Luther had, in fact, described faith as a divine work which kills the Old
Adam and fashions the believer into a totally different person. More than
once, Luther had called faith a living, powerful thing which transforms a
person's heart, soul and mind.[43]   And yet, there are some significant
differences between the perspective of these Lutherans and the basic
assumptions which prevail in Luther's later theological writings.   While
Luther acknowledged the importance of spiritual growth, he consistently
noted that believers must always take refuge in the alien righteousness of
Christ. The Christian is *simul justus et peccator*, at the same time justified
and still a sinner. Luther increasingly preferred to view the Christian life as
a continuous process of beginning again.[44]

None of the seventeenth century devotional writers would have
denied that Christians remain sinners to some extent throughout earthly
life, but they could not believe that God did not act to diminish the power
of sin in the lives of those who had the gift of true faith. This expectation
encouraged careful scrutiny of the observable signs of holy living and the
prescription of ways to promote continued growth. Luther, by contrast,
was averse to such preoccupation with empirical piety. From his point of
view, the progress of sanctification was not a clear object of psychological
observation. To look for signs of growth and to depend on techniques of
spiritual development ran the risk of promoting a return to self-
preoccupation and self-assertion. Whereas for Luther the Christian is a

---

[42] Phillip Jacob Spener, *Die evangelische Lebens-Pflichten in einem Jahrgang der
Predigten* (Frankfurt: J. D. Zunner, 1707).

[43] WA *Deutsche Bibel*, 7:10.

[44] It should be noted that there are disagreements among Luther scholars about the
degree to which he expected spiritual growth to take place in this life. See the
contrasting assessments of Regin Prenter, *Spiritus Creator*, trans. John Jensen
(Philadelphia: Muhlenberg Press, 1953): 64-100, and Axel Gyllenkrok, *Rechtfertigung
und Heiligung in der frühen evangelischen Theologie Luthers* (Wiesbaden: Otto
Harrasowitz, 1952): 99-111.

convalescent sinner who trusts in the physician's promise that healing will take place despite the absence or clear signs of recovery, the seventeenth century spiritual writers expected to find evidence of restored health however slowly it might sometimes appear.

These leaders in the effort to promote piety also turned away from the preoccupation with strict standards of doctrinal orthodoxy evident in the orientation of Luther and the most prominent of his theological disciples. Their spiritual advice moved instead in the direction of establishing precise norms of religious experience and behavior. This trend had the potential of reintroducing the problem of spiritual despondency which the Reformation had sought to overcome. Their encouragement of intense self-examination and scrupulous avoidance of all forms of worldliness was also capable of degenerating into petty legalism. The presence of these traits can be observed in some of the most zealous admirers of these authors, particularly among some Pietists in the eighteenth and nineteenth century. In the seventeenth century, however, the major writers of Lutheran devotional literature felt little need to speak out, at length, about these dangers, for they were convinced that complacency or indifference were the more pressing problems to be confronted.

9

The Sense of God's Presence: Spiritual Vision and Discipline in the Early Wesleyan Witness

DAVID TRICKETT

Literature having to do with the phenomenon now commonly identified as "spirituality" is rapidly increasing in accumulative bulk. As one scans the wide range of articles and books now available, it becomes rather clear that there is probably not yet any genuine consensus as to what constitutes an adequate vision of the subject. The perspective offered here suggests that a fruitful way to comprehend spirituality is to think in terms of a vision of the world and the significance that vision has for one's embodiment of faith. Spirituality has to do with the formation of character, with the shaping of one's identity as a disciple of a tradition. It is, as it were, a path which one is led to follow in a disciplined way. Though certainly involving one's intellectual capacities, it also requires the employment of one's conative and affective senses. The now-unknown author of *The Cloud of Unknowing* has left us another text, sometimes called *A Letter of Private Direction*; in it, one can discern counsel toward this end: "the path . . . demands that you constantly insist on bare consciousness of your own self, always offering your being—the most valuable sacrifice you can offer—to God. . . . of course it is right to say that a human being

naturally wants to know, but it is also true to say no one can experience
God—tasting him in spirit, that is—by any means other than grace, no
matter how much natural or acquired knowledge he or she possesses."[1]

Though there are remarkable parallel developments in spiritual
disciplines representative of all the world's major religious traditions, it
remains the case that the distinctive histories of these various strains of
faith have helped to shape a number of spiritualities. Within the spectrum
of the Christian witness, one of the rays of spiritual light that is now coming
into clearer focus than ever before is a movement tied to certain persons
and events of the eighteenth century, first in England and later in North
America and ultimately—in our own day—found all around the world. This
is the stream of spiritual vision and discipline known variously as the
Methodist movement or the Wesleyan witness. Yet, as no one would be
inclined to deny, this distinctive witness did not spring into being *sui generis*;
it began as something of a reform movement within the Church of England,
and it is within the rich Anglican heritage that many of its roots can be
found.

John Wesley (1703-91), *paterfamilias* of the Methodist movement,
was reared in a household wherein biblical, as well as both Anglican and
Puritan, spiritual insights were part of daily life.[2] Over the course of time,
his spiritual nourishment included not only the Edwardian homilies and
immersion in the Book of Common Prayer, but also a number of quite
significant devotional writings that have influenced other people as well.[3]
Several of these works seem to stand above the rest: Jeremy Taylor's *Holy
Living* (1650) and *Holy Dying* (1651; in subsequent years, this was printed

---

[1] *A Letter of Private Direction* (New York: Crossroad, 1981): 73.

[2] For studies of Wesley's earliest years, see, for example, the first volume of Robert
Southey, *Life of Wesley* (London: Longman, Hunt, 1920); volume one of Luke Tyerman,
Life and Times of the Rev. John Wesley, M.A. (New York): Harper and Brothers, 1872);
and the first volume of Martin Schmidt, *John Wesley: A Theological Biography* (London:
Epworth, 1962). Though I shall not pursue the Puritan influence on Wesley (especially
in connection with the sense of "inward assurance"), it is nonetheless an important factor
upon his thought. See, for example, Robert Monk, *John Wesley: His Puritan Heritage*
(Nashville: Abingdon, 1966). Other useful pertinent studies include Albert C. Outler's
introductory essay in the new critical edition of *The Works of John Wesley. Volume I:
Sermons I: 1-33* (Nashville: Abingdon, 1984): 1-100; Thomas A. Langford, *Practical
Divinity: Theology in the Wesleyan Tradition* (Nashville: Abingdon, 1983); and David
Lowes Watson, "Methodist Spirituality," in *Protestant Spiritual Traditions*, ed. Frank C.
Senn (New York: Paulist, 1986): 217-273.

[3] For a list of Wesley's readings between 1725 and 1734, see Appendix I in V.H.H.
Green, *The Young Mister Wesley. A Study of John Wesley and Oxford* (New York: St.
Martin's, 1961): 305-19. Further data are available in the dissertations (at Duke
University) of Steve Harper and Richard P. Heitzenrater.

together with the earlier work); *The Imitation of Christ*, usually attributed to Thomas à Kempis (and likely written in the first quarter of the fifteenth century); and two works by a contemporary, William Law: *A Practical Treatise Upon Christian Perfection* (1726) and *A Serious Call to a Devout and Holy Life* (1728). About a half-century after what he thought to have been an especially rich formative period in his spiritual pilgrimage, Wesley recorded the significance of his discovery of this body of literature; though the perspective is that of an old man remembering himself when young and struggling with the nature of discipleship, there is no doubt an element of significant continuity between 1777 and 1725. Because this reminiscence is quite illumining, it is quoted at some length:

> In the year 1725, being in the twenty-third year of my age, I met with Bishop Taylor's 'Rule and Exercises of My Holy Living and Dying'. In reading several parts of this book, I was exceedingly affected; that part in particular which relates to purity of intention. Instantly I resolved to dedicate all my life to God, all my thoughts, and words, and actions; being thoroughly convinced, there was no medium; but that every part of my life (and not some only) must either be a sacrifice to God, or myself, that is, in effect, to the devil. . . .

> In the year 1726, I met with Kempis's 'Christian Pattern'. The nature and extent of inward religion, the religion of the heart, now appeared to me in a stronger light than ever it had done before. I saw, that giving even all my life to God (supposing it possible to do this, and go no farther) would profit me nothing, unless I gave my heart, yea, all my heart to him.

> I saw that 'simplicity of intention, and purity of affection', one design in all we speak or do, and one desire ruling all our tempers, are indeed 'the wings of the soul,' without which she can never ascend to the mount of God.

> A year or two after, Mr. Law's 'Christian Perfection' and 'Serious Call' were put into my hands. These convinced me, more than ever, of the absolute impossibility of being half a Christian; and I determined, through his grace (the absolute necessity of which I was deeply sensible of [sic],) to be all-devoted to God, to give him all my soul, my body, and my substance.[4]

These major writings in spiritual direction helped to stir Wesley in such a way that considerations such as vision, intention, sacrifice (and its implicit correlate, discipline), inward experience, and single-mindedness became absolutely crucial rather early on in his life. They were present in the spiritual climate of the "holy club" in Oxford, and they remained important elements in the subsequent Methodist revival.

---

[4] Thomas Jackson, ed., *Works of the Rev. John Wesley, M.A.* (1831), 11: 366-67.

Among the other aspects of his religious heritage that contributed to the spiritual formation of Wesley, another book is worthy of special mention: *The Whole Duty of Man*. This work appeared anonymously in 1657, and by the time Wesley appeared on the scene it had exerted a profound influence on many parts of the Anglican communion. One student of Anglican devotional literature claims that "it was the dominant book of religious instruction throughout the eighteenth century, going almost hand in hand with the Bible and the Prayer Book."[5] The work is relatively simple, and focuses upon what it may mean for people to live the faith they verbally profess. Expounding sections of the Book of Common Prayer and the decalogue, it attempts to help communicants discern their responsibilities ("duties") to God and their neighbors. It stresses accountability, which is a theme that has a fundamental role within the early Wesleyan witness. This accountability is given significant depth by the book's keeping before its readers the liturgical insight that a person exercises his or her discipleship while communing with God and one's neighbors; one's embodiment of faith is without question lived in the presence of God and a community of fellow human beings. By regular participation in, say, the eucharistic liturgy, men and women are existentially "centered" in such a way that they are empowered by the spirit of God within them to live courageously, to persevere, and to embody authentically their "whole duty."

Perhaps a word of caution should be interjected here. The web of influential sources that affected John Wesley is actually considerably more complex than has been indicated thus far. Those who have studied his life and thought with care have come to see that Wesley undertook a regular programme of such wide-ranging reading that in addition to his own immediate Anglican traditions and certain Puritan sources, he knew quite a number of patristic authors (and, indeed, was especially sensitive to certain major themes from orthodoxy, perhaps the most important of which is the idea of "participation"), something of the Continental reformers, and the like. The account given here has had to be selective. Wesley also turned to a significant number of authors who tend to be overlooked by many today. Three of this company are worthy of brief mention here. Robert Nelson helped to form Wesley's sense of importance of the relationship between liturgy and spiritual disciplines such as fasting and prayer—all viewed from

[5] C.J. Stranks, *Anglican Devotion. Studies in the Spiritual Life of the Church of England Between the Reformation and the Oxford Movement* (London: SCM, 1961): 125.

the communal ecclesial perspective.[6]   Among other things, William Beveridge taught Wesley to see the power of prayer not only in the high holy festivals of the church but also in all the "common" moments of an individual's and of the community's life—and that the two go together. Beveridge hammered home the point that "[you] will soon be convinced by your own Experience, that Weekly Sacraments, and Daily Prayers, are the greatest Blessings you can have on this side of Heaven, and the best Way to bring you thither. . . ."[7]   The third influence is Daniel Brevint, whose understanding of the Eucharist made a tremendous impression upon Wesley. Brevint claimed that the service of holy communion is a means of grace, a pledge of happiness and glory yet to come in its fullness, a sign of the present divine graces sustaining the pilgrim people of God, and a participatory memorial of the suffering and death of Christ.[8] Each of these emphases was important for the spiritual life of the Wesleyan witness for most of the eighteenth century.

Though (as with many men and women) it took some time for John Wesley's own spiritual journey to lead him through a stage of genuine struggle and let him emerge with a certain kind of resolution, there is no gainsaying that toward the end of 1738 or in the first months of 1739 Wesley's ministry took a new form. It would appear to be the case that Wesley experienced a profound transformation of his own vision and sense of mission (and certain texts of his own authorship tend to confirm this judgment), and that this experience (often linked to his evening in Aldersgate Street) led him to seek new ways of communicating to the people of his homeland—increasingly, the common people—the transformed understanding of the life of faith that represented for him a new hope for humankind. Of course, the rich spiritual heritage that had had a role in shaping his identity was retained, though he appropriated it afresh.[9] The new feature was Wesley's changed perspective; he had been freed from what somewhat loosely can be termed a "works-righteousness" stance toward the embodiment of faith, for he had come to have an inward assurance that God-in-Christ had freed him from himself for a new life of

---

[6] Cf. Robert Nelson, *A Companion for the Festivals and Fasts of the Church of England: With Collects and Prayers for Each Solemnity* (London: W. Bowyer, 1712).

[7] William Beveridge, *The Great Necessity and Advantage of Public Prayer, and Frequent Communion. Designed to Revive Primitive Piety* (London: R. Smith, 1708): 109.

[8] Daniel Brevint, *The Christian Sacrament and Sacrifice, By Way of Discourse, Meditation, and Prayer, Upon the Nature, Parts, and Blessings of the Holy Communion* (Oxford, 1673), passim.

[9] That Wesley in no way broke from his spiritual rootage is seen both in his own sermons and in his production of *A Christian Library*.

liberty-in-service. Discipleship became for him something slightly different (but the slight difference made a world of difference!) from what it had been earlier in his life; rather than being primarily a "good work" to be done, it became a matter of living doxologically, of seeing that "Christian life is *devotio*, the consecration of the whole man in love to God and neighbor in the full round of life and death."[10] As he travelled the length and breadth of the kingdom with his renewed proclamation of the Christian gospel, Wesley began to have more and more auditors, a significant number of whom also became his followers and supporters. It is to the vision that Wesley shared with these people, those who formed the early Wesleyan movement, and to the spiritual disciplines enjoined upon them, that this discussion now turns.

If one is asked to identify the heart of the "renewed" Wesley's vision, how ought one reply? Before responding, one should remember that it stood squarely within the continuous stream of Christian spirituality that spans the entire history (or better, perhaps, histories) of the church. Yet it also represents a distinctive mode of witness that blossomed in eighteenth-century England, a time and place where some think the established church "was not only lax in the ordering of worship and in pastoral over-sight. At the higher levels of church government there was little co-ordination of responsibilities; ecclesiastical authority had become an empty show, and spiritual initiative dissipated itself in political manoeuvoring."[11] Even if this assessment of the quality of spiritual life in the Anglican Church of Wesley's day is not altogether accurate, it would nevertheless seem to be the case that the period in which Wesley grew to majority was not itself one of the high-water marks of Anglican spirituality. This may in part account for the rise of religious societies in general, and the explosive growth of the Wesleyan witness in particular, during the period. The so-called "evangelical revival" met the spiritual hungers of people, especially the common people, in such a way that the people were enabled anew to sense the presence of the living God in the world abroad and in their own lives. Two metaphors with a venerable history in the literature of spirituality help to characterize basic dimensions of this whole movement, of which the Wesleyan element is of direct concern here: the revival led men and women to *hear* the divine word of grace-with-judgement that justifies, and also to *see* a path of righteousness that leads to sanctification, to a new mode of participating in the divine life (and hence also in the world). A

---

[10] Albert C. Outler, ed., *John Wesley* (New York: Oxford U., 1964): 7.
[11] Frank Baker, *John Wesley and the Church of England* (Nashville: Abingdon, 1970): 3.

distinctive combination of proclamation, evangelism, and nurture, of spiritual formation, lay at the center of this evangelical vision of the Christian witness.

Of recent scholars who have addressed this matter, none has stated better than Albert Outler the heart of the Wesleyan focus of this vision. In his Library of Protestant Thought volume on John Wesley, Outler claims that, according to Wesley's more mature understanding:

> faith is the primary reality in Christian experience but not its totality. It is . . . a *means*—a necessary means—to a still higher end: "Faith . . . is only the handmaid of love. . . ." The goal of the Christian life is holiness, "the *fullness* of faith." This means the consecration of the whole self to God and to the neighbor in love. This, in turn, involves a process of corporate discipline and effort, guided by the motives of "devotion," by which [Wesley] meant the delivering up of one's *whole life* to God. The outcome to be expected in this endeavor is the renewal of the *imago Dei*, mutilated by sin and ruined by waywardness. But our aspiration of holiness is as truly a function of faith as justification itself is. The faith that justifies bears its fruits in the faith that works by love.[12]

At some point after his return to England from Georgia, Wesley came to see that earlier in his life he had perhaps known all (or at least many of) the right words (the outward "show") but had not yet been given the tune (the inward vivifying assurance) in order most effectively to bear witness to the grace of the divine mystery that brings life from death; from that point on, though, he became an ardent supporter of the view that God's grace undergirds every part of the universe, and that it can actually make a difference *firsthand* in the lives of men and women. He claimed that at various stages along life's way, men and women encounter this grace in its several modes: prevenient and preventing, justifying and saving, sanctifying and sacramental. This grace is not an intervention from a God who is utterly outside the realm of human experience; Wesley took with great seriousness the insight he had gleaned from the biblical witness and elsewhere, according to which grace is understood as cooperative. God works with and within people.[13] By thus viewing human life as a response to and cooperation with the activity of God, Wesley mediated two strains of spirituality sometimes thought to be at odds with one another: the "holy living" tradition and the "salvation by (grace through) faith" tradition.

Wesley claimed to be a *homo unius libri*; though this is an accurate assertion only in a certain sense, it does seem to be the case that for most

---

[12] Albert C. Outler, ed., *John Wesley*, 28.
[13] See, for example, Philippians 2:12-13, and the sermon Wesley preached upon this text: "On Working Out Our Own Salvation."

of his life he was grasped by a biblical notion, namely, that people are to be single-minded in their devotion to God, and that those who are will grow in their understanding of the divine mystery.   Such single-mindedness required that there be no major confusion of the creator with the creation; in his articulation of this point, Wesley in some ways prefigured certain figures of more recent times who have defended the "Protestant principle." Nevertheless, even as he maintained that it is only *God* who is to be revered as God, his position also included within itself the embrace of what can be termed the principle of catholicity.   This dimension of his spiritual vision stressed both the absolute inclusiveness of God's grace and the presence of God in the world (which entailed his belief that creatures participate in the creator's life).[14] What might be identified as a mystical element in Wesley's spiritual sensibility can be seen at this point; it often came to expression most clearly in his reflections upon the sacraments, perhaps best of all in his affective attachment to, say, part of the prayer of humble access in the eucharistic liturgy: "that we may for ever more dwell in him, and he in us." One can see also bits of it in Wesley's argument for the reality of perfection in love in a person's life.[15]   In order to live so that these manifestations of God's grace can be efficacious in one's life, however, a person must be committed to a life of discipleship.   Such discipleship is a gift of God, but it is costly.   It requires the transformation of one's life.   In a letter sent to Richard Morgan shortly after the latter's son—a member of Wesley's little band at Oxford—had died, Wesley revealed his understanding of the all-encompassing claim upon one's allegiance that a life of true discipleship makes; here he spoke of discipleship in terms of "religion": "I take religion to be, not the bare saying over so many prayers morning and evening, in public or in private; not anything superadded now and then to a careless or worldly life; but a constant ruling habit of the soul; a renewal of our minds in the image of God; a recovery of the divine likeness; a still-increasing conformity of heart and life to the pattern of our most holy Redeemer."[16]

To make progress in one's path of discipleship, Wesley found, was to make the spiritual journey with other pilgrims.   One of the most effective vehicles of spiritual discipline Wesley ever encountered was the small group meeting.   Any number of accounts of his early experiments at Oxford are

---

[14] For a recent effort to hold both principles together, see Avery Dulles, *The Catholicity of the Church* (Oxford: Clarendon, 1984).

[15] See, for example Albert Outler's introductory essay in *The Works of John Wesley. Volume I*, 55f.

[16] Cited in Richard P. Heitzenrater, *The Elusive Mr. Wesley. Volume One: John Wesley His Own Biographer* (Nashville: Abingdon Press, 1984): 70.

extant, some of them recounting his own memories while others come from different pens. Several years after Wesley's death, John Gambold published a memoir he had written many years earlier, a piece entitled "The Character of Mr. John Wesley." Since having eventually broken with the Methodists, Gambold had also left Anglican orders for the Moravian ministry. Over the course of time, he had been selected to exercise episcopal oversight among the Moravians in England. Despite his divergent spiritual trek, Gambold retained real admirations for the vision and spiritual disciple he remembered in Wesley during the early days of their adulthood. Recalling the vital meetings of the little band in the university community, Gambold told how the group met in one of their member's rooms in college, how they prayed together, how they had a simple meal with one another, how often they sang, and then how they turned to their "chief business," which was "to review what each had done that day, in pursuance of their common design, and to consult what steps were to be taken next."[17] He related how members of the society undertook a variety of social projects, for they saw outreach to the larger community around them to be a basic feature of the faithful life. They fasted regularly, celebrated the Eucharist, and participated in regularly set services of worship outside as well as within the university community. Gambold maintained that at least John Wesley "thought prayer to be more his business than anything else . . . ," though of course this practice was to be cultivated by each group member in the course of his daily routine.[18] As things turned out, Wesley's sense of vocation (and the sense of the group) led him to become the spiritual guide of the little club. Since it was this function that he was largely to have when the Methodist movement left the university cloisters, it will be instructive to see just how it was that Wesley sought to provide spiritual direction for his earliest comrades-in-faith.

Themes later to be crucial—among them, the strict adherence to a disciplined pattern of life that would enable one to "redeem time"—were already present in Wesley's Oxford days. According to Gambold, Wesley "earnestly recommended" that all members of the small group adopt a "method and order" in all that they said and did.[19] A plan for daily conduct included morning devotions (usually at an hour before the sun rose for much of the year!), the determination of what use ought to be the various

---

[17] John Gambold, "The Character of Mr. John Wesley," reprinted in Richard P. Heitzenrater, *The Elusive Mr. Wesley. Volume Two: John Wesley as Seen By Contemporaries and Biographers* (Nashville: Abingdon, 1984): 39.
[18] Ibid., 40.
[19] Ibid., 41.

segments of time in the day (no "trifling" employment is countenanced), the observation of fasts, the visitation of the poor, imprisoned, or ill people, the regular participation in the Eucharist (especially on Sunday), the careful study of the Bible, the transcription of one's daily expenditures of time and energies into a diary, the regular practice of prayer, and the continual meditation upon the riches of divine mystery.[20] Anyone aware of the subsequent history of the Methodists can sense here adumbrations of the general rules for the united societies. It was not in rules as such, however, that Wesley was ever interested; what was most important for him was the nurture of the experience of living in a genuine community, a *koinonia*. In the little holy club in Oxford, Wesley experimented with various means of spiritual formation that he believed to be of service to the *ordo salutis*. Seeds were planted; though it took some time, fruit eventually appeared in the larger Wesleyan revival.

Not long after John Wesley returned from his apparently disastrous (but actually spiritually important) mission to Georgia, he began the extraordinary itinerant ministry for which he is usually remembered; people from London, Newcastle, Bristol, the West Country, and spots in between began to heed his proclamation of the Christian gospel. What, though, was the nature of the spiritual identity and discipline found in this early Wesleyan witness? How were principles and practices that had been employed in a small group of university men adapted for a much larger constituency? It is one thing to oversee a handful of Oxford friends, and quite another to attempt shepherding thousands of men and women, many of whom had never had much—if any—formal education. How would one attempt to convey the vivifying sense of God's presence in human life when the community with which one were called to work is vastly larger than—and in some respects clearly qualitatively different from—the *koinonia* within which one's spiritual guidance had thus far been exercised?

For one thing, at least in a certain respect Wesley had no confusion about what he was trying to do; his efforts for the common folk were aimed at helping them participate actively in the fellowship he knew as the body of Christ, which always remained for him the Church of England. Wesley wanted in no way to start a new church. He took very seriously Article XIX of the Anglican communion's Articles of Religion, which states that "the visible Church of Christ is a congregation of faithful men, in which the pure Word of God is preached, and the Sacraments be duly ministered according to Christ's ordinance in all those things that of necessity are

---

[20] Ibid., 41ff.

requisite to the same," even though he seems to have treated the last qualifying clause in a way that has raised some eyebrows.[21] Wesley's hope was that his societies should serve within the Church of England as an "evangelical order defined by their unique *mission*: 'to spread scriptural holiness over these lands.'"[22] In a number of places, Wesley made a case for an understanding of the Methodist movement that places it within its larger ecclesial context, rather like the notion of an *ecclesiola in ecclesia*. He wanted people to sense that fundamental unity can encompass diversity, and in this conviction he revealed a genuinely ecumenical sensitivity. In his sermon "Of the Church," for example, Wesley used Ephesians 4:1-6 as his text, which in part asserts that Christian people who heed their vocation given them by God are to forbear "one another in love; endeavouring to keep the unity of the Spirit in the bond of peace. There is one body, and one Spirit, even as ye are called in one hope of your calling; one Lord, one faith, one baptism, one God and Father of all, who is above all, and through all, and in you all."[23] Wesley argued for the widespread acceptance of the idea "church" that would include his societies within the one, holy, catholic, apostolic body of Christ. In a related sermon entitled "On Schism," he set forth a view of schism that plays upon a distinction between diversity and disunity, with the Methodists clearly not falling into the latter category. One can also note that even within the Methodist societies Wesley went to considerable lengths to encourage his followers to remain in full communion with Canterbury; he formulated preaching services, for example, that were "liturgically insufficient," so that men and women would not begin to think that he somehow approved of any break with the Church of England.[24]

So it was from within a larger ecclesial framework that Wesley exercised his function as spiritual guide, or mentor, of the Methodists. This ecclesial setting for his work encompassed a historical dimension as well; in part because of his strong sense of identity within the universal body of Christ, he was aware of living amidst a vast cloud of Christian witnesses whose respective pilgrimages had been completed, but who still had a presence that was spiritually instructive for the current generation of faithful persons. Wesley learned from this collective body a vision of

---

[21] Article XIX, "Of the Church." Articles of Religion, Book of Common Prayer.
[22] Albert C. Outler, "Do Methodists Have a Doctrine of the Church?" Dow Kirkpatrick, ed., *The Doctrine of the Church* (Nashville: Abingdon Press, 1964): 14.
[23] John Wesley, "Of the Church," reprinted in Albert C. Outler, ed., *John Wesley*, 308.
[24] Albert C. Outler, "Do Methodists Have a Doctrine of the Church?" 13. It is also possible, for example, to grasp the force of the message in Wesley's sermon "On the Duty of Constant Communion" as being pertinent in this connection.

ordered discipleship, the abiding aim of which vision was always to produce holy living—particularly "inward righteousness, attended with the peace of God; and 'joy in the Holy Ghost'"—never separated, of course, from the setting of a community of believers.[25] "Discipline" was the overarching concept Wesley used to characterize the requirements of the spiritual path his people were to follow; he believed that if one were to maintain a properly ordered embodiment of faith (necessarily grounded in divine grace), it would be possible to live a sanctified life. This being the case, the effective employment of various "means of grace," the means by which one carries out disciplined living, became absolutely essential.

In a sermon on "The Means of Grace," Wesley attempted to set straight those of his followers who had endorsed a certain Moravian interpretation of "outward observances" as either unnecessary or dangerous in one's spiritual life. He countered the "quietism" of those men and women by developing an idea he based upon Malachi 3:7, "Ye are gone away from mine ordinances, and have not kept them."[26] Though it is true, Wesley said, that the observance of outward and visible religious acts ("ordinances") ought never be confused with "religion of the heart," people should see that both are vehicles of divine grace and that they properly go together in the authentic embodiment of faith. Indeed; in contrast to certain evangelical Christian interpretive schemes, Wesley's vision held certain "outward signs, words, or actions" to be ordained by God precisely in order to serve as the "*ordinary* channels whereby he might convey to men preventing, justifying, or sanctifying grace."[27] Wesley then specified some of the more significant of these means of grace, and one can see from Wesley's list that there can be no question but that he saw himself to stand within the mainstream of Anglican spiritual tradition, "prayer, whether in secret or with the great congregation; searching the Scriptures (which implies reading, hearing, and meditating thereon) and receiving the Lord's Supper, eating bread and drinking wine in remembrance of him. . . ."[28] These acts of disciplined spiritual life (as well as at least two others—fasting and the close encounter with fellow Christians that Wesley called "Christian conference") are instituted means of grace, and are conducive to a person's spiritual nourishment because the living spirit of God is present "in and by

[25] John Wesley, "A Plain Account of the People Called Methodists," cited in Gerald O. McCulloh, "The Discipline of Life in Early Methodism Through Preaching and Other Means of Grace," Dow Kirkpatrick, ed., *The Doctrine of the Church*, 169.
[26] John Wesley, "The Means of Grace," in *The Works of John Wesley. Volume I: Sermons I: 1-33*, ed. Albert C. Outler, 378.
[27] Ibid., 382.
[28] Ibid.

them."[29] Even if a person does not have a personal inner assurance of God's saving love, he or she is called to wait patiently for the dawn of that inward sense *while participating in these means of grace.* God's spirit can and will work within people even if they are not clearly aware of it.

As he argued thus against the proponents of spiritual quietism, Wesley had also to protect himself against the charge that he was putting forth a programme of "works-righteousness." In a number of his sermons, including some quite early ones, he plainly claimed that human beings are saved only by God's grace, as mediated through faith. "All the blessings which God hath bestowed upon man," he asserted, "are of his mere grace, bounty, or favour: his free, undeserved favour, favour altogether undeserved, man having no claim to the least of his mercies."[30] In fact, though one can employ any number of "outward signs" of a fully faithful life (and should not be discouraged from doing so), if that person has not the awareness that he or she stands justified and free by virtue of the divine grace, then that person can be no more than an "almost Christian." Though there is real hope for persons in this position, they can become utterly pathetic creatures if they do not eventually come genuinely to know that it is God who works within them to bring them to freedom from bondage. A major difficulty arises if a person confuses his or her role with God's in the *ordo salutis,* and this is rather easy to do, for those who earnestly employ certain means of grace tend to reflect in their lives "a real design to serve God, a hearty desire to do his will. It is necessarily implied that a man have a sincere view of pleasing God in all things: in all his conversation, in all his actions, in all he does or leaves undone. This design, if any man be 'almost a Christian,' runs through the whole tenor of his life. This is the moving principle both in his doing good, his abstaining from evil, and his using the ordinances of God."[31] The more zealous one is in working out his or her salvation, the greater the tendency to misperceive his or her real role in the process. What people are to do is straightfowardly sense that it is the divine presence that is the prime agent of salvation; it is God's grace that awakens people and leads them to respond to the divine embrace, not only by serving God but also by showing commitment to neighbors. And the various means of grace are instrumental in helping to guide souls toward this vision and its disciplined embodiment.

---

[29] Ibid., 382. See also "The Large Minutes," *The Works of John Wesley, Volume VIII,* 322ff.

[30] John Wesley, "Salvation By Faith," *The Works of John Wesley Volume I: Sermons I,* 117. See also Wesley's sermon on "Justification By Faith," in the same volume, 181-99.

[31] John Wesley, "The Almost Christian," ibid., 136.

These instituted means of grace were intended to help weave together one's spiritual life within both the church and the much smaller and more intimate societies that the Methodists formed.   Prayer, for instance, was to be employed by a person in all places where he or she was to be found; if one prayed regularly, both in the strict privacy of one's own devotional moments at, say, the beginning of the day, and in the increasingly more public settings of one's family, one's society fellowship, and the gathered community of the church, one would in some fruitful sense be found by God.   Whether in the form of petition, intercession, thanksgiving, or contemplation, prayer was believed to open a person to God in such a way that he or she would be able to discern a reconciling, healing power in his or her life.   This presence, God's spirit, could eventually transform one's vision, thereby increasing one's growth in wisdom. Such was to be prepared for new and increased responsibilities in one's life of disciplined faith. As things developed, in the early Wesleyan witness prayer and hymnody were often very closely related to one another; indeed, one of the literary legacies left by the Wesleys and their followers is a large body of hymns, many of which have served as sung group prayers.

In conjunction with prayer, the Methodist people were enjoined to "search" the Scriptures, by which term Wesley meant that they should hear it when rightly proclaimed (one can sense here that an important responsibility was placed upon the preacher, and that is right; preaching was an important part of the early Wesleyan movement), as well as that they should regularly read the Bible and meditate upon it.[32] No matter what was one's status in the *ordo salutis*, a careful engagement with biblical texts (under the guidance of a right-minded mentor) was deemed to be spiritually enriching.   The matter of being guided in one's study was important; in order to prevent aberrant interpretations of the gospel from popping up, a system of accountability in the context of the small group was established.

The most important of the various instituted means of grace for the early Methodists was the Eucharist. Wesley maintained that "all who desire an increase of the grace of God are to wait for it in partaking of the Lord's Supper."[33] By communicating regularly (Wesley preferred to refer to "constant communion"), and by doing it "in remembrance" of Christ in such a way that the anamnesis is participatory, a person's vision of the Eucharist can shift sufficiently so that when a man or woman consumes the elements

---

[32] John Wesley, "The Means of Grace," 387.
[33] Ibid., 389.

he or she can sense that he or she is brought to an awareness of really participating in the divine life, that, as it were, he or she is consciously re-membered into the body of Christ by being "made conformable to the death of Christ" and the life-giving grace it conveys.[34] This early Wesleyan understanding of the efficacious channelling of divine grace through the Eucharist is evident in this representative selection from a volume entitled *Hymns on the Lord's Supper*, which John and Charles Wesley issued in 1745 as a companion to their people's worship:

> Come, Holy Ghost, thine Influence shed,
>   And realize the Sign,
> Thy Life infuse into the Bread,
>   Thy Power into the Wine.
>
> Effectual let the Tokens prove,
>   And made by Heavenly art,
> Fit channels to convey thy Love
>   To every Faithful Heart.[35]

The theme of divine-human interaction, or cooperation (synergism), which lies at the heart of John Wesley's theological perspective is envisioned in the above excerpt from a hymn as mediated by the sacramental means of grace present in the Lord's Supper. It was in part this understanding of the relationship between God and human beings that led Wesley to see the Eucharist as paradigmatic of all the means of grace, and therefore to urge "constant communion" to his people. In a sermon on "The Duty of Constant Communion," Wesley stated that "it is the duty of every Christian to receive the Lord's Supper as often as he can."[36] Beyond the fact that sharing in the sacrament can lead persons to see afresh their participation in the life of God, its practice also conveys to those who worthily take the elements "the forgiveness of our past sins" and "the present strengthening and refreshing of our souls."[37] It provides rich spiritual nourishment, so, as the body requires nourishment constantly in order to function properly, the "true rule" that is to guide one's spiritual discipline is this: "so often are we to receive [the Eucharist] as God gives us opportunity."[38] If one does anything less, he or she shows an inadequate

---

[34] Ibid.

[35] "Hymn LXXII," John and Charles Wesley, *Hymns on the Lord's Supper. With a Preface Concerning the Christian Sacrament and Sacrifice, extracted from Doctor Brevint* (Bristol: Felix Farley, 1745): 51.

[36] John Wesley, "The Duty of Constant Communion," in *John Wesley*, ed. Albert C. Outler, 335.

[37] Ibid.

[38] Ibid. 336.

grasp of the significance of Christ's command regarding the sacrament (cf. Luke 22:19: "Do this in remembrance of me") and of the real communication of grace mediated through the Eucharist.[39]

Wesley saw that it simply would not do merely to tell people they ought to partake of the instituted means of grace. In order for spiritual fruit to appear, men and women must "trust" the means of grace.[40] To trust them was to seek within them the blessing of God, to believe that "if I wait in this way I shall attain what otherwise I should not."[41] Thus to speak of trusting the instituted means of grace was to raise the question of the "*order*" and the *manner*" of their employment.[42] Building upon his fundamental conviction that one is ripe for nurture if only one has "a desire to flee from the wrath to come," Wesley saw that a person could be led to trust the means of grace, a step at a time, while undertaking a spiritual pilgrimage within a relatively small group. Other people have a vital role in each person's spiritual development. It is here that Wesley showed his grasp of a profound insight: growth in grace is an intensely personal experience, but it is never truly private. One is to grow toward spiritual maturity within a social setting that does not ignore the individual needs of the persons making up the group, and yet (as he had found earlier in Oxford) a group that is sensitive to its constituent members must also have operating principles, and rules, that help bring the individuals together into a coherent group. That the early Wesleyan witness was able to hold together the necessarily personal dimension of spiritual direction with sensitivity to the demands of group process is no mean accomplishment.

To provide for this two-fold (i.e., individual and social) model of spiritual nourishment, Wesley championed what he called the exercise of prudential means of grace along with the instituted means. Some five years after the Methodist societies had begun in earnest, the first Annual Conference was held; in the minutes of that series of meetings in 1744, one finds recorded the consensus of those gathered that the process of submitting oneself to the judgment of others within one's society, and the pledge to keep strictly confidential whatever transpired within the group meetings, were actually spiritually significant principles.[43] Among other

---

[39] For a discussion of the role of the Eucharist in the early Wesleyan witness, see John C. Bowmer, *The Sacrament of the Lord's Supper in Early Methodism* (London: Dacre, 1951). A related treatment is found in John R. Parris, *John Wesley's Doctrine of the Sacraments* (London: Epworth, 1963).

[40] John Wesley, "The Means of Grace," 390.

[41] Ibid. 391.

[42] Ibid. 393.

[43] "Minutes" of the First Annual Conference, Albert C. Outler, ed., *John Wesley*, 136.

things, they helped to engender the trust that was necessary for people to grow together in grace. But it had also become clear that different group configurations were needed, for not all people had begun their spiritual journeys at the same existential point, nor had they proceeded at the same pace. Wesley's original "united society," begun in 1739, had been "a company of men having the form and seeking the power of godliness, united in order to pray together, to receive the word of exhortation, and to watch over one another in love, that they may help each other to work out their salvation."[44] But it had been only a short time before the Wesleyan revival had found it crucial to subdivide its organ of mutual trust and accountability into several kinds of bodies: not only were there to be the united societies, but also bands, select societies, and groups known as "the Penitents."[45] Within this network of groups, Wesley set aside some people as representative leaders (while allowing certain others to emerge from the group dynamic), and for each of the several categories of discipleship he set up a system of accountability. In "The Large Minutes" there is an extended statement focusing upon aspects of the respective responsibilities and encouragements given seekers at different stages of spiritual maturity.[46] Wesley was aware, however, that certain kinds of organizational structure can at best only *aid* spiritual development. God is the one who works in the souls of men and women, so Wesley saw that it is possible for a person to participate for a time within a society and do so without bearing fruit in any obvious way.[47]

Even while holding this view, Wesley believed that the exercise of some of the prudential means of grace (as with the instituted means) cannot help but be of benefit in any person's life—"namely, watching, denying ourselves, taking up our cross, [and the] exercise of the presence of God."[48] Armed with this conviction, Wesley put together series of questions that were to be asked of those persons who participated in the Methodist revival. The aim of the disciplined engagement with this kind of query was to build up each individual's witness to the reality of divine grace in his or her life and to strengthen the collective witness of the group itself. Questions included matters such as these: "Do you steadily watch against the world, the devil, yourselves, your besetting sin? . . . Do you deny yourself every pleasure of sense, imagination, honour? Are you temperate

---

[44] "The Rules of the United Societies," Albert C. Outler, ed., *John Wesley*, 178.
[45] "Minutes" of the First Annual Conference, 143.
[46] "The Large Minutes," cited in David Lowes Watson, "Methodist Spirituality," 239.
[47] Ibid.
[48] Ibid.

in all things? . . . Wherein do you 'take up your cross daily?' Do you
cheerfully bear your cross (whatever is grievous to nature) as a gift of God,
and labour to profit thereby? . . . Do you endeavour to set God always
before you; as to see his eye continually fixed upon you?"[49]

Questions such as these could be asked of any spiritually "awakened"
person (Being thus "awake" was the criterion for inclusion in the societies).
The various societies were divided into classes of about a dozen people
each; there, once a week under one of their own who had been appointed
to serve as their leader, class members were advised, reproved, comforted,
and exhorted in order that "their souls prosper."[50] In addition to asking
after the state of each person's soul, the class leader also collected
contributions of money which were used for poor relief, and also met with
ministers regularly in order adequately to care for their flock. To continue
in membership within a class required some evidence of a person's desire of
salvation, which not only entailed regular attendance (which before very
long was monitored by the issuance of tickets of admission, quarterly
examinations, and even trial memberships) but also adherence to three
basic rules (illustrated with a number of examples); first, one was to do no
harm, and was enjoined to avoid "evil in every kind; especially that which is
most generally practised."[51] Second, one was to do good, "by being in every
kind merciful after their power; as they have opportunity, doing good of
every possible sort, and as far as is possible, to all men. . . ."[52] Third, one
was to use the instituted means of grace ("by attending upon all the
ordinances of God"), which in this list of rules were identified as "the public
worship of God; the ministry of the word, either read or expounded; the
Supper of the Lord; private prayer; searching the Scriptures; and fasting, or
abstinence."[53] Clearly, the class within the society was a source of mutual
nurture, wherein members made covenant with one another and God to
build up each other in a way of faith that could transform their lives.
Believing that their chief purpose was to bear witness to God's love and be
"fellow-labourers" with that mysterious presence, the early Methodists
struggled with one another in their class meetings to embody a discipline
that would free them from resistance to the efficacy of the means of grace.[54]

---

[49] Ibid., 239-40.
[50] "The Rules of the United Societies, 178.
[51] Ibid.
[52] Ibid., 179.
[53] Ibid.
[54] In this connection, see two volumes by Leslie F. Church: *The Early Methodist People*
(London: Epworth, 1948), and *More About the Early Methodist People* (London:
Epworth, 1949).

Those within the societies who were "supposed to have remission of sins" were given additional matters with which to deal; they were grouped into bands. Those others who seemed "to walk in the light of God" were gathered into still smaller groups, the select societies. And those who had "made shipwreck of their faith" were called aside to meet as "penitents."[55] Members of the bands and select societies were to continue in their regular weekly class meetings as part of the societies even as they undertook more rigorous soul-searching in their respectively smaller units. It was expected that as one moved ahead in the pursuit of holy living, demands placed upon one would increase.

The chief end of the band meeting was to fulfill the biblical command in James 5:16, namely, "confess your faults to one another, and pray for one another, that ye may be healed." Meeting once a week, beginning with prayer or singing, the agenda moved under the guidance of a leader who emerged naturally from within the group. Each person in turn, "Freely and plainly," was able to address the "true state" of his or her soul, specifying faults that had been committed ("in thought, word, or deed"), and any temptations faced, since the last band meeting.[56] The meetings were rather emotionally intense, for prior to a person's admission to a band he or she was not only given scrutiny about the present state of his or her soul, but also told that in band meetings one must expect probing inquiry into one's awareness of whether he or she had "the forgiveness of sins" and whether "the love of God [is] shed abroad in your heart." More than this, though, persons were asked these questions: "do you desire to be told of all your faults, and that plain and home?" and "do you desire we should tell you whatsoever we think, whatsoever we fear, whatsoever we hear concerning you . . . [and] that, in doing this, we should cut to the quick, and search your heart to the bottom?"[57] Trust, confidentiality, and mutual accountability were vital to the functioning of the bands; only within such an environment was the regular agenda capable of being discussed fruitfully:

1. What known sins have you committed since our last meeting?
2. What temptations have you met with?
3. How were you delivered?
4. What have you thought, said, or done, of which you doubt whether it be sin or not?
5. Have you nothing you desire to keep secret?[58]

---

[55] "Minutes" of the First Annual Conference, 143.
[56] "Rules of the Bands," Albert C. Outler, ed., *John Wesley*, 180.
[57] Ibid., 180-81.
[58] Ibid. 181.

It was from this body, not from the larger class meeting of the societies, that the "penitents" tended to come. It was believed that a person "on the way," as it were, and not merely "awakened" as a relatively immature spiritual seeker, was much more likely to have the possibility of experiencing a "shipwreck" of faith. When a person fell, by one or another willful transgression of a command of God (as seen, for example, in the various sets of principles and rules having to do with the employment of the means of grace), he or she was taken aside for special instruction, advice, and other forms of nurture. As things seemed to turn out, those who "recovered the ground they had lost" were usually much more sensitive to the awareness of human frailty and every person's need for divine grace than they had been previously, so they seemed to work ever more diligently for the experience of the fullness of love in their lives. It was from this group that membership in the select societies tended to be drawn.[59]

The select societies were those groups wherein the Wesleyan vision of sanctified living bore witness to the "best rule of all" that was sensed to be present in the hearts of their members. In addition to the guidelines that informed the activities of the bands, the select societies had only three others: "1. Let nothing spoken in this Society be spoken again; no, not even to the members of it. 2. Every member agrees absolutely to submit to his minister in all indifferent things. 3. Every member, till we can have all things common, will bring once a week, *bona fide*, all he can spare towards a common stock."[60] It was here that the fullness of faith, the "true circumcision of the heart" (by which term Wesley meant "the distinguishing mark of a true follower of Christ . . . a right state of soul—a mind and spirit renewed after the image of him that created it"[61]), could be discerned among the Methodist disciples of the Christian gospel. The way of holy living and dying, the path toward perfection in love, was most powerfully sought by these, the relatively few members of the select societies.

When viewed as complementary (as they should be), the societies and their classes, the bands, the select societies, and even the groups of penitents, are seen to have worked as various organic parts of that member of the Anglican communion known as the Wesleyan, or Methodist, witness. These groups were instruments, or vehicles, through which the various

---

[59] For a recent discussion of the various patterns of group-organization found in the early Wesleyan witness, see David Lowes Watson, *The Early Methodist Class Meeting: Its Origins and Significance* (Nashville: Discipleship Resources, 1985). For a treatment of "penitents," see esp. 121.

[60] "Minutes" of the First Annual Conference, 144.

[61] John Wesley, "The Circumcision of the Heart," *The Works of John Wesley. Volume I: Sermons I: 1-33*, 402.

means of grace could be mediated through a communal setting to pilgrims at various stages of their journeys in disciplined faith. A conviction of the catholicity of God's grace suffused the whole movement, along with the sense that the proper vocation given men and women—by God's grace, in which they participate—was to embody gratitude and benevolence. Gratitude was to be given God and benevolence to their neighbors-in-existence. An epitome of this basic spiritual vision, showing as it also does the ultimate aim of the spiritual discipline of the early Wesleyan witness, is found in the 1780 volume, *A Collection of Hymns, For the Use of the People Called Methodists*. It also provides a fitting conclusion to this discussion of the sense of God's presence in the eighteenth-century Methodist pilgrimage of faith:

> Love divine, all loves excelling,
>   Joy of heaven, to earth come down,
> Fix in us thy humble dwelling,
>   All thy faithful mercies crown!
> Jesu, thou art all compassion,
>   Pure, unbounded love thou art;
> Visit us with thy salvation!
>   Enter every trembling heart.

* * *

> Finish then thy new creation,
>   Pure and spotless let us be;
> Let us see thy great salvation
>   Perfectly restored in thee;
> Changed from glory into glory,
>   Till in heaven we take our place,
> Till we cast our crowns before thee,
>   Lost in wonder, love, and praise.[62]

---

[62] "Hymn 374," The Works of John Wesley. Volume VII: *A Collection of Hymns for the Use of the People Called Methodists*, ed. Franz Hildebrandt and Oliver A. Beckerlegge, with James Dale (Oxford: Clarendon, 1983): 545, 547.

10

The Visions of Margaret Mary Alacoque from a Rahnerian Perspective

ANNICE CALLAHAN, R. S. C. J.

In this paper, I want to discuss the visions of Margaret Mary Alacoque with the help of Karl Rahner's insights into their authenticity, their historical relevance, and their theological significance. First, I want to evaluate these visions of Margaret Mary Alacoque in the light of contemporary theological principles. Second, I want to account for their historical place in the formulation of one form of devotion to the Sacred Heart that was affected by these visions. I have decided to use Karl Rahner's reflections on these visions as a vehicle for evaluation not only because he has addressed these particular points in a credible way, but also because his other writings on the Sacred Heart give this topic a larger context of devotion to the Sacred Heart and of Christian spirituality in general.

The visions of Margaret Mary Alacoque are difficult to gauge in terms of their authenticity, their historical relevance, and their significance in shaping a form of devotion to the Sacred Heart. To evaluate their authenticity, we must distinguish the divine origin of these visions from Margaret Mary's subjectivity. To estimate their historical relevance, we ought to keep in mind that the situation at the time was marked not only by

The author has incorporated this material into her book *Karl Rahner's Spirituality of the Pierced Heart: A Reinterpretation of Devotion to the Sacred Heart* (1985). Used by permission of University Press of America.

Jansenism but also by a secularization which parallels that of Christians in today's world. To determine the theological significance of these visions, we can examine their importance in contributing to the form taken by Sacred Heart devotion which developed afterwards. In addition, we can make qualifying remarks about certain practices connected with this form of the devotion which seem to contradict church doctrine.

On December 27, 1673, Margaret Mary Alacoque (1647-90), a Visitandine living at the convent in Paray-le-Monial, France, claimed to have experienced Christ's revelation of the secrets of his Heart to her. In an apparition to her, he called her his beloved disciple, and expressed his desire to entrust to her the mission of spreading the love of his Heart for humanity.[1] Margaret Mary related that the next year, possibly on the Friday within the octave of Corpus Christi, she saw his Heart as a burning furnace of love, and heard him ask her to carry out two of his designs: a Communion of reparation on the First Friday of every month, and a weekly Holy Hour of reparation on Thursday nights.[2] Sometime later, Margaret Mary reported that she saw the disembodied Heart of Jesus as it had been pictured in the propagation of the cult with a wound mark in it, a crown of thorns around it, and a cross on top.[3] Most likely on June 16, 1675, Margaret Mary said she experienced what was later called the "Great Apparition," during which Jesus asked that the First Friday after the octave of Corpus Christi be dedicated to honor his Heart and that Communion be received on that day in reparation for the insults against the Blessed Sacrament exposed on the altar.[4] According to Margaret Mary's account, on July 2, 1688, Christ appeared to her as a disembodied Heart, together with Mary, mother of the Lord, Francis de Sales (1567-1622), her founder, and Claude de la Colombière (d. 1682), her trusted confessor.[5]

AUTHENTICITY

The visions of Margaret Mary Alacoque can be considered imaginative visions.[6] It is hard to evaluate their authenticity because:

---

[1] Auguste Hamon, *Histoire de la Dévotion au Sacré Coeur* (Paris: Beauchesne, 1924): 1, 140-1.

[2] Ibid., 150.

[3] Ibid., 140-41.

[4] Ibid., 173, 430.

[5] Jean-Joseph Languet, *La Vie de la Vénérable Mère Marguerite-Marie*, ed. Léon Gauthey (Paris: Librairie Poussièlques Frères, 1890): 330-31, n. 1.

[6] For example, see Karl Rahner, S. J., *Visions and Prophecies, Quaestiones Disputatae 10*, trans. Charles Henkey and Richard Strachan (London: Burns & Oates, 1966): 32. (Hereafter cited in the text as *Visions*.) Earlier he reflects on the three kinds of visions

"almost all their thought and imagery can be found in earlier published books and especially in the traditions of her order" (*Visions*, 63, n.63). Allegedly, visions of the Sacred Heart had been granted to Juana Benigna Goyos, a contemporary of Margaret Mary, to Anne Marguerite Clément fifty years before the Paray-le-Monial visions, and to Anne Marie Rosset sixty years prior.[7]

God's interior work of grace leads to a contact with him that lies deeper than that coming from sense perception alone. However, the mystical process can be influenced not only by knowledge gained through the senses, but also by the visionary's individual characteristics and by the historical situation in which she finds herself.[8] Hence the content of the imaginative vision is a combination of divine influence and a visionary's subjective dispositions (*Visions*, 55-63).

One must distinguish the authenticity of visions emanating from the divine, from the visionary's subjectivity, which can affect the content of any vision in terms of "historical inaccuracy, theological distortions, errors, partiality, or bad taste" (*Visions*, 64). This explains why a great deal of uncertainty surrounds the content of visions. In other words, the mystical experience may be genuine even though there is error in the imaginative content of the vision. The divine influence only indirectly causes the

---

which mystical doctors recognize: the corporeal, the imaginative, and the purely intellectual. In corporeal visions which are properly called "apparitions," an object is experienced by the external senses. In imaginative visions, bodily features are imagined. Intellectual visions are by definition without images. Rahner writes that the mystical doctors view the imaginative type as more exalted than corporeal and he gives Teresa of Avila's imaginative visions as his example. He concludes that the imaginative vision is the normal case, because all those in popular and ecclesial piety are assumed to be imaginative. Cf. earlier versions of this book in Karl Rahner, "Über Visionen und verwandte Erscheinungen," *ZAM* 21 (1948): 179-213; and "Les Révélations Privées: Quelques Remarques Théologiques," *RAM* 25 (1949): 506-14.

[7] Karl Rahner reports that Francis de Sales is said to have begun the "tradition of the Sacred Heart." On June 10, 1611, the First Friday after the Octave of Corpus Christi, this co-founder of the Visitandines wrote a letter to Jane Frances de Chantal in which he suggests that a heart pierced by two arrows and surrounded by a crown of thorns could be the arms of the new order. (See François de Sales, *Oeuvres complètes* 7: 198ff.: Lettre à Madame de Chantal sur les armoires des monastère de la Visitation [10 juin 1611], cited in *Visions*, 63).

[8] On the point that mystical experiences differ from normal Christian existence not because they are of a higher nature but because their natural substratum is different from the psychological circumstances of every-day life, see Karl Rahner, "Religious Enthusiasm and the Experience of Grace," *Theological Investigations* 16, trans. David Morland, O. S. B. (New York: Seabury, A Crossroad Book, 1979): 35-51; and "Mystical Experience and Mystical Theology," *Theological Investigations* 17, trans. Margaret Kohl (New York: Seabury, A Crossroad Book, 1981): 90-99.

imaginative vision. One example is the theological problem caused by the "Great Promise" given to Margaret Mary Alacoque.[9]

HISTORICAL RELEVANCE

Rahner explains that the situation to which the message of Paray-le-Monial spoke was marked not only by Jansenism, but also by secularization which characterizes modern times. People today do not live in a Christian world, but rather in the world of an "absent God." This situation, Rahner recalls, was characteristic of Gethsemane and Golgotha in the life of Jesus, "in a situation where life lies in death, where abandonment means the deepest proximity to God, where powerlessness is the manifestation of the power of God."[10] In this context, Rahner observes, one is able to understand the message of Paray-le-Monial and its connection with a particular situation in the history of the church.

Rahner treats the question of the dependence of the Sacred Heart devotion on its time. First, he observes in the seventeenth-century form of this devotion the lack of a Trinitarian context and a lack of emphasis on the mediatorship of Christ. He argues that these forms of dependence on a particular time are not essential to this devotion and can be remedied.

---

[9] See *Visions*, 68, and the next section. Cf. Paul Wenisch, S. J., *Promises of Our Lord to St. Margaret Mary: A Textual, Theological and Pastoral Study* (Tamil Nadu, India: The National Office of the Apostleship of Prayer, 2978): 1, for the text of the edited form of "The Promises of Our Lord to the Persons devoted to his Sacred Heart":
1. I will give them all the graces necessary for their state of life.
2. I will establish peace in their families.
3. I will bless every home where the image of my Sacred Heart shall be exposed and honored.
4. I will console them in all their difficulties.
5. I will be their refuge during life and especially at the hour of death.
6. I will shed abundant blessings on all their undertakings.
7. Sinners shall find in my Heart a boundless ocean of mercy.
8. Tepid souls shall become fervent.
9. Fervent souls shall rise speedily to great perfection.
10. I will give priests the power of softening the hardest hearts.
11. Those who propagate this devotion shall have their names written in my Heart, never to be effaced.
12. I promise you that, in the excessive mercy of my Heart, my all-powerful love will grant to all who communicate on the First Friday of the month for nine consecutive months, the grace of final repentance; they shall not die in my displeasure nor without their sacraments; my divine Heart shall be their safe refuge in their last moments.

[10] Karl Rahner, "Some Theses for a Theology of Devotion to the Sacred Heart," *Theological Investigations* 3, trans. Karl Rahner and Boniface Kruger (New York: Seabury, 1967): 340. (Hereafter cited as *TI* 3.)

Second, he grants that the individual elements of this devotion are elements of dogma and as such remain valid for all periods of Christianity.

Third, he observes that the Sacred Heart devotion of Paray was relative to a situation that will exist for a long time, and so this devotion is relevant. That it has suffered a setback in our century is not because it is irrelevant, but rather because it was not rightly preached, or because rejection of it is a sign of "love growing cold." Hence Rahner defends the devotion, not its time-conditioned elements.

Fourth, he admits that no one can foresee whether the present state of this devotion will last until the end of time, so whoever can humbly and willingly surrender to the guidance of the Holy Spirit can become an "agent and apostle of Sacred Heart devotion without being possessed of the fanaticism of the 'definitive' and 'unsurpassable'" (*TI* 3: 341).

Rahner observes that the theological situation of the Church in the seventeenth century was marked by a Jansenistic pessimism about salvation (*Heilspessimismus*) which was convinced that many souls were damned to hell for their sins and only the chosen few were saved.[11] This view reflected a certain interpretation of Augustine's theory of the *massa damnata* and led to an unhealthy anxiety about salvation (*Heilsangst*).[12] At the same time, the theological situation in the church was becoming increasingly influenced by secularization. This secularization continues to affect the situation of the church in the world. Rahner sees the consideration of secularization as critical in establishing the relevance of this devotion in the contemporary church. The nineteenth century witnessed a clear upsurge of devotion to the Sacred Heart that was strongly encouraged by the popes in the writing of encyclicals, by the establishment of the Feast of the Sacred Heart for the universal church, and by the writing of an act of consecration to the Sacred Heart to be recited by the church at large. Numerous religious congregations (including my own, the Society of the Sacred Heart of Jesus) were founded in the nineteenth century and consecrated in one way or another to the Sacred Heart. At the time, the church still reflected a Jansenistic *Heilspessimismus* and had to keep coming to grips with increasing secularization.

Vatican Council II articulated a significant change in attitude from one of pessimism to optimism concerning universal salvation

---

[11] See Karl Rahner, "Die Bleibende Bedeutung der II. Vatikanischen Konzils," *Schriften zur Theologie* 14 (Cologne: Benziger, 1980): 314-18. This reference was first brought to my attention by Professor Rahner in a private interview on February 25, 1982. On tape.

[12] Rahner, "Bleibende Bedeutung," 315.

(*Heilsoptimismus*).[13] It encouraged a biblical and liturgical spirituality. In this atmosphere, the church in the twentieth century has witnessed a marked decline in outward forms and practices of devotion to the Sacred Heart.

THEOLOGICAL SIGNIFICANCE

In his article entitled "Some Theses for a Theology of Devotion to the Sacred Heart," first written in 1954, Rahner agrees with the claim that today's Sacred Heart devotion is based on the private revelations of Paray-le-Monial and so is not derived directly from scripture and tradition. He argues that a private revelation which includes a mission to the church is not so much a new communication as a mandate to follow a particular course of action. This mandate contains what is most urgently needed to be done *here and now* according to the general principles of the faith. If this is so, then Rahner claims, a private revelation must be interpreted according to the universal principles of theology and in light of the historical situation of the church and of the world (*TI* 3: 338-39). The Roman Catholic phrase "private revelations" can be used to describe religious impulses and experiences that have sent so many in our Christian tradition to preach new ways to follow Jesus, for example, the experience of John Wesley when he heard Martin Luther's commentary on the Romans.

Characteristics

Rahner notes three characteristics of the Sacred Heart devotion of Paray: inwardness, belief in the presence of the love of God in a world marked by sinfulness and godlessness, and reparation. First, he distinguishes a genuine inwardness (the nurturing of an interior life of faith and love without the aid of an external Christian society) from a false inwardness which is "the individualistic luxury of a religious introversion" (*TI* 3: 340). Second, he observes that faith in the love of God stands over and against the world in which God's dominion seems to be entering an hour of darkness in society and in individual persons. Third, he sees expiation as "a suffering to the bitter end of this godless situation with and in the Son of Gethsemane and Golgotha as a share in consummating the seemingly wasted love of Christ for the sinful world" (*TI* 3: 340).

---

[13] Ibid.

Reparation and Promises

Rahner takes care not only to reflect on the private revelations of Paray-le-Monial in general, but also to discuss particular aspects connected with these visions, that is to say, reparation, consoling the Lord by means of a Holy Hour, and the promises of Paray-le-Monial. With regard to the first aspect, the theology of reparation in the form of the devotion, he points out that the honoring of this Heart implies "reparation" regarded as "an equal sharing in the accomplishment of this redemptive love and its fate in the world!" (*TI* 3: 345).[14] What does "reparation for the sin of the world" mean? For Rahner, it consists "primarily and essentially in the trusting, obedient, and loving acceptance of a share in the fate of the Lord, in a taking upon oneself of the appearance of sin in the world: body, darkness, persecution, distance from God, death" (*TI* 3: 345). Therefore, reparation participates in faith in the destiny of Christ. The expiatory significance of every good work need not be explicitly intended nor taught, especially to those who have a tendency toward religious introversion and to being "sacrificial souls." The one to whom the Christian makes reparation is the Father in union with Christ. Thus, one can add nothing to the reparation Christ has made. Rather by prayers and practices of reparation, the Christian enters into the sacrifice which Christ offered to his Father, "in the sacrificial love of his Heart obedient unto death" (*TI* 3: 347).

With regard to the second aspect, consoling the Lord by means of a Holy Hour, Rahner asks what this means. He begins to treat the question by insisting on the efficaciousness of contemplating the sufferings of Jesus in such a way as to make them present to oneself. Such contemplation tends to eliminate the time-gap between the one who prays and the Passion of Christ. Its significance lies not in one's ability to be *now* an active participant in events in the life of Jesus which happened *then*. Rather it means that the contemplative tries to grasp how these events have made Jesus what he is *now* and how Christians can open themselves to let the life, suffering, and death of Jesus permeate their lives *now*.

The link for such contemplation is the mystery of the Heart of Christ which enables us to remember that the glorified Lord is not merely an abstract God-man without a history, "but the one in whose concrete reality the most original source and the most real effect of his own history (in fact the 'heart'!) is an eternally valid present" (*TI* 3: 348). Therefore, Rahner

---

[14] The expression "equal sharing" is a mistranslation of the German expression "angleichender mitvollzug" which suggests rather the idea of being conformed to Jesus Christ through the re-enactment of his redemptive love.

insists, Christian prayer now is to Christ who *has* suffered but who is *now* glorified. This theological truth does not exclude that Jesus could know in his Passion, by means of his infused knowledge and direct vision of God, the co-suffering of people throughout the ages, "and could by this knowledge draw from this loving share in his suffering consolation for his human Heart. Therefore, when we suffer with his 'today,' this consoled him 'already then'" (*TI* 3: 349).

In order to clarify this point, Rahner adds three notes of explanation. He raises the question as to whether and how Jesus was consoled in his suffering by this knowledge since there is a possibility that the depth of his inner suffering at the God-forsakenness of this world obscured any consoling vision of victory. Furthermore, were people's good deeds "consoling" to Jesus? Rahner asks, "For an infinite love, is it not in a certain sense a disappointment even to be accepted and reciprocated in a very finite way" (*TI* 3: 349)?

The second note Rahner adds is that all deeds performed in love and grace could have consoled Jesus, not only those consciously intended to console him. Thus the "consoling" of Christ does not depend essentially on a conscious intention to do so.

The third note Rahner adds is to ask how helpful it is to encourage the ordinary Christian to perform mental gymnastics in order to console the Lord *then* by good works *now*, even though Christians know that the glorified Christ to whom they *now* pray has no need of their consolation. Rahner argues against such a practice as too complex. He underlines the value of accepting suffering in faith with Christ.

The last point that Rahner treats in this article is the promises of Paray-le-Monial.[15] He writes that they are subject to the usual rules of interpretation of private revelations. He observes that in general they do not promise anything other than what was promised by Jesus in the Gospel to those who believe. Hence, Rahner concludes, the new element is not the promises but the circumstances which specify them within devotion to the Sacred Heart. He would interpret these promises in the same way he would interpret the promises in scripture, not as technical directions for controlling God, but as gifts to those who surrender themselves in faith and love to the will of God. He addresses the question of interpreting the "Great Promise" which promises salvation to one who receives Communion on nine consecutive First Fridays. Preachers should do so in such a way that it does not become "for many people the occasion at least *after* the

---

15 See n. 9 of this text for a list of these promises.

novena of First Fridays, of sinning by thoughtlessness or presumption against the mercy of God" (*TI* 3: 352).[16]

COMMENTS AND QUESTIONS

Rahner's skepticism about private revelations stimulates further comment and new questions. The following is meant to be an attempt to contribute to a critique of the visions at Paray-le-Monial.

Authenticity

In light of Rahner's reflections, one can conclude, first, that Margaret Mary Alacoque's visions were prophetic since they contained a message for the church at large. Second, they were imaginative rather than corporeal or purely intellectual.[17] This imaginative aspect is an important point to clarify, especially in trying to evaluate her vision of the disembodied Sacred Heart. Nonetheless, a critical and sober skepticism makes one wonder about aspects of these visions and about some of the visions themselves. For example, as Rahner points out, others before or contemporary with her life also claimed to have received visions of the Sacred Heart (*Visions*, 63). Did she know about them? If so, in what way did they influence her? In what way were hers unique? Moreover, Rahner himself is highly suspicious of private revelations which urge a devotion in such a way as to overestimate its significance in the spiritual life and growth of those in the Church (*Visions*, 85). He insists that the context of all private revelations must be gauged in light of the public revelation given by God in Jesus

---

[16] In his published study of the promises which Margaret Mary Alacoque claims that Christ made, Paul Wenisch, S. J., distinguishes between the edited form of the promises and the promises in their authentic wording as found in the writings of Margaret Mary. He concludes that the tabular form appeared for the first time in 1863 on the cover page of a booklet published in Le Puy, France, and again in 1882 when Philip A. Kemper, a businessman of Dayton, Ohio, printed the first eleven promises on a picture of the Sacred Heart which was distributed around the world. Instead, Wenisch prefers to reflect on what he calls the authentic promises which the nuns at the Visitation Monastery, Paray-le-Monial, are now starting to call benefits (*bienfaits*). Concerning the controversial Twelfth Promise, which assures the grace of final perseverance to those who receive Communion on nine consecutive First Fridays, Wenisch unknowingly meets Rahner's objection by explaining that it is not intended to foster a presumption about salvation. He takes the position that Christ asked Margaret Mary to promote the reception of Communion on every First Friday, not on nine consecutive First Fridays. See Wenisch, *Promises of our Lord*, 1-9, 43-52, and 63-73.

[17] It is difficult to distinguish the psychological mechanism of imaginative visions from that of pseudo-hallucinations. See Joseph Maréchal, S. J., *Studies in the Psychology of the Mystics*, trans. Algar Thorold (London: Burns Oates & Washbourne Ltd., 1927): 168-70.

Christ. Do her visions suggest an overemphasis on this devotion to the Sacred Heart or an urging of others to use concrete means to adore the humanity of Christ, central to Christianity?

In light of such considerations, one can grant that Margaret Mary Alacoque experienced prophetic imaginative visions which led her to promote the public liturgical cult of devotion to the Sacred Heart. Not all her visions can be considered genuine (*Visions*, 81). Nor can it be proved that all aspects of all of these Paray revelations were genuine.

Even though Margaret Mary claimed to have heard Jesus speak to her, this assertion does not authenticate the visions she says she received, since what she heard may indeed have been the product of her subconscious. One would have to go back to books published in France prior to her visions and to the traditions of the Visitandines in order to trace carefully the thought and imagery of her visions. But the fact that she received the images and symbols from others does not rule against the authenticity of her visions since uniqueness is not the criterion. One cannot verify the divine character of private revelations. Rather one can only try to detect signs of appropriateness or inappropriateness.

One is not likely to doubt her personal honesty, integrity, or piety, although some of her superiors and members of her own community certainly did so. Nor could one call her insane or hysterical. She was known to be a normal, shy, prayerful individual who did not like to attract attention to herself. She experienced bad physical health at times. Due to her painful childhood and the extraordinary events of her religious life, her mental health has been considered questionable by some (See below, nn. 30-31). These aspects are valid criteria for determining whether or not the visions she claims to have received were authentic (*Visions*, 76-78).[18]

It is not possible to estimate the depth and intensity of Margaret Mary's interior life. "Miracles of confirmation" accompanied her visions and these assured her superiors of their authenticity. Her canonization by the church attests that at least a few miracles were believed to have occurred after these visions. But one cannot gauge whether these miracles reported as proofs of her sanctity were "miracles of mercy" or "miracles of confirmation" directly connected with the authenticity of the apparitions she claimed to have received (*Visions*, 103, n. 131).

---

[18] One might also consider the amazing coincidence of William Harvey's discovery that the heart is a blood-pumping muscle in the same century in which Jean Eudes and Margaret Mary experience the Heart of Christ as a burning furnace of love. See Frans Josef van Beeck, S. J., *Christ Proclaimed: Christology as Rhetoric* (New York: Paulist, 1979): 523-47, for a brilliant development of this connection.

To establish the authenticity of her vision of the disembodied Heart of Christ is particularly difficult. Persuasive evidence either way is not available. But one can satisfy one's doubts and reservations to some reasonable acceptance or non-acceptance. They may also reflect the opinion that this imaginative vision was heavily conditioned by Margaret Mary's personality, temperament, background, and life-situation. One cannot overlook the fact that she was a seventeenth-century French Visitandine living monastic spirituality in a cloistered existence in the rustic secluded town of Paray-le-Monial. It seems appropriate to raise a few questions: When did Margaret Mary first see an image of the disembodied Heart of Christ? Could she have seen one in a spiritual book, a seventeenth-century emblem book, or in a pamphlet? Could she have imagined this disembodied Heart more for the details she noted about it, for example, its crown of thorns and the cross? Could this image have been the only part of the vision which she remembered, since there had to have been an interval between her experience and her recording of the experience? Is it possible that what she meant to convey was an overwhelming conviction of the centrality of this image in her spirituality and in this particular vision, even though in fact the Heart may not have been disembodied at all? Could she have imagined seeing the disembodied Heart of Jesus as a way of describing something going on at a much deeper level of her awareness, a mystical union which joined her so closely to Jesus in his suffering and death that she began actually to imagine what that must have been like in concrete terms? Could her interior mystical experience have been so intense that all she remembered was this image which may indeed have appeared?

Historical Relevance

How essential are the visions to the devotion? Is the relationship between them causal, conditioning, or accidental?[19] The Paray-le-Monial visions were not causal to devotion to the Sacred Heart, since the devotion existed long before the visions were experienced. Nor do these visions condition this devotion since it has flourished in several different forms. Perhaps it can be said that these visions condition one form of this devotion, the form that continues to foster Holy Hours and First Friday Communion. One can conclude that these visions are accidental to this devotion which would have continued without them. On the other hand, would this devotion have received papal approval and a public liturgical

---

[19] Rahner private interview.

cult in the Roman Catholic Church without the stimulus of Paray-le-Monial? The image of the disembodied Heart may be a repellent and unacceptable aspect for some. It need not color or qualify one's estimate of the validity of the Paray-le-Monial revelations taken as a whole. The church was ready to move from a private cult of the Sacred Heart, practiced mostly by individual mystics and monks, to a popular devotion. It needed an impetus to universalize certain customs being practiced, for example, an annual celebration of a Feast of the Sacred Heart, an act of consecration to the Sacred Heart, and a growing attraction for reparation. The church's readiness to make this devotion popular was probably an influence contributing to its acceptance of these visions. The church has approved private revelations negatively, in the sense that it has said one *may* believe.[20] The church is aware that authentic visions sometimes contain inauthentic elements.

Theological Significance

One can evaluate the famous "Twelfth Promise" which Margaret Mary claims to have received from Christ in the light of the other promises connected with this revelation, in light of the promises of Jesus recorded in the New Testament, and in light of the cultural and historical situation of Margaret Mary Alacoque[21]. The twelve promises focus on the deepening and strengthening of faith. To this extent, they suggest means of helping one live a life of greater faith, hope, and love. The Twelfth Promise as it has been transmitted to us might be considered a false promise if it is interpreted to mean that anyone can be certain of salvation. The tradition of the church has been very clear on this point.[22]

Rahner adds that one dare not presume on God's mercy by simply receiving Communion on nine First Fridays without at the same time making efforts to respond more fully, freely and faithfully to God's love in everyday life. It could be that Christ gave eleven promises and Margaret Mary made up the twelfth as a natural consequence of the others. It could be that the Lord never dictated these promises to her, and that they were

---

20 *Visions*, 13-17, and K. Rahner, "Revelation. IV. Private Revelation," K. Rahner and A. Darlap, eds., *Sacramentum Mundi: An Encyclopedia of Theology* 5 (New York: Herder, 1968), 358-59. Cf. Avery Dulles, S. J., "Revelation, theology of," *New Catholic Encyclopedia*, 1976 ed. To the best of my knowledge, the church has not pronounced specifically on the Paray-le-Monial visions, although it has condoned adoration of Christ's humanity, in particular, devotion to his Sacred Heart. For example, see *DS* 2661-63, 3353, 3922-26.

21 Wenisch, *Promises of our Lord*, 1-8.

22 *DS* 1532.

solely the product of her imagination. It could also be that these promises were her deductions from her spiritual experiences, conscious or unconscious. Or it could be that Christ did make several promises in a vision or series of visions and that Margaret Mary remembered them differently afterwards when she wrote them down. Perhaps she remembered certain details of this experience accurately and other details incorrectly. Maybe she recorded them at different times as descriptions of what the nuns in her convent today call "benefits."

One must take into account the anxiety for salvation which prevailed in France in the seventeenth century, largely because of the influence of Jansenism. This anxiety provoked an unhealthy fear of God's punishment and a preoccupation with currying God's favor. One did not extend the benefit of the doubt to the dead who had tried to lead prayerful, charitable lives. Those who had not led lives of piety and service were imagined with great certainty to be suffering the pains of hell and damnation. This distorted, inaccurate eschatology came out of and led to a distorted and inaccurate ecclesiology which still held tenaciously and triumphantly to a narrow and uncritical understanding of the formula *extra ecclesiam nulla salus.* This perspective not only affected the Roman Catholic attitudes toward Protestants in Europe at the time, attitudes that encouraged disdain. It also fed the exaggerated Jansenistic stress on God's justice that was strangely separated from his mercy. In this climate of distrust and despair, the Twelfth Promise might have been received like "a balm in Gilead."

Today, however, in face of an optimism about the possibility of universal salvation, the Twelfth Promise strikes Catholics as more problematic than consoling, especially in light of the slow steady steps being taken toward productive ecumenical dialogue. How indeed could a Protestant, a Jew, or a Buddhist begin to find it helpful or meaningful to learn that salvation can be assured by a regular full participation in the Eucharist on nine consecutive First Fridays?[23] Such an assertion could cause a needless setback in non-Catholics' efforts to reach a fuller understanding of this devotion. Perhaps the most that an educated Roman Catholic can venture to say about the Twelfth Promise is the little that Rahner has written. He is willing to grant that the promises of Paray-le-Monial are part of visions which may be accepted by those whose religious culture or personal experience disposes them to accept.

---

[23] For example, see Rosemary Haughton, *Transformation of Man: A Study of Conversion and Community* (Springfield, IL.: Templegate Publishers, 1980): 180-241, which is excellent on characteristically Catholic and Puritan emphases.

In fact, one may find the vision of the disembodied Heart of Christ and the Twelfth Promise totally unacceptable, and still believe that Margaret Mary experienced some genuine supernatural revelations. One may reject all her visions as inauthentic or unacceptable, and still be a firm believer and a faithful member of the church.

CONCLUDING REMARKS

Summary

Karl Rahner's reflections on the private revelations of Margaret Mary Alacoque offer balance and perspective. He is aware of the ambiguity in trying to clarify how much can be attributed to the divine influence and how much to the visionary's imagination. He has a healthy critical skepticism with regard to all private revelations, while at the same time he acknowledges their possible role in nourishing a life of faith.

Karl Rahner "demytholigizes" the private revelations at Paray-le-Monial. He finds it possible to consider the authenticity of some of these visions. But at the same time he observes that their thought and imagery can be traced to books written before 1673 and to the traditions of the Visitation Order to which Margaret Mary Alacoque belonged. He insists that the message of Paray-le-Monial concerns not only the Jansenism of the seventeenth century, but also secularization which continues to affect the church in the world. He underscores three relevant elements of this , message: interior life, belief in God's love, and reparation. He criticizes the Paray-le-Monial form of devotion to the Sacred Heart for its lack of emphasis on Christ's mediatorship, trying to remedy these lacks by his own reflections.

Rahner has excelled in offering an interpretation of this devotion which has nothing to do with sentimentality or individualistic piety. If anything, he is most interested in whatever can help educated twentieth-century Christians believe, hope and love more. He considers the symbol of the pierced Heart of Christ to be relevant in a world ravaged by heart-suffering and strife of every kind. He is not convinced that practices presently associated with this devotion can endure into the future. Even at present they seem meaningless to the majority of Roman Catholics. Unfortunately, even the terminology of "devotion to the Sacred Heart" grates on people's sensibilities. They would prefer to speak of their personal relationship to Jesus Christ or of their response of love to Christ's love.

Reflecting on the theological foundations of this devotion, Rahner attests that it is rooted in scripture and tradition, and not merely in the private revelations which Margaret Mary claimed to have received.[24] He discerns that these revelations are prophetic visions having historical relevance and theological soundness. He observes that Margaret Mary Alacoque's revelations brought nothing new in terms of insight into God's revelation in Jesus Christ, but they did help to make that revelation accessible to Catholics in modern times; and they promoted a set of practices which strengthened the corporate and liturgical dimensions of devotion to the Sacred Heart.

At the same time, Rahner brings his theological understanding of doctrine to bear on particular practices connected with this form of the devotion, namely, reparation, consolation of Jesus suffering, and the reception of Communion on nine consecutive First Fridays. Without ridiculing or rejecting these practices, he explains what is theologically valid in each practice and points out what needs to be more carefully understood.

First, he affirms that only Jesus Christ can make reparation. He points out that the Christian does so by participating in the reparation Christ has made in dying on the cross. Second, Rahner insists that Jesus Christ is no longer capable of suffering in his glorified humanity. At the same time, Rahner stresses the permanence of Jesus' having suffered. Hence, we console the Lord by means of a Holy Hour *now* for suffering he experienced *then* in his earthly existence. Rahner emphasizes the importance of accepting suffering in faith with Christ. Without rejecting the practice of consoling the Lord, he argues that it is not a constitutive element of devotion to the Sacred Heart. Third, he relativizes the promises of Paray-le-Monial by regarding them as made to all those who believe in God's love without presuming on his mercy.

Critique

I have attempted to evaluate and reinterpret the visions of Margaret Mary Alacoque using Karl Rahner's valuable questions and clarifications. The strength of his reflections is that they pinpoint theological difficulties

---

[24] For examples which demonstrate this point, see Annice Callahan, R. S. C. J., *Karl Rahner's Spirituality of the Pierced Heart: A Reinterpretation of Devotion to the Sacred Heart* (Lanham, MD.: University Press of America, 1985): 3-36.

connected with certain aspects and propose ways of resolving these difficulties in the light of contemporary principles of the faith.   The weakness of his reflections is that they do not include an investigation into the history of seventeenth-century French spirituality, the history of Margaret Mary Alacoque's psychological development, or her "victim soul" spirituality.   Her description of her visions must be evaluated in terms of her experience of the church in seventeenth-century France and of the Visitandine Order at this time.   Her personality and background must have heavily influenced the thought-patterns and imagery described in her visions.   Her sense of herself as a "victim soul" sacrificially offered with Christ to the Father in reparation for others may help one understand her stress on reparation and consoling the Lord.   I shall conclude by indicating references for exploring these three areas of possible future research.

In treating the visions of Margaret Mary Alacoque from a Rahnerian perspective, one needs to ask what Rahner means by seventeenth century "secularization" in France.   Does he mean the rejection of the "cruel God" underlying the revolt against Christianity that began in seventeenth-century Europe?   Does he mean the lukewarmness that eventually changed to hostility toward the church in the eighteenth century?   Or is he referring to the industrialization and urbanization that developed in the nineteenth century?[25]   It is easier to discuss secularization in France at the time of the Enlightenment, or in the nineteenth and twentieth centuries after the French Revolution.

One must take into account the change in the mid-seventeenth century from a mystical to an ascetical or moralizing approach to the spiritual life in France.   In the context of this shift, one could almost call Margaret Mary anachronistic in her own time since her visions and spirituality reflect a mystical approach.   On the other hand, her devotedness to the Heart of Jesus seems particularly understandable in an age of moralism and individualism when devotions had to substitute for the lack of biblical and liturgical foundations for spirituality.   From this point of view, Margaret Mary is truly a woman of her time.   In the seventeenth and nineteenth centuries, devotion to the Sacred Heart served the very important function of placing Christ at the center of people's consciousness.   In fact, the future of this devotion is questionable in light of

---

[25] For an investigation into these developments, see Jean Delumeau, *Catholicism Between Luther and Voltaire: A New View of the Counter-Reformation* (Philadelphia: Westminster Press, 1977): 203-230. Cf. Paul Hazard, *The European Mind (1680-1715)*, trans. J. Lewis May (New York: The World Publishing Co., Meridian Books, 1967): 119-154, 198-216, and 304-318.

the biblical, liturgical, and Christological developments of the twentieth century. One area that needs research and development is the history of seventeenth-century French spirituality. In this context, it would be invaluable to investigate Margaret Mary's socialization in the Visitandine Order, her theological education, and possible earlier parallels to her visions.[26]

Louis Biernaert, a French Jesuit psychiatrist,[27] has written a note on the possible psychological connections of the symbol of the Heart of Jesus which Margaret Mary described. He conjectures that she might have been attracted to this wound in the side out of which blood and water flowed from personal experiences of acute pain in her own side as a young girl, and possibly, too, from persistent hunger and thirst from which she suffered all her life.

Second, the image of the Heart of Jesus as the secret dwelling where one finds welcome and regeneration could be rooted in her childhood attraction for a little corner where she would not be seen or remembered. A third theme of the Heart of Jesus as the furnace, the flame, the sun, spoke to her ardent desire of consuming and being consumed.[28] Another area that needs research and new insight is that of the psychological dimension of Margaret Mary's growth and well-being.

Since suspicions are sometimes raised regarding the possibility of some sort of psychopathology, it would be helpful to find out how well-grounded these are. For example, her stress on reparation might have come from her need to appease a sense of neurotic guilt and inferiority.[29]

---

[26] For further research, see William A. Clebsch, *Christianity in European History* (New York: Oxford University Press, 1979): 177-228; Henri Bremond, *La vie chretienne sous l'Ancien Régime*, vol. IX of *Histoire littéraire du sentiment religieux en France* (Paris: Colin, 1968): 45-128; and Jacques Le Brun, "France: VI. Le grand siècle de la spiritualité française et ses lendemains," *Dictionnaire de spiritualité ascétique et mystique*, 5: 940-944. For example, reparation for offenses made against the Eucharist was widespread in seventeenth-century France. This attitude sprang from the emphasis of the Council of Trent on the Real Presence of Jesus Christ in the Blessed Sacrament and the actual desecration of Roman Catholic churches by the Hugenots during the wars of religion. Eucharistic adoration, with reparation as its primary motive, was a feature of a number of reformed or new religious orders. See Le Brun, *Dictionnaire de spiritualité* 5: 940-941, and Bremond, *Histoire littéraire du sentiment religieux en France*, 9: 207-219.

[27] Rahner brought this author to my attention in private interview.

[28] See Louis Beirnaert, S. J., "Note sur les Attaches Psychologiques du Symbolisme du Coeur chez Sainte Marguerite Marie," in *Le Coeur: Études Carmélitaines* (Toulouse: Desclee, 1950): 228-33.

[29] For this example, I am indebted to Professor Joseph E. Byrnes of Oklahoma State University for allowing me to read his unpublished paper, "Mystical Vision as Personality Integration: The Case of St. Marguerite-Marie Alacoque, (1647-1690)," 1-16.

Friedrich von Hügel criticizes the "psycho-physical abnormality and morbidity" in the life of Margaret Mary Alacoque, though he respects greatly the healing mystical element in her life.[30] William James remarks that the only "good fruits" of these revelations which he can see in Margaret Mary's life are "sufferings and prayers and absences of mind and swoons and ecstasies."[31] Reflecting on both of these critics, Harvey Egan adds a note of warning in judging the spirituality of what he calls a "victim soul":

> Although one must be very cautious in discerning what is at work in the life of a "victim soul," one must beware of judging authentic mystical life according to the principles of American pragmatism or self-actualization. Granted that authentic contemplation can be judged in many cases by the attractive, personal integration and life-style of the mystic, the authenticity of the life of a victim soul must be discerned with the eyes of faith. Christ's Passion and shameful death, his disgrace, his loneliness and isolation on the cross, his being misunderstood and his entombment were part of his redemption of the world. The Christian mystical heritage indicates that some have been called to incarnate in their own lives the "suffering servant" aspects of Christ's salvific life.[32]

This aspect of spirituality hearkens back to a theology of martyrdom prevalent in the early church.[33] Perhaps yet another area that needs theological investigation and reflection is this "victim soul" spirituality which could shed valuable light on the spirituality of Margaret Mary Alacoque and on the private revelations which she claims to have received.

---

[30] See Friedrich von Hügel, *The Mystical Element of Religion* (Westminster: Christian Classics, 1961) 2: 57-61.

[31] William James, *The Varieties of Religious Experience* (New York: New American Library, 1958): 268-69, 317.

[32] Harvey D. Egan, S. J., "The Clouds of Unknowing and Pseudo-Contemplation," *Thought* 54 (1979): 172.

[33] W. H. C. Frend, *Martyrdom and Persecution in the Early Church* (New York: Doubleday, 1967): 58-76.

11

Jesus, Mary and the Rosary:
The Spirituality of Louis de Montfort

EDWARD L. SHIRLEY

One of the major currents of Catholic spirituality in the seventeenth and eighteenth centuries involved a fresh impetus and new direction given to Marian devotion by members of the French School: Cardinal Berulle, Jean-Jacques Olier, and Jean Eudes, among others. Probably the foremost and most enduring manifestations of this Marian spirituality was found in the writings of Louis Marie Grignion de Montfort (1673-1716). Montfort's spirituality can be summed up in three words: Wisdom, Cross and Virgin,[1] and involves a type of mysticism through which the Christian becomes intimately united with Christ, the Eternal Wisdom of the Father, through absolute surrender to and union with the Virgin Mary.

This paper will be presented in three primary sections. The first will briefly examine the life of Louis de Montfort, focusing on the elements which influenced his spiritual vision. This section does not pretend to be a complete biography, nor even a detailed analysis of the complex relationships among Gallicanism, Jansenism and the French School; it simply intends to mention some of the major movements which influenced Montfort's time, and, hence, Montfort himself. The second and main section of the paper will be an examination of his spiritual doctrine: union

---

[1] George Rigault, *St. Louis de Montfort: His Life and Work* (Port Jefferson, NY: Montfort Fathers, 1947): 139.

201

with Christ through Mary, particularly through devotion to the Rosary. The concluding section will present some suggestions concerning the relevance of Montfort's spirituality for today.

THE LIFE OF LOUIS DE MONTFORT

Louis de Montfort's life was marked from the beginning with elements which were to exercise profound influence upon his spiritual vision. Born Louis Grignion in 1673 at Montfort-la-Canne in France, he lived his life in a France permeated by both the spirits of Gallicanism and Jansenism, which had formed an uneasy alliance against Rome. Both of these influences were to become a cross for Montfort in his later years, particularly after Pope Clement XI, who saw Montfort's spirituality as a means for combatting Jansenism, appointed him Apostolic Missioner to France.

His early life was marked by a childlike devotion to the Virgin Mary, a devotion which he carried to his death. At his confirmation, he took the name "Marie," and later dropped his family name, wishing simply to be known as Louis Marie de Montfort. In 1786 he began the phase of his education which was to form him intellectually and spiritually, beginning with seven years of studies under the Jesuits at the school of St. Thomas in Rennes. Here he received a liberal education, nourished on the Classics as well as the Scriptures, drank in Jesuit theology, and began his own spiritual formation under the direction of a Father Bellier.

Afterwards, Montfort continued his theological education for seven years at Saint-Sulpice, a seminary which only forty years before had been at the center of the Jansenist controversy when a curate of the seminary had refused absolution to Duke de Liancourt because of the latter's affiliation with Port-Royal. During this period Montfort came in contact with the French School of spirituality, which had strong ties with Saint-Sulpice through such figures as Cardinal Berulle, Jean-Jacques Olier, Jean Eudes and Francis de Sales. He also studied the Church Fathers, the Scholastics, and, in particular, enjoyed the works of Bernard of Clairvaux.[2] It was here that his earlier devotion to the Blessed Virgin took its concrete shape.

Judged an eccentric by superiors at Saint-Sulpice, Montfort was dismissed from the seminary. Years later when told of Montfort's heroic sanctity, one of them remarked with a touch of irony, "You see I do not know a saint when I see one."[3] Ordained in 1700, Montfort had difficulty

---

[2] Ibid., 25.
[3] Ibid., 33.

finding his pastoral niche, for this reaction seemed to follow, not always without reason. It is reported that once he heard a street singer performing a bawdy song. Though living on alms at the time, Montfort bought every copy of the song he could find and destroyed them in front of the singer. Even those devoted to him could not help but notice the odd forms his apostolic zeal could take. It is reported that on numerous occasions he would, without warning, take his companion to a brothel, kneel and say a Hail Mary, and then preach to the ladies and their clients. This produced the at least short-term result of reducing the women to penitential tears and the men leaving in shame.[4]

In addition to these personal reactions, Montfort had further crosses to bear. Much of the French clergy was permeated by either a spirit of indifferentism or Jansenistic rigorism. To the former, Montfort represented a threat to their luxurious lifestyles; for the latter, the antagonism was even more pronounced. In 1706 he was commissioned as Apostolic Missioner to France by Pope Clement XI for the express purpose of combatting the Jansenist heresy. Indeed, his doctrine of unlimited atonement, personal cooperation with grace, and divine mercy contradicted the Jansenist doctrine of limited atonement and irresistible grace, as well as their picture of Christ as the severe judge. In commissioning Montfort for this task, however, Clement was also mindful of the political climate in France. Not wishing to alienate the French bishops, whose relations with Rome were already strained because of the Gallican controversy, Clement stipulated that Montfort needed the ordinary's permission to preach a mission in a diocese. For this reason, he was forbidden in many places and suffered cold reception in others. When in 1707 he preached in his home town, the bishop placed severe limitations on his ministry.[5]

His preaching was Christ crucified, and consecration to the Virgin Mary, termed in the custom of his day the "Holy Slavery of Love." The spiritual exercise he advised was the Rosary; indeed, he seems to have fashioned himself after the model of St. Dominic who, at the time, was believed to have combatted the Albigensian heresy through the Rosary, a prayer revealed to him by the Virgin herself.

There were many attempts on his life, and in 1711 he was poisoned by Calvinists at La Rochelle, an attack from which he never fully recovered. After several years of repeated illnesses, he retired to the motherhouse of the Daughters of Wisdom in St. Laurent-sur-Sevre where, after kissing his

---

[4] Ibid., 119.
[5] Ibid., 77-78.

statues of Jesus and Mary, and with their names on his lips, he died on April 28, 1716.

In his sixteen years as a priest, Louis de Montfort labored tirelessly to spread the Gospel through devotion to Mary and the Rosary. He founded two congregations, one for women, the Daughters of Wisdom, and one for men, now known as the Montfort Fathers. He wrote the rules for both congregations, 23,400 verses of hymns, and several books, among which are *The Love of Eternal Wisdom*, *The Secret of the Rosary*, and *The Secret of Mary*. However, his renown as a writer and theologian came posthumously when in 1842 an untitled manuscript was found which was called *True Devotion* by the first editors (also known under other titles such as *True Devotion to Mary* and *True Devotion to the Blessed Virgin*).[6] It is to these teachings that we now turn.

SPIRITUAL DOCTRINE

As previously stated, the spiritual theology of Louis de Montfort can be summed up in three words: Wisdom, Cross and Virgin. In fact, the formula "to Jesus through Mary" expresses his entire life. It is important to remember that the term of devotion, the focal point of Christian growth toward union, is always the Crucified and Risen Christ, never the Virgin herself. Unfortunately Montfort is often misunderstood on this point, as it is his work *True Devotion* for which he is best known. It is ironic that his reputation is based on a work which lay hidden for 126 years, a work which can be understood only in light of his lesser known *The Love of Eternal Wisdom*, and which is, in fact, simply a continuation of the theme of the last chapter of *Wisdom*.

This section of the paper will be divided into three main themes of Montfort's teaching. The first deals with mystical union with Christ, spoken of as Eternal Wisdom. The second theme is devotion to the Blessed Virgin, considered by Montfort to be the surest means for union with Divine Wisdom. And the third theme is the place of the Rosary as the spiritual exercise leading one to union with Jesus through Mary.

Eternal Wisdom

Drawing upon the writings of the Church Fathers, Montfort identifies the pre-existent Wisdom of the Old Testament with the Johannine Logos,

---

[6] *God Alone: The Collected Writings of St. Louis Marie de Montfort* (Bayshore, NY: Montfort Publications, 1987).

and, hence, with Jesus himself, the "Word made Flesh." All wisdom, natural and supernatural, revolves around Jesus Christ, Uncreated Eternal Wisdom. To know and to possess Wisdom is the proper end of human endeavor:

> *To know Jesus Christ, eternal wisdom, is to know enough; to know everything and not to know Him, is to know nothing.* What does it avail an archer to know how to hit the outer parts of the target, if he does not know how to hit the center?[7]

Montfort asserts that Wisdom is the parent, not simply the maker, of all of Creation, for parenthood expresses a loving relationship. In the act of Creation, Wisdom came to dwell within that very Creation, much the same way the Fathers envisioned the seminal logos as the seed of all Creation. The diverse forms one sees in Creation are manifestations of the richness contained in Wisdom itself: "This ineffable play of Divine Wisdom is apparent in the diversity of His creation." This is why those to whom Wisdom has been given, namely the saints, can see the "beauty, sweetness, and the order displayed in Eternal Wisdom in even his smallest creatures," and are thus "rapt in ecstasy" (*Wisdom*, 14).

Yet, surpassing even the glory of Wisdom found in Creation as a whole is the manifestation of Wisdom in humanity, the "divine masterpiece, living image of His own beauty and perfections, . . . and his sole representative on earth." Indeed, humanity seems to contain the fullness of the rest of Creation, for Wisdom "summarized in [humanity] all the various perfections of the Angels, the animals, and other creatures" (*Wisdom*, 14-15). Thus, for Montfort, humans are a type of microcosm.

Sin, however, darkened the soul of humanity, so that the presence of Wisdom was no longer apparent. Sin made humanity the slave of the devil, the object of the wrath of God, and the prey of hell. Heaven was closed, and there was no one to open it; hell was open, and there was no one to close it (*Wisdom*, 17).

At this point, Montfort presents what he himself indicates is an imaginative scene, with the Trinity as a heavenly council, debating the fate of humanity. Though the justice of God demands that humankind share the punishment of the fallen angels in the same way that they have shared their disobedience, Wisdom pleads the cause of humanity, offering

---

[7] Louis de Montfort, *The Love of Eternal Wisdom* (Bayshore, NY: Montfort Publications, 1980): 3. Hereafter this work is cited in the text as *Wisdom*.

ultimately to become human, suffer and die to satisfy Divine justice and calm Divine anger. His offer is accepted (*Wisdom*, 18).[8]

Slowly preparing the way through the revelations of the prophets, Wisdom finally built himself a house, and in the womb of St. Anne, Mary was fashioned. If humanity as a whole is the summation and masterpiece of Creation, Mary seems to be the summation of humanity, possessing the fullness of grace, and is the "Masterpiece of the Most High" (*Wisdom*, 54). In fact, Montfort says, God took even greater delight in forming her than He did in creating the Universe.

God is portrayed here as a lover who has lost his heart to his beloved; Gabriel is the messenger who takes the proclamation of love to the beloved in the Angelic Salutation, and awaits her response. She says yes, and her fiat is the moment long awaited by the whole world, the angels, and even the Trinity itself. Out of the pure blood of Mary's heart, God fashions a perfect body, with which he unites the most perfect soul ever created. It is with this perfect humanity that Eternal Wisdom unites himself in the hypostatic union, and the Word becomes flesh (*Wisdom*, 56).

Montfort paints a picture of a Christ who endured sufferings in every aspect of his being. Here he echoes the kenosis hymn of Philippians. Though he was Divine Wisdom, he gave up his majestic glory to become human. His wisdom was derided, for people thought him mad; his power impeached, for they thought him possessed. His reputation was smeared, he was called a sinner, his body was torn. However, all of this was simply preparation for the Cross, which Montfort calls "the greatest mystery of Eternal Wisdom" (*Wisdom*, 88). It is the Cross to which Christ was drawn, step by step, from village to village, throughout his ministry; it is the summation of his entire life. At last, Montfort says, he was satisfied, and Jesus died in the embrace of his friend, the Cross.

For Montfort, the Cross is so essential to his spiritual vision that he claims that the Resurrection should not be thought of as a denial or relinquishment of the Cross. Rather, Christ

> united himself so closely to it and became, as it were, so incorporated with it, that no angel or man, no creature in heaven or on earth can separate Him from it. Their bond is indissoluble; their union is eternal. *Never the cross without Jesus; nor Jesus without the cross* (*Wisdom*, 91).

---

[8] Though the image of Divine wrath might not set well with people today, and though the image of the Trinity as a council is not the most theologically accurate, if one can accept this as a creative myth, the spiritual truths come through. One should not dismiss such fanciful imagery too quickly, particularly today when myth and story are again being accepted as valid means of conveying theological truth.

In fact, Montfort claims that Jesus has so fully identified himself with the Cross that one can say, *"wisdom is the cross, and the cross is wisdom"* (*Wisdom*, 98). Here we see that Montfort speaks of a union of Christ and the Cross which seems analogous to the hypostatic union of his humanity and divinity: there is no separation possible.

The Cross of Jesus is the cross of Christians; that is, the crosses we bear daily are our participation in, our possession of the Cross of Christ. Montfort states that Peter and Paul, the Apostles and Martyrs all sought and embraced the Cross. In fact, Montfort maintains, they preferred their sufferings to the gift of miracles and the graces to convert others. It would seem that Montfort's experience of rejection may have contributed to his particular sensitivity on this point. Yet, the Cross is also the source of unspeakable joy, being the sign of God's love for us and our loving response to Him.

This vision of the Cross as identical with Divine Wisdom, around whom revolves all other wisdom and truth seems to echo the Bonaventurian meditation on St. Francis' vision of the six-winged seraph at La Verna. Whether one approaches God through contemplation of Creation, within the soul, or God in Himself, the focal point, the goal of all contemplative wisdom, is the Crucified Christ.[9]

Yet, the Cross of Montfort does not lead to Jansenistic despair or demand severe penances because of the utterly corrupt nature of humanity. Rather, Montfort sets before us "a Christ whose arms are outstretched more widely than the Crucified of whom Port Royal taught."[10] Montfort's Christ wishes to give himself to humanity, for *"wisdom is for man and man is for wisdom"* (*Wisdom*, 31). Montfort holds that everything about Jesus is gentle: his looks, his words, his actions. Even after his death and Resurrection, Christ goes out of his way to remain ever close to us in the Eucharist, not hiding himself under the sign of a diamond or precious stone in order to dwell with us in a purely external manner, but "under the appearances of a morsel of bread, . . . so that being received by man He may dwell also in his heart, and there take his delight" (*Wisdom*, 35). It is clear here that McBrien's presentation of Montfort's Marian spirituality as an attempt to "get by [a severe Christ's] weak side" is a misrepresentation.[11]

---

[9] Bonaventure, "The Soul's Journey into God," in *Bonaventure*, trans. Ewert Cousins. *The Classics of Western Spirituality* (New York: Paulist, 1979).
[10] Rigault, *Louis de Montfort*, 145.
[11] Richard McBrien, *Catholicism* (Minneapolis: Winston Press, 1980), 2: 878.

The Effects of Wisdom

Among the effects of Divine Wisdom in the souls of those who possess Him, Montfort enumerates the ability to know the truth (that is, enlightenment), the ability to make the truth known, the purest joy and consolation, and the spiritual strength and motivation to persevere.

Enlightenment can take many forms. Solomon, for example, had the gift of a keen intelligence and a spirit of discernment. Wisdom can also communicate to humans the knowledge of sacred and natural sciences: Solomon knew the true knowledge of our nature, much of which was unknown before him. Jacob, on the other hand, knew the "science of the saints" (*Wisdom*, 45). This was the Light which also guided the great doctors of the Church, of whom Montfort singles out Thomas Aquinas. Furthermore, this knowledge is not dull and lifeless, but also satisfies the heart through a spirit of piety.

The second effect of Wisdom on the soul is the ability to make this truth known to others. He loosened Moses' tongue, spoke through the prophets, and gave the apostles the ability to preach the Gospel and proclaim God's marvelous deeds. The words given by Divine Wisdom are "piercing words," which touch the heart, and Montfort laments how few of the preachers in his day could say with St. Paul, "We speak the wisdom of God." Perhaps it might serve us well to reflect on the implications for our own time.

The third effect of Wisdom is joy and consolation. The person will begin to desire only those things which are of God, and will as a result experience peace which transcends his or her most difficult trials. It is in this context that Montfort places the virtues: theological (faith, hope and love), cardinal (temperance, prudence, justice and fortitude), and moral (religion, humility, meekness, obedience, detachment, mortification, and prayer) (*Wisdom*, 48-49).

The final effect of Eternal Wisdom on the soul is to motivate and activate it, because Wisdom is "more active than all active things." (Wisdom of Solomon 7:24) He sets souls aflame and enables them to do great things for God. They are also given the strength to persevere. Though Wisdom allows these souls to undergo severe temptations by the devil, triumph by their enemies, and desertion by their friends; though he allows illness or poverty, and will load them down with reproach and sadness, it is this furnace in which He purifies the gold of their souls, and through which He receives them as a sacrifice (*Wisdom*, 49-50).

Montfort names four means necessary to obtain Divine Wisdom: ardent desire, persevering prayer, universal mortification, and devotion to the Blessed Virgin. Concerning ardent desire, he states that one must covet Wisdom, and that through meditation on God's commandments, God will give one a heart and desire for Wisdom. Even Solomon, the wisest human to have lived, received Wisdom only after he had desired, sought, and prayed for a long time.

"Seek and you shall find" (Mt. 8:7). Prayer for Wisdom must be persevering, just as the world had beseeched God for Wisdom since the time of Adam, and Mary's womb was prepared through her prayers. One must persevere in the darkness of faith, not seeking consolations, visions, or revelations, for pure faith is both the cause and effect of Wisdom in the soul (*Wisdom*, 102).

Since Jesus is inseparable from the Cross, the mortification of the Cross is the only means of attaining Him. One must carry one's cross daily, burying oneself in Christ, fleeing the values of the world, patiently bearing bodily ailments, fasting, and mortifying the will through obedience. Though the world considers such practices useless, they are the way to true Wisdom.

Devotion To The Blessed Virgin

The greatest means of all, however, the surest means for attaining Eternal Wisdom, is true devotion to the mother of Eternal Wisdom, the Virgin Mary (*Wisdom*, 113). Montfort maintains that just as she once conceived and brought forth Eternal Wisdom in the Incarnation, so she now conceives and gives birth to him in the souls of Christians. She is a "secret magnet," drawing Wisdom toward her. Through her intercession, one can quickly and surely possess Him. She is the key to the gifts of the Holy Spirit, for He fills the soul with His Presence in the same proportion to which He finds His spouse present.

Montfort, drawing upon the Fathers, uses several Scriptural images to speak of Mary: she is the "sealed fountain and the faithful Spouse" of the Holy Spirit, the earthly paradise wherein the New Adam took flesh, the Tree of Life bearing the Fruit of Life, the City of God, and the New Eve, mother of the faithful (*Wisdom*, 118).[12] Montfort divides devotion to Mary into two categories, "General" and "Perfect."

---

[12] See also Montfort, *True Devotion to the Blessed Virgin* (Langley Bucks, England: St. Paul, 1973): 2, 20. Hereafter this work will be cited in the text as *True Devotion*.

General Devotion

General devotion is that which is required of every Christian, and is based on the intimate union of Mary and Jesus and her central role in the salvation of the world. Montfort speaks of Mary's role in the Incarnation, in the sanctification of souls, and in the Parousia, the Second Coming of Christ.

Though compared to God Mary is nothing, and though He had no actual need of her, God has chosen to work through her to bring salvation to the world. Citing Augustine, Montfort states that the world was unworthy to receive Christ directly, so God gave His Son to Mary, who gave Him to the World. She is present and active in Jesus' ministry from the Annunciation to the Cross, as He sanctified John the Baptist from her womb and performed his first miracle at Cana through her intercession. It is on this basis in the economy of salvation that Montfort builds his Marian doctrine, for, he says, God does not change his methods from century to century. The Incarnation of Christ through Mary assumes an anagogical role which runs through Montfort's doctrine (*True Devotion*, 9-10).

Just as Mary was God's instrument for giving His Son in the Incarnation, so, too, is she the instrument through which He communicates His Son to the human soul. Just as in creation God gathered the waters together and called it the sea, so, too, has He gathered His graces together and called it Mary. As the ocean of His graces, she has been made also the dispenser of those same graces (*True Devotion*, 13).

Grace builds on and perfects nature. Therefore, just as Jesus was Mary's son on earth, so is he still her son in heaven. This is not to be taken as an abasement of Christ, for he remains infinitely greater than Mary. As Montfort states, "she is not even His equal—it would be blasphemous to say so" (*True Devotion*, 14). However, as she is perfectly transformed in God, she does not will anything contrary to the will of God; hence, it may be said that Christ continues to be persuaded by her wishes. In this sense, then, she is legitimately called Mistress of Eternal Wisdom and Queen of Heaven.

Just as she is the mother of Christ, the head of the Mystical body, so is she also the mother of the members of that Mystical Body. That is to say, she is the mother of Christians (*Wisdom*, 118). Just as the natural order stems from two parents, so, too, the order of grace. Again citing Augustine, Montfort states that the elect on earth are hidden in the womb of Mary and conformed to the image of the Son of God. At death, she gives them birth into eternal glory (*True Devotion*, 20).

Mary's role in the Second Coming of Christ is simply a continuation of the role which Montfort sees her performing in the Incarnation and the sanctification of souls; through her, salvation has begun, and through her it will be consummated. Yet, whereas she has a hidden role at the Incarnation (so as not to detract from Christ himself, Montfort maintains), at the eschaton her role will be more manifest, for the historical conditions necessary for her to remain hidden at the beginning no longer exist (*True Devotion*, 29-30).

Not only will her role be widely known, but Montfort also predicts that her "special devotees" will be more visibly active in the world. This is for two reasons. First, there is a direct correlation between the degree to which she is visible and the visibility of Christ. When Christ was born in a stable and revealed only to a few, she also had a hidden role. However, when he is manifested to the entire world, she will also be manifested. The second reason her devotees will be more visibly active in the world is that there is a parallel between her seed and that of Satan, who will unleash special attacks against her devotees, for he dreads her more than anyone, in a sense more than God Himself, for defeat from a mere mortal wounds his pride more than direct defeat from God.

In the last days, Montfort predicts, there will arise saints with a special devotion to Mary who will appear like thunder clouds, unattached to earthly things, blown by the Holy Spirit, thundering against sin and raining God's word upon the earth.

> They will bear on their shoulder the blood-stained standard of the Cross, their right hand supporting it while in their left hand they hold a Rosary. The sacred Names of Jesus and Mary will be written on their hearts (*True Devotion*, 37).

Perfect Devotion

There are many spiritual practices which the faithful undertake to give honor to Mary under the heading of general devotion; however, perfect devotion goes beyond this. Perfect devotion consists of consecrating oneself totally to Mary so that one may belong entirely to Christ. This involves giving Mary everything to which one may legitimately lay claim: body and soul, our material and spiritual treasures. To consecrate oneself in this manner goes beyond even religious vows, for religious forsake the goods of fortune, body and will, but not the right to dispose of their own graces.

True and perfect devotion is based upon five truths which Montfort names. First, Jesus Christ is the final end of all devotion, for he is "our only Master . . . our only Lord . . . our only Head . . . our only Model . . . our only Physician . . . our only Way . . . Truth . . . Life" (*True Devotion*, 40). Devotion to Mary is a sure way to union with Christ because of the intimate union which they share: they are as inseparable as the light from the sun or heat from fire. To those who object that veneration of Mary detracts from worship of Christ, Montfort states that she does not keep any love or devotion to herself, as evidenced at the Visitation: when Mary was praised by Elizabeth, Mary passed the praise on to God in the Magnificat.

The second truth is that we belong to Jesus already. Before baptism, we were slaves of Satan; at baptism we became slaves of Jesus, held by a bond of love. Here Montfort is simply using the language of St. Paul. A servant, Montfort says, works a few hours for benefits and wages, and may leave an employer at any time. A slave, on the other hand, belongs to the master totally and forever, and depends on him for everything. Using the dictum that whatever is Jesus' by nature is Mary's by grace, Montfort reasons that we are her slaves as well. Consecration to Mary is, then, simply a renewal and deepening of the bonds of baptism. When Montfort speaks of slaves of Jesus in Mary, it must be understood in this context, and not as a type of inhuman self-abasement.

The third truth is that we must strip ourselves of self-interest. By placing ourselves in the hands of Mary, we remove ourselves from the possibility of acting in self-interest, for she is in control of our spiritual goods.

The fourth truth is that we need a Mediatrix with Jesus, not so much from God's point of view as from ours. Jesus is the unique Mediator, Montfort reminds us, and no one can approach God outside of the merits of Christ. Yet, Montfort fears that one might lose respect for Christ, or that one might fear Christ because of his majesty or one's sins. "If . . . we are afraid . . . let us boldly seek the aid and intercession of Mary" (*True Devotion*, 60). It can be seen here that the nature of Mary's mediation is different from that of Christ; Montfort says that Christ is the Mediator of Redemption, leading us to the Father, while Mary is the Mediatrix of Intercession, leading us to Christ.

The fifth truth is that we are weak, and are thus in danger of losing our spiritual treasure. This danger stems primarily from pride, in which one relies too much on one's own strength. This is compounded by the corruption of the world in which we live. If we place our treasure in Mary's hands, she will not lose it.

Montfort warns that one must not suppose that a false and totally exterior devotion to Mary will suffice. Those who claim to rely on her while willingly continuing to live sinful lives are presumptuous and hypocritical. One cannot rely on false devotion to save, nor should one approach Mary in self-interest. This calls to mind some of the abuses of Marian devotion lampooned by Erasmus: a businessman going on a trip prays to the Virgin that his mistress be faithful, robbers pray for a fat haul, and a prostitute prays for rich customers.[13] Montfort condemns these attitudes: "There is nothing so damnable in Christianity as this diabolical presumption" (*True Devotion*, 71). True devotion, on the other hand, is interior, holy, constant, and disinterested.

Perfect devotion is, then, for Montfort, the conscious renewal of one's baptismal vows and placing oneself totally in the hands of Mary. One relies totally on her to watch after one's spiritual and temporal interests. Consecration of this sort is complete and without reserve, thus rendering the greatest service to God. In becoming slaves to Mary, we imitate Jesus, who, Montfort says, imprisoned himself as a slave in her womb. Not to be outdone in generosity, she can be counted on to care for our interests even better than we can ourselves.

Every offering to God is thus purified, for she adds her own merits to ours. This leads quickly to union with God: crosses and dark nights are not so difficult as with other paths, there is little chance for going astray, and it is short. Montfort points out that in a short lifetime lived in submission to Mary, Jesus undid the Sin of Adam, who lived over 900 years.

Such devotion gives increased interior liberty, freeing one from scruples and fears, and leads to greater perseverance. In this last regard, Montfort compares Mary to the Ark of Noah, who will not let the waters of sin drown her devotees. Though our vessels and coffers are cracked and defective, she is the sure container to preserve our spiritual treasure. It should be remembered that perseverance is one of the virtues necessary to obtain Eternal Wisdom.

Montfort compares the relationship between Mary and her devotees to that of Rebecca and Jacob. He sees Esau as a type of the world, one who will compromise and sell his baptismal grace for worldly goods, and yet still wants the blessing of heaven. Esau, Montfort points out, trusted his own strength, never stayed at home (that is, ignored the interior life), and did not care for his mother.

---

[13] Hilda Graef, *Mary: a History of Doctrine and Devotion*, Part II (Westminster: Christian Classics, 1985): 2.

Jacob, on the other hand, remained at home (that is, attended to his interior life) and was subject to his mother in all things. When she commanded him to bring two kid goats, he did not question her. Devotees offer Mary the two kids of body and soul, which she kills and strips of self-love. She then clothes them in a way which is pleasing to their Heavenly Father who, though they have no natural right for His blessing, sees their garments and senses the odor of sanctity, and recognizes His Son, Jesus. Like Rebecca, Mary loves, provides, directs, protects and intercedes for her children.

The effects of perfect consecration to Mary are seven-fold. First, it leads to knowledge of self, as one sees one's metaphysical and moral nothingness. Second, one participates in Mary's faith: pure, full and solid. Third, it delivers devotees from fears and scruples, for they are no longer led by fear, but by love. Here, again, one must notice the anti-Jansenistic tone of this devotion. Fourth, one loses false pride in oneself and gains confidence in Mary and in God. Fifth, there is a mystical communication with the soul and spirit of Mary who, in a sense, replaces those of the devotee, and proclaims her magnificat in him or her. This is the mystical union with Mary of which Garrigou-Lagrange writes.[14] Sixth, Mary, as the Tree of Life, produces Jesus in the soul. Montfort compares Mary to a mold in which Jesus is formed. More accurate and easier than sculpting, pouring a mold is not as easily ruined. However, only molten liquid can be poured into the mold, so the Old Adam must be melted down and refined to cast the New Adam. And seventh, this devotion gives even greater glory to God.

In all of this, it must be noticed that, for Montfort, there exists a parallel between the effects of perfect consecration to Mary and the possession of Eternal Wisdom discussed earlier. Enlightenment and self-knowledge, the desire to make known the doctrine concerning Mary, the joy and consolation of depending upon her, and the strength of perseverance all find their echo in the effects of Divine Wisdom on the soul. This should not be surprising, for Montfort repeatedly insists that the final end of true devotion is union with Christ himself, Eternal Wisdom.

Montfort then discusses the particular practices which mark this devotion, distinguishing between interior and exterior practices. Interior practices consist of a disposition of the will whereby all actions performed are done through, with, in, and for Mary. Through Mary in that the soul is

---

[14] Reginald Garrigou-Lagrange, *The Mother of the Saviour and Our Interior Life* (St. Louis: Herder, 1959): 264-270.

inhabited by her, and mystically united to her. With her in imitation of her virtues. In her insofar as she is the Paradisical Garden where the New Adam dwells, and within which one finds the Tree of Life and its fruit, Jesus. And all actions are done for Mary as the devotee is her slave. The slave defends her and draws others to her service. Montfort again reminds the reader that Mary is not the final end of service, for she passes the service on to Jesus Himself. These interior practices are especially recommended when receiving the Eucharist, and Montfort suggests some concrete ways to recollect oneself before, during and after Communion.

Exterior practices are so-named, says Montfort, not because they lack interior qualities, but because they have some external element and are not wholly interior. Montfort mentions just a few: recitation of the Crown of the Blessed Virgin, wearing a small blessed chain as a symbol of slavery, and devotion to the Feast of the Annunciation and to the Magnificat. He also advises a three week program designed to help one gain knowledge of self, the Virgin Mary, and Christ. In many ways, this three week program is reminiscent of the week-by-week process of the Ignatian exercises.

The Rosary

The practice which Montfort most strongly advises, however, the practice which forms the perfect link between exterior practice and interior disposition, is devotion to the Rosary. Montfort points out that the Rosary consists of vocal and mental prayer: vocal prayer consisting of the Creed, Our Father, and Hail Mary (to which he adds his own recommendation of the Glory Be) and mental prayer being the meditation on the Life, Death and Resurrection of Jesus.

Montfort states that the Apostles' Creed is a summary of Christian truths, yet the most potent phrase of the entire prayer is "I believe in God." It is this faith which is the key to the Mysteries of the Rosary; it is faith alone which suffices, a faith which must be constant and informed by love.

The Our Father, Montfort claims, is the most perfect prayer, for it was composed by Jesus Himself. In it are contained all of the duties a Christian owes to God. Citing Tertullian and Thomas á Kempis, Montfort calls the Pater a summary of the Old Testament and a condensation of all the psalms and canticles. It is from this fountain spring that all other prayers stream: It blesses God as Absolute fullness, admits our poverty before Him, asks forgiveness, expresses a love for neighbor, and begs deliverance from temptation and evil.

Modern Christian Spirituality

The Hail Mary, which Montfort loves to call the Angelic Salutation, is, for him, shrouded in mystical ineffability, and is a concise summary of all authentic Mariology.   These are the words which signalled the greatest event in history, the Incarnation, and it is this connection which gives this prayer its potency.   By these very words, Montfort says, God became human, sins were forgiven, the sick were healed, and the dead were raised.[15] These are the words God spoke through Gabriel to win the heart of the Virgin, and it is through these same words that the Fruit of Life sprang up in a barren world.   By the same token, these words cause the Fruit of Life to germinate in the soul.[16] Here again we see the anagogical interpretation of a historic event: God acts in the soul in the same manner through which He acted in the Incarnation.   We also notice the repetition of a familiar theme: Mary gives birth to Eternal Wisdom in the soul, and this is done through the instrumentality of the Angelic Salutation.   For this reason, Montfort calls the Hail Mary the "New Song" proclaimed in Psalm 144:9.   This song blesses both Jesus and Mary and, though sung principally to Mary, is returned to God in the same manner that Elizabeth's salutation was passed on to God Himself.

The second element of the Rosary is mental prayer, that is, meditation on the fifteen Mysteries of the lives of Jesus and Mary. Without the Mysteries, Montfort claims, the Rosary is like a body without a soul. Meditation not only pleases God by adoration, but transforms us through imitation: the virtues of Jesus and Mary are etched on the soul. If the Jews were continually to remember what God did for them at Sinai, how much more should Christians remember what Jesus has done for them?   In fact, Montfort, accepting the legendary connection of St. Dominic to the Rosary, draws a parallel between God giving the Law to Moses and the Virgin giving the Rosary to Dominic (*Rosary*, 19).

Montfort does not treat this meditation so much as a discursive reflection, as spiritual writers following a more Ignatian model often do, but rather speaks of the Mysteries as "tableaux," implying a type of visualization, a simple gazing upon the scenes as one would gaze at an icon. Both the learned and the uneducated can benefit from this practice, which Montfort speaks of as "active" contemplation, placing oneself in the Presence of God, which may lead to a deeper and more "infused" or passive contemplation (*Rosary*, 63).   Hence, it is clear that the Rosary, for

---

[15] Louis de Montfort, *The Secret of the Rosary* (Bayshore, NY: Montfort, 1975): 43. Hereafter this work cited in the text as *Rosary*.

[16] *True Devotion*, 182.

Montfort, cannot be dismissed simply as popular piety, but is rather an advanced tool for mystical union with God.

When Montfort discusses the effects of praying the Rosary, he largely does so by way of anecdotal illustrations: parishes are reformed, sinners converted, demons put to flight, and the sick are healed. He reproduces several versions of the Theophilus legend, whereby grace is obtained for conversion or a pact with the devil broken. The power of the Rosary over demons is, of course, rooted in the power of God working through the Blessed Mother. Indeed, in one anecdote, demons are forced to declare that they fear Mary most of all the saints, and that those who are faithful devotees of the Rosary are never conquered (*Rosary*, 78-79).

One particularly interesting account demonstrates Montfort's faith in the efficacy of the Rosary: it reforms people before they have any idea of what is happening. Montfort tells of a monastery in which one young nun was devoted to the Rosary, and for this was considered a fanatic by her fellow nuns, who were accustomed to a luxurious and lax lifestyle. Her confessor saw in a vision that the monastery was filled with demons who fled her room and hid in the cells of the other nuns. The priest then bought several ornate Rosaries and told the nuns that if they prayed them, he would not make them reform. Willing to strike such a bargain, and attracted by the beauty of the beads, the nuns accepted. Within the year, they asked to have their monastery reformed (*Rosary*, 82).

Again, the effects of faithfully praying the Rosary echo the effects of true devotion to the Blessed Virgin and the possession of Eternal Wisdom in the soul: it gives a perfect knowledge of Jesus Christ, purifies souls, makes virtue easy, gives victory over enemies, and supplies spiritual riches in abundance. Sins are forgiven, souls refreshed, the sorrowful consoled, and the ignorant instructed (*Rosary*, 65, 86).

The dispositions necessary to recite the Rosary also echo those found above. Intentions must be pure, that is, the devotee must have the determination to give up mortal sin. Though the Rosary is a cure for ills, prayed hypocritically it would become a poison. It must be prayed with attention, that is, with no voluntary distractions. Montfort counsels against scrupulous concern for involuntary distractions; these are natural and the Mysteries are designed to help alleviate this. But willful distractions are another story, for the devil plays on our inattentions and tries to induce the devotee to abandon the practice. To combat distractions, Montfort recommends pausing before each decade to reflect on the Mystery, asking for particular graces, and slow recitation, with pauses. It is better, he says, to recite one decade recollectedly than thousands of Rosaries in a rush and without attention.

To aid in the struggle against distractions, and to strengthen the effects of the Rosary, Montfort advises group recitation, for united prayer is powerful and Jesus is in the midst of that union (Mt. 18:20). In fact, to recite it responsorially in two groups, in "choir," as it were, is the most effective means. It keeps one more alert, as well as making up for individual deficiencies. One gains the merits of not one, but many Rosaries, for "this is the law of public prayer" (*Rosary*, 97).

The Rosary is a way to fulfill Jesus' command to keep watch and pray always. Because the disciples did not heed this command, they fell into temptation. This is, again, a walk in the darkness of faith, for it involves humility and confidence, even in dryness; one should not rely on "warm feelings." The Rosary is a means to persevere in prayer, to continue to knock and ask. To aid in this perseverance, Montfort says it is helpful to ask for some particular grace. "Most of all you should ask for divine Wisdom which is an infinite treasure" (*Rosary*, 104). And the thesis has come full circle.

RELEVANCE FOR TODAY

The primary purpose of this section is simply to raise some issues; this paper does not pretend to name every relevant issue, nor to explore any one of them in depth. Such a task is beyond the scope of this work. The issues to be raised are three-fold: women's issues in spirituality, Creation as the sacrament of God's presence, and the rediscovery of the Christian mystical tradition, particularly in light of the encounter with non-Christian traditions.

The importance of feminist issues in theology and spirituality is only today beginning to be appreciated; in fact, the surface has barely been scratched. To use the words of St. Francis, "Let us begin, for up to now we have done nothing." Issues such as the femininity of God, sexually inclusive language, the maleness of Jesus, and the role of the Spirit (as the feminine *ruah*) are just some of the areas being discussed. Jungian psychology has also suggested that everyone, men as well as women, have a "feminine" side. It would seem that a proper understanding of the centrality of Mary's role in the economy of salvation, as portrayed in the Gospel of Luke, where she is viewed as the first Christian disciple, and a proper understanding of Mary's role as Woman and mother in the Gospel of John, a theme carried forward by the Church Fathers when they assigned Mary the title of "New Eve," should lead to a greater appreciation of the feminine in general.

The relevance of Mariology to feminine issues is evidenced in four recent books. The first is Rosemary Radford Ruether's *Mary: Feminine Face of the Church*. Ruether identifies three areas in which a better understanding of feminine symbols, particularly in regard to Mary, might result in a better understanding of relationships with God. The three areas are: an aspect of God at work in Creation (for example, Spirit, Presence, Wisdom), which can be understood as feminine; the believing community as God's feminine companion; and the feminine as the soul's openness and receptivity toward God.[17] The second work is Robert Faricy's *The Lord's Dealing: The Primacy of the Feminine in Christian Spirituality*, which is based on Teilhard de Chardin's vision of Mary as the feminine in Creation.[18] The third work is Leonardo Boff's *The Maternal Face of God: The Feminine and its Religious Expressions*. Boff sees Mary as the symbol for the feminine depths of the psyche, Creation, and of God Himself (Herself?).[19] And, finally there is a wonderful work entitled *Mary according to Women*, which examines the role of Mary as woman in light of peace and justice issues (that is, spirituality in action).[20]

Another major current in spirituality today is the attempt to become more rooted in Creation, to become conscious of the fact that nature and people mediate God's presence to us. This should not be seen as detracting from the unique mediation of Christ; rather, it expands our understanding of his mediation. Raimundo Panikkar asserts that every created being is a christophany, a manifestation of Christ, and Matthew Fox heralds the "coming of the Cosmic Christ." This is a rediscovery of the Logos Christology of the Fathers, who saw the seed of the Logos in every creature, and takes seriously the Franciscan view of Creation as the sacrament of the encounter with Christ.

If it is true that Creation in general is the sacrament of Christ's presence among us, how much more so for the one Wordsworth called "our tainted nature's solitary boast"? As mentioned above, Ruether, Faricy and

---

[17] Rosemary Radford Ruether, *Mary: the Feminine Face of the Church* (Philadelphia: Westminster, 1977).

[18] Robert Faricy, *The Lord's Dealing: The Primacy of the Feminine in Christian Spirituality* (Mahwah, NJ: Paulist, 1988).

[19] Leonardo Boff, O.F.M., *The Maternal Face of God: The Feminine and its Religious Expressions*, trans. Robert R. Barr and John W. Diercksmeier (San Francisco: Harper and Row, 1987).

[20] Carol Francis Jegen, B.V.M. (ed.), *Mary according to Women* (Kansas City: Sheed and Ward, 1985).

Boff all see Mary as the living symbol of the Presence of Christ in Creation. She is, in Teilhard's view, Creation transformed and caught up into the life of God himself. If, as Montfort states, humanity is in a sense a summation of Creation (a statement echoed by Teilhard), and if Mary is a summation of humanity (Boff states that she is the pinnacle of the evolution of the Old Creation, who enables the birth of the New), does she not become a sacrament of our own earthly existence? And if a sacrament of our earthhood, then also a sacrament of our eschatological hope, which is the fullness of Christ Himself. Hence, along with Teilhard, Ruether, Faricy and Boff, perhaps we too can see Mary as the perfect symbol, the sacrament, of Creation transformed, divinized, assumed into the Divine Life.

The final area in which Montfort's spirituality can have relevance for today is the "rediscovery" of the Christian mystical tradition. The Jesus Prayer has become popular in Western Christian circles, largely through the translation of *The Way of a Pilgrim* and the writings of Jesuit Father George Maloney. Centering Prayer, a modernized version of a prayer method mentioned in the fourteenth century mystical work *The Cloud of Unknowing* has also become popular. Everywhere one turns, there are workshops on creative visualization. Much of this impetus has come about through the infusion of Eastern meditation techniques into the West, from Transcendental Meditation to the "Hare Krishna" movement, from Zen to Tibetan Buddhism. One must raise the question of the place Montfort's spirituality, particularly his teaching on the Rosary, might play in this creative encounter.

Unfortunately, there seems to be a tendency in contemporary scholarly circles to relegate Marian spirituality, and in particular Louis de Montfort's Marian devotion, to the realm of popular piety. In the Crossroads Press series on World Spirituality, for example, Orthodox writers spend a great deal of time discussing the Jesus Prayer and the hesychist tradition, but there is no corresponding discussion of the Rosary from Catholic writers. It is barely mentioned, and then only as a "popular devotion." This seems odd, especially in light of the fact that the Rosary has been a means of prayer and meditation used by popes and peasants, monks and laity for centuries. It has been one of the most democratic of all prayers of the Christian West. Certainly its use was more widespread among Western Christians of all walks of life than the Jesus Prayer was in the East, and accounts of sanctity attributed to the Rosary are numerous. And while Marian devotion gets some attention in the series, it is never explored as a mystical path as Montfort portrayed it. Indeed, Montfort is never mentioned at all, which is strange considering the wide-spread influence he exercised over Marian spirituality.

We have seen that Montfort's spiritual method is an attempt to lay out a very deep mystical path. His spiritual vision is like a mandala, having a circular rather than linear movement. One begins by seeking union with Divine Wisdom, which necessitates perseverance in prayer. Consecration to Mary helps to attain Divine Wisdom and to persevere. And the Rosary, the most excellent prayer to Mary, is a way of persevering in prayer, particularly if one asks for Divine Wisdom. Much like the physical Rosary itself, Montfort's spirituality comes full circle: the beginning and the end are the same. Yet, there is progression, and themes repeat, as was seen in the case of the effects which possessing Wisdom, devotion to Mary, and praying the Rosary have in the soul. There is a sort of spiral effect, constantly circling, constantly touching familiar ground, constantly renewing itself.

The presence of non-Christian meditation methods has spread through the West over the course of the past three decades. Certainly there is much to learn from these traditions, and in the spirit of dialogue, it is hoped that the Christian tradition has something to offer back. At a time when mantra chanting and visualization meditation are becoming more popular, it would seem strange to ignore the contribution which Montfort's spirituality could make to this encounter. It is ironic that at a time when Catholicism in the West has tended to downplay certain traditional forms of spirituality such as the Rosary or prayer before the Blessed Sacrament, young Westerners are seeking ancient wisdom from other traditions which promote individual and group chanting, silent meditation, and praying before shrines. The fact that many of these young people are former Catholics has caused one contemporary spiritual writer to wonder if this is where some of our vocations are going. As the Christian West continues to rediscover its own mystical tradition, and as we continue to dialogue with non-Christian spiritual traditions, certainly the mystical theology of Louis de Montfort must play a role.

12

Holiness as Spirituality: The Religious Quest of A. B. Simpson

BILL PITTS

The holiness and Pentecostal groups are probably the two most important expressions of Christianity to appear in the past century.[1] They both emerged in the U. S. and have enjoyed phenomenal growth here as well as among the younger churches of South America, Africa, and Asia. This paper examines the spirituality of A. B. Simpson, founder of the holiness group called the Christian and Missionary Alliance.

The holiness tradition focuses especially on the doctrine of sanctification. Simpson uses the phrase "deeper life" as a shorthand expression for his vision of the full-fledged follower of Christ. His spirituality is neither sacramental nor meditative; instead, it centers on understanding Christ residing within the individual, making possible a holy life.

Albert Benjamin Simpson (1843-1919) was reared near Chatham, Ontario, Canada. His father was an elder in the Presbyterian church who trained his children in religion by having them stand in a row and answer questions from the Shorter Catechism. Simpson reflected that the religious knowledge "crammed" into his mind furnished him with doctrinal beliefs in

---

[1] For a general survey, see Vinson Synan, *The Holiness-Pentecostal Movement in the United States* (Grand Rapids: Eerdmans, 1971) and Robert Mapes Anderson, *Vision of the Disinherited: The Making of American Pentecostalism* (New York: Oxford, 1979).

later life. Simpson's mother was also deeply religious. She trained him to "take everything to God in prayer." One of his earliest memories was praying to find a lost knife; he found it, and this result created a pattern of praying about everything. Simpson decided early to enter the ministry. Local ministers tutored him in Greek and Latin, thereby preparing him for his college and seminary work. He went to Knox College in Toronto in October, 1861. In 1865 Simpson accepted his first pastorate at Knox Church in Hamilton, Ontario. He was immediately ordained. He also married in that same year.[2]

Simpson remained in Canada until 1870, at which time he moved permanently to the United States. He pastored the Chestnut Street Presbyterian Church in Louisville, Kentucky, where he stayed from 1870-1879. In 1879 Simpson moved to the Thirteenth Street Presbyterian Church in New York City. Simpson wanted to be a catalyst to change existing churches, but since he did not get the response he desired, he resigned his Presbyterian pulpit in 1881 and established the independent Gospel Tabernacle. By 1887 he had become the reluctant founder of a new denomination—the Christian and Missionary Alliance.

Simpson insisted that he was not establishing a new church. This is the reason for his use of the term "Alliance" for the movement and "Branches" for local groups. He drew both terms from the English Evangelical Alliance. His original idea was therefore to create associations of Christians who would continue to function within their own denominations.[3]

In 1884 he began a series of annual preaching conventions where he set forth his distinctive teachings. Out of these meetings grew the Christian Alliance. Another convention was organized at Old Orchard, Maine for 1886. The theme was missions in Tibet. The message of W. E. Blackstone deeply stirred Simpson's interest in missions. In 1887 he guided the formation of the Evangelical Missionary Alliance. Instructions were given to combine the two Alliances;[4] the actual name was changed in 1897 to the Evangelical and Missionary Alliance.

The current Christian and Missionary Alliance is a missionary church with a membership of about two million. It has about 238,000 members in

[2] A. E. Thompson, *The Life of A. B. Simpson* (Brooklyn, NY: Christian Alliance Publishing, 1920): 9-42.

[3] Louis L. King, "Agents of Change, Not It's Victims," *Our Help and Our Hope: 1987 General Council* (Nyack: The Christian and Missionary Alliance, 1987): 3.

[4] Robert L. Nicklaus, John S. Savin and Samuel J. Stolsz, *All for Jesus: God at Work in the Christian and Missionary Alliance Over One Hundred Years* (Camps Hill, PA: Christian Publications, 1986): 68-79.

the U. S. A.,[5] but larger churches in Indonesia (485,850), Zaire (305,000), the Philippines (281,200) and Vietnam (250,000).[6] The growth has been spectacular in the past ten years.

The Christian Missionary Alliance has held firmly to Simpson's major message of a four-fold gospel. This is very clear in a restatement of faith adopted in 1987 called "New Century Affirmation of the Christian Missionary Alliance" and in a new centennial history called *All for Jesus*.[7] The denomination's log represents the four major emphases in Simpson's teaching. This paper will examine the four strands in Simpson's understanding of the Christian faith and thereby suggest a holiness approach to spirituality.

Simpson's thought was greatly popularized in the 1940s through the extensive publications of A. W. Tozer.[8] Tozer's influence spread well beyond the Christian Missionary Alliance into many evangelical circles. Simpson's spirituality seems to be well established and significant today, thanks to rapid mission growth, popularization by writers such as Tozer, and reaffirmation by the denomination itself. His spirituality is not a relic of 1900; it is a significant option in current Protestantism.

Four-Fold Gospel

Simpson was a prolific author. The Library of Congress lists seventy-eight titles under his name. Many of his books are collections of sermons, taken by dictation for newspapers and later gathered together as small volumes clustered around a common theme. New ideas emerge in most of his writings. But there are common themes or motifs which appear to control his thought in publication after publication. He writes over and over of the four-fold gospel. He sees Jesus as Savior, Sanctifier, Healer and Coming Lord. And he has a deep commitment to the missionary enterprise. Since these grand themes comprise the essence of the faith for him, it is not surprising that they surface again and again. In fact, they shape the structure of many of his sermons and books, and even his hymns.

---

[5] The earliest concentrations of members were in New York and Pennsylvania. Now the largest constituencies are (in order) California, Pennsylvania, Ohio, New York and Florida. ("Statistics," *Our Help and Our Hope: 1987 General Council*, 25. This report will hereafter be cited as *OHOH*. The seminary is located at Nyack, New York; the headquarters have recently been moved to Colorado.)

[6] "The Measure of Missions," *OHOH*, 9-10.

[7] "New Century Affirmations of the Christian and Missionary Alliance," *Alliance Life* 122 (July 22, 1987): 16.

[8] A. W. Tozer, *The Root of Righteousness* (Harrisburg: Christian Publications, 1955), and numerous other publications.

The inner meaning of Christianity is brought together for Simpson in the combination of these grand themes.

Each of Simpson's four emphases were common in American Protestantism by 1900. For one hundred fifty years revivalism had been established as a powerful tradition.[9]　Millennialism had produced the Seventh Day Adventists, had permeated many Protestant circles, and would grow even more popular through the work of Simpson's friend, C. I. Scofield.[10]　Missions had captured the Protestant imagination in the nineteenth century.[11]　John R. Mott was leading the Student Volunteer Movement for Christian Missions, which recruited and placed thousands of missionaries from college campuses; and Hudson Taylor, much admired by Simpson, had established the largest of the missionary enterprises.[12] Sanctification had a powerful heritage in church history through monasticism and in Protestantism through John Wesley. Phoebe Palmer had recovered the teaching for Methodists in the nineteenth century and Charles G. Finney popularized it in his revivals. But it became a driving force for reform and renewal so powerful that it broke the old wineskins of established denominations and produced numerous new groups whose message was the sanctified life. Divine healing was practiced in a variety of groups of the day, and would become a regular feature in twentieth century holiness and Pentecostal groups. Simpson was remarkably open to this rich variety of currents in the church. He often spoke of "the present truth." He meant by this the inner core of the relationship with God. For him it was best expressed not merely in conversion, but in conversion plus three more Biblical themes: sanctification, healing, and millennialism.

Simpson believed reform was essential because of two basic factors. On the one hand secularism had begun to undermine religious traditions. Simpson points to the issues of evolution and higher criticism as examples of the growing influence of rationalism in modern society.[13]　Materialism and self-interest are common: "Men live for what they can get out of one

---

[9] William G. McLaughlin, *Revivals, Awakenings and Reform* (Chicago: U of Chicago, 1978).

[10] Thompson, *Life of Simpson*, 98. See Robert G. Clouse, ed. *The Meaning of the Millennium: Four Views* (Downers Grove: Intervarsity, 1977).

[11] Kenneth Scott Latourette, *A History of the Expansion of Christianity* (New York: Harper, 1939-1945). Volumes 4, 5 and 6 are devoted to the nineteenth century.

[12] Kenneth Scott Latourette, *A History of Christianity* (New York: Harper, 1953): 1325.

[13] A. B. Simpson, *Ernests of the Coming Age and Other Sermons* (New York: Christian Alliance Publishing, 1921): 15ff. Also see Simpson, *Danger Lines in the Deeper Life* (Harrisburg: Christian Publications, c. 1898, reprint 1966 and 1975): 116-119.

another."[14] Secularism has been called "the greatest problem for spirituality in the twentieth century.[15] Simpson felt keenly the challenges posed by growing secularity.

Moreover, within the church itself there were powerful forces of "cold traditional, theological rationalism" working against renewal.[16] It is standard historiography to explain the origins of the holiness groups as a reaction to complacent parent bodies (mostly Methodist) overtaken by a deadening formalism. This theme recurs in Simpson's writings. Simpson wrote a book on Judges which he called *Danger Lines*. He interprets the book as a picture of "spiritual declension after great spiritual blessing . . . failure after entering the land of promises." To him Judges stands as a picture of the declension of the church after the apostolic age. He finds a parallel application in the individual who backslides.[17] Simpson laments a church "filled with apathy, indifference, and selfishness."[18] And again, "Outwardly the world has been conformed to the will and government of Christ, but inwardly it is to be feared that multitudes have not really been converted."[19] Simpson pointed out that the church had made the mistake of emphasizing externals: doctrine, rules, creeds, confessions and doctrinal principles. This left him cold. It was a "Spirit-less" church: "We say that even the Bible without the Holy Ghost is not sufficient for the church of the Christian."[20]

In his book *Christ Life* Simpson draws a sharp contrast between nominal adherence which he calls "the Christian life" and the level of commitment he is seeking which he calls the "Christ life." The Christ life is a "vital and divine experience through the union of the soul with the Living Christ Himself." In the Christian life one tries to keep the commandments, but "the Christ life is the incarnation of Jesus Himself in your own life. It is the Christ re-living His life in you and enabling you to be and to do what, in

---

[14] A. B. Simpson, *The Challenge of Missions* (Harrisburg: Christian Publications, n. d., reprint 1965): 12. Hereafter all secondary citations of Simpson's works will give just title and page.

[15] Ewert Cousins, "Preface to the Series," in *Christian Spirituality 1: Origins to the Twelfth Century*, eds. Bernard McGinn and John Meyendorff, World Spirituality: An Encyclopedic History of the Religious Quest, vol. 16 (New York: Crossroad, 1985): xii.

[16] A. B. Simpson, *The Gospel of Healing*, (New York: Christian Alliance Publishing, 1915): 11.

[17] *Danger Lines*, 7, 20-21.

[18] *The Challenge of Missions*, 29.

[19] A. B. Simpson, *The Gospel of the Kingdom: A Series of Discourses on the Lord's Coming* (New York: Christian Alliance Publishing, 1890): 314.

[20] *Danger Lines*, 50.

your own strength, you could never accomplish."[21] Alton Bynum studied
Simpson's hymns in a dissertation and concluded that Simpson's whole life
"was centered around knowing Jesus Christ as a personal being who could
be intimately known."[22]

According to Simpson, in the Reformation era Luther recovered
justification, but not the whole gospel. The fullness of the gospel includes
also healing, the power of Christ, and the message of the millennium.[23]
Simpson is clearly setting forth a fuller agenda than hitherto practiced in
the Protestant heritage.

Hymns and other forms of devotional literature come nearer
expressing the heart of spirituality than do theological reflections. One of
the best known of Simpson's 167 published hymns is "Jesus only . . . Jesus
even, all in all." Recently retired President of the Christian and Missionary
Alliance, Louis L. King, sees "Jesus Only" as the organizing center of the
Christian Missionary Alliance—and he finds this in the thought of Simpson.
But this is a very broad statement; it needs further refinement, and
Simpson provided further definition with his repeated restatement of the
four-fold gospel.   The hymn summarizes his spirituality beautifully by
combining "Jesus only" and the four-fold gospel.

> Jesus only is our Message, Jesus all our theme shall be;
> We will lift up Jesus ever, Jesus only we will see.
> Jesus only is our Savior, All our guilt He bore away,
> All our righteousness he gives us, All our strength from day to day.
> Jesus is our Sanctifier, Cleansing us from self and sin.
> And with all His Spirit's fullness, Fitting all our hearts within.
> Jesus only is our Healer, All our sickness He bare.
> And His risen life and fullness, All his members still may share.
> Jesus only is our Power, His the gift of Pentecost.
> Jesus, breathe Thy power upon us. Fill us with the Holy Ghost.
> And for Jesus we are waiting, Listening for the Advent Call:
> But 'twill still be Jesus only, Jesus ever, all in all.
>   REFRAIN
> Jesus only, Jesus ever, Jesus all in all we sing,
> Savior, Sanctifier, Healer, Glorious Lord and Coming King.

Jesus as Savior

The conversion experience is for Simpson the beginning of the
spiritual journey. He describes his own conversion in some detail. Simpson
suffered intense desolation of spirit and fear of dying before he received

---

[21] A. B. Simpson, *The Christ Life* (New York: Christian Alliance Publishing, n.d.): 28.
[22] Alton C. Bynum, "Albert B. Simpson, Hymn Writer, 1843-1919," *The Hymn* 30 (April, 1979): 111.
[23] *The Gospel of the Kingdom*, 10.

assurance of salvation. He was terror-stricken and prayed repeatedly for delay of his death for yet another day so that he could receive salvation. Several events accentuated his spiritual crisis. (1) He reports three brushes with death—a fall from scaffolding, being thrown from a horse, and escaping drowning. (2) The preaching of visiting evangelist H. Grattan Guiness deeply moved Simpson. He was further terrified one day, as he was walking in the woods, when he came upon the gruesome sight of desecrated Indian graves. It was a terrible reminder of his mortality.[24]

At length one day when he was in his pastor's study, he came across Marshall's *Gospel Mystery of Salvation*. This book said that the reader's first good work is to "believe on the Lord Jesus Christ." "This sentence opened for me the gates of eternal life," Simpson wrote. The book continued, "The moment you believe you will pass into eternal life . . . [this was] like light from heaven . . . I prayed . . . and assurance came. I had sought assurance without believing."[25]

Again, devotional literature strongly influenced Simpson when he read Philip Doddridge's *Rise and Progress of Religion in the Soul*. He followed Doddridge's recommendation to enter into a written covenant with God.[26] At age 17 Simpson set aside a day of prayer and fasting to write the nine-hundred-word document which he titled "A Solemn Covenant: The Dedication of Myself to God."[27] He confessed his unworthiness, affirmed his belief in Christ, and appealed to God to ratify the covenant. The purpose of the covenant was to assure his own everlasting life. He asked for a special blessing of the Spirit of God in his life. Simpson closed by asking God to support him and make him neither poor nor rich, "but thy will be done." This document is dated Jan., 1861. It was renewed in 1863 with the note "backslidden" written beside it. College life—especially the influence of a roommate—had taken its toll. Simpson renewed this covenant of commitment again in 1878.[28]

A revival held in Louisville in 1875 was another very influential event in Simpson's life. It reinforced the centrality of conversion in his mind. The London Evangelical Alliance had for several years encouraged Christians to dedicate the opening week of each new year to prayer. People in Louisville gathered for this purpose at the Walnut Street Baptist Church in January, 1875. The churches of the city had planned for a

[24] Thompson, *Life of Simpson*, 11-12, 16, 26.
[25] Ibid., 16.
[26] Ibid., 19.
[27] Nicklaus, Savin, and Stolsz, *All for Jesus*, 24.
[28] Thomspon, *Life of Simpson*, 22.

revival meeting to follow the prayer meeting.   It was led by Chicago evangelist Major Whittle and the singer, P. P. Bliss.   Simpson was greatly moved by this experience, and he wanted it to continue.   Simpson rented public halls and continued to preach in the evenings.[29]

His goal was to reach the unchurched masses who would not come into the established churches.[30]   He was deeply disturbed by the social exclusivism represented by pew rentals in the Louisville church which effectively excluded blacks and lower classes.[31]   Simpson therefore sought to build a vast tabernacle which would seat 2,500 (the capacity of his church was 650).   His church supported him, but he wanted a simple structure which would cost $75,000; the church spent $105,000 for a nicer building, but when they entered it in 1878, they were in debt.[32]   Simpson had just had his eyes opened (in 1877) to the needs of the world mission, and he urged that the church must remain free of debt "if it is to be unselfish and missionary."[33]   He refused to dedicate the unpaid tabernacle.

Again in New York, Simpson's compassion for the masses became evident.   His parishioners were not happy with his approach to evangelism. When Simpson asked the session to bring 100 converts into the church from the Italian quarter, he was refused.   This is probably the event that caused him to leave his church.[34]

Simpson retained a deep desire to preach to the masses.   He resigned his church in 1881, and based his last sermon on the text, "The Spirit of the Lord is upon me because he has anointed me to preach the gospel to the poor."[35]   Simpson began meeting with followers in homes and rented halls. He started his independent church with seven people and by 1883 he had 247 in morning services and 700 in night services.[36]   He stressed that services were free in every respect.   He wanted rich and poor to sit side by side in worship, following the model of Spurgeon's Tabernacle in London.[37]

The concept of the new birth has been central to American revivalism since Whitefield.   Simpson finds the clue to understanding salvation in the gospel of John.   Other New Testament writings speak of

---

[29] Ibid., 54.
[30] Ibid., 71.
[31] Nicklaus, Savin, and Stolsz, *All for Jesus*, 13, 51.
[32] Ibid., 13.
[33] Thompson, *Life of Simpson*, 58.
[34] Nicklaus, Savin, and Stolsz, *All for Jesus*, 36.   He also came to a position of adult believer's baptism in 1881 and was privately rebaptized. Ibid., 43.
[35] Ibid., 44.
[36] Thompson, *Life of Simpson*, 93.
[37] Nicklaus, Savin, and Stolsz, *All for Jesus*, 51.

truth and righteousness, and the Sermon on the Mount tells what an ideal life should be. But the gospel of John tells the secret of how these ideals may become reality. It talks about the secret of the New Birth, where life begins.[38] Simpson describes the new birth as man entering into union with Christ by trusting him. "This saves us from judgment . . . this is the first result of being in Christ.[39]

Simpson's development of this doctrine is very traditional. Nevertheless it is the beginning point of spiritual formation. Gordon Wakefield says that justification is the basis for all Protestant evangelical spirituality.[40] Simpson writes that salvation means that people are saved from the guilt of sin, the wrath of God, the curse of the law, an evil conscience, an evil heart, fear of death, Satan's power, eternal death. On the other hand, salvation brings forgiveness of sins, justification in the sight of God, the favor and love and acceptance of God, a new heart (regeneration), grace to live, eternal life, and so forth.[41] There is no attempt to develop new theological emphases here. He is simply reaffirming justification by faith as the starting point of his theology.

Simpson, in a long list, explains the steps by which salvation is received. First comes conviction of sin and turning from it. Then there is apprehension of Jesus as Savior and turning to him. Next one must accept Jesus as Savior, believing that he has accepted us. Then one must confess Christ and abide in him. With that, salvation is complete.[42]

Simpson abandoned the Calvinistic heritage of predestination. He said that salvation is for everyone, and every man's salvation is dependent upon his own choice and free will. One voluntarily chooses it or rejects it.[43] To believe is to be saved; to fail to believe is to be damned.[44]

Simpson's diary shows that he considered becoming a full-time evangelist.[45] Throughout his career he was concerned with preaching "Jesus as Savior." However, he thought most of Protestant Christianity had stopped precisely here. There was much more to the Christian faith: "Salvation opens the way for all blessings that follow it. It is the stepping-

---

[38] *Christ Life*, 10.

[39] Ibid., 44.

[40] Gordon S. Wakefield, "Spirituality," *The Westminster Dictionary of Christian Spirituality* (Philadelphia: Westminster, 1983): 363.

[41] A. B. Simpson, *The Four-Fold Gospel* (Harrisburg: Christian Publication, n.d.): 8-16.

[42] Ibid., 18-20.

[43] Ibid., 22-23.

[44] A. B. Simpson, *A Larger Christian Life* (Harrisburg: Christian Publications, 1979): 5.

[45] Nicklaus, Savin, and Stolsz, *All for Jesus*, 34.

stone to sanctification and healing . . . from this first gateway the prospect opens out boundlessly to all the good land we may go on to possess."[46]

Jesus as Sanctifier

The unique contribution of holiness groups is their focus on the doctrine of sanctification. This idea reached the height of its popularity in the 1880s.[47] Simpson summarizes its essence succinctly: "There is a place for man's obedience as well as for man's faith."[48]

In 1867 John Inskip and other Methodist ministers formed the National Camp Meeting Association for the Promotion of Holiness.[49] It renewed interest in camp meetings and helped spread the holiness movement beyond both denominational and national bounds.[50] In England an important parallel movement was established at Keswick in 1875.[51]

In 1874 Simpson discovered W. E. Boardman's *The Higher Christian Life* (1858), which deeply affected his life. The message of Boardman was that Jesus who justifies also seeks to sanctify. This little book was destined to have widespread influence.[52] It was critical for Simpson. Reading it convinced Simpson of the possibility of sanctification and provided the occasion of his own sanctification. This was the second decisive turning point in his spiritual journey.[53] Simpson had previously interpreted the doctrine of sanctification to mean the last step before entering heaven. Now he saw it as the basis for a life of service to God. One is consecrated to God, and sanctification follows; the Holy Spirit is the agent in this experience.[54] At this point, Simpson says, Jesus took up residence in him.[55] He uses the analogy of entering a house and beginning to live in it. Further, sanctification is an "attitude of ceaseless growth, not an instant attainment. . . . There must be constant yielding and constant receiving."[56]

---

[46] *Four-Fold Gospel*, 15-16.

[47] Synan, *The Holiness-Pentecostal Movement*, 43.

[48] *Danger Lines*, 65.

[49] Charles Edwin Jones, *Perfectionist Persuasion-The Holiness Movement and American Methodism, 1867-1936* (Metuchen, NJ: Scarecrow, 1974): 19.

[50] Nicklaus, Savin, and Stolsz, *All for Jesus*, 32.

[51] John C. Pollock, *The Keswick Story* (London: Hodder and Stoughton, 1964).

[52] Melvin Easterday Dieter, *The Holiness Revival of the Nineteenth Century* (Metuchen, NJ: Scarecrow, 1980): 56-67.

[53] Nicklaus, Savin, and Stolsz, *All for Jesus*, 7.

[54] Thompson, *Life of Simpson*, 66.

[55] Nicklaus, Savin, and Stolsz, *All for Jesus*, 7.

[56] Ibid., 8. Gerald McGraw's exhaustive study of Simpson's doctrine of sanctification argues that his view should be distinguished from both Wesley and Keswick. He favors the image of the "habitation" of Christ in the life of the individual. Gerald E. McGraw,

Simpson notes that stress on holiness is a current phenomenon in the life of the church:

> The prominence given to the subject of Christian life and holiness is one of the signs of our times. . . . No thoughtful person can have failed to observe the turning of the attention of Christians to this subject within the past quarter of a century.[57]

Many questions were raised about Simpson's teaching concerning both sanctification and healing. He therefore developed a method of dealing with the many objections to and misconceptions of his views: He would set forth "what it is not," and follow with "what it is." Simpson defines sanctification first by saying that it is not regeneration or morality or a person's work of gradual attainment, or the struggle at death nor self-perfection nor a state of emotion (ecstasy).[58]

Simpson turned to the Biblical basis for his message. He finds holiness used in three distinct ways. First, it means "to separate." It does not mean that evil is destroyed. Rather, "sanctification" is an act of the will by which we renounce evil in every form. It is to be a sharp and definite break—like a divorce or a death. Secondly, "sanctification" means "dedication;" not only does one separate from, but also separates to."[59] This is the desire to please God, and to take the position, "Thy will be done."[60] Thirdly, it means "filling." Christ fills the sanctified person with his own presence.[61] The image is of an empty vessel which is filled by God. In some traditions sanctification is treated as a moment of transformation after conversion; in others, it is treated as a process of growing more holy. In Simpson's thought, sanctification involves a twofold process. It includes both a moment of separation from sin and an ongoing gradual process of being filled by God. Simpson summarizes: "Sanctification is progressive, and yet it has a definite beginning."[62]

Simpson says that sanctification should not be confused with regeneration. Regeneration is the beginning, "the germ of the seed, but it is not the summer fullness of the plant."[63] "Justification brings us peace *with*

The Doctrine of Sanctification in the Published Writings of Albert Benjamin Simpson (Ph.D. dissertation, New York University, 1986).

[57] A. B. Simpson, *Wholly Sanctified* (Harrisburg: Christian Publications, 1925): 7.

[58] *Four-Fold Gospel*, 27-33.

[59] *Wholly Sanctified*, 13-18.

[60] *Four-Fold Gospel*, 34.

[61] *Wholly Sanctified*, 21.

[62] *A Larger Christian Life*, 53.

[63] *Four-Fold Gospel*, 28.

God, sanctification the peace *of* God."[64] "Many Christians are converted and stop there. They do not go on to the fullness of their life in Christ."[65]

> Germany brought in the grand truth of justification by faith through the teachings of Martin Luther but he failed to go on to the deeper teachings of the Christian life. What was the result? Germany today is cold and lifeless, and the very hot-bed of rationalism and all its attendant evils. How different it has been in England! The labors of men like Wesley, and Baxter, and Whitfield [sic], who understood the mission of the Holy Spirit, have led the Christian life of England, and America, her offspring, into deeper and more permanent channels. You will find that the men and women who do not press on in their Christian experience to gain the fullness of their inheritance in Him, will often become cold and formal.[66]

Simpson finds in Ezekiel 36 a paradigm to explain the relationship of regeneration to sanctification:

> 'I will sprinkle clean water upon you.' That is forgiveness; old sins are all blotted out. 'A new heart also will I give you;' that is regeneration. 'I will put My Spirit within you, and cause you to walk in My statutes and ye shall keep My judgments and do them;' ah! that is something more than regeneration and forgiveness. It is the Living God come to live in the new heart. It is the Holy Spirit dwelling in the heart of flesh that God has given, so that every movement, every thought, every intention, every desire of an whole being will be prompted by the springing life of God within. . . . Thus only can man enter completely into the life of holiness. As we are thus possessed by the Holy Spirit we are made partakers of the Divine nature.[67]

In his commentary on Judges, Simpson takes the life of the Nazirite as a type of separation from God: "this [separation] is one of the profoundest principles of God's whole plan of redemption."[68] He recounts long lists of Biblical characters who were to be "separate" from the world, and he concludes that the command: "Come ye out and be separate" applies to the present. God must have separated vessels (holy people) today.[69] Simpson finds in the modern church a complete breakdown of all the barriers between the church and the world.[70] He attacks ritualism,

---

[64] *Wholly Sanctified*, 10.

[65] *Four-Fold Gospel*, 28.

[66] Ibid., 28-29.

[67] Ibid., 40.

[68] *Danger Lines*, 97.

[69] Ibid., 97-98. The holiness reform sentiment was held within Methodism for several years, but in the 1880s and 1890s many ministers began to separate or "come out" from the established denomination. These "come-outers" founded the new holiness denominations. See Timothy L. Smith, *Called Unto Holiness* (Kansas City: Nazarene Publishing, 1962): 27ff.

[70] *Danger Lines*, 97.

formalism and human traditions. He criticizes without mercy: "our worship is sustained at an enormous cost by trained performers who belong to the world, flesh and the devil for six days, and for a consideration give a few hours to the Lord on the Sabbath." He recognizes the manipulation common in revivalism: "our revivals are gotten up by careful organization and artificial mechanism."[71]

Sanctification is not just personal improvement but also acceptance of Jesus into life: "He does not improve us, and make us something to be wondered at, but He just comes in us. . . ."[72] Simpson makes the point over and over that what happens at sanctification is that Christ (God/Holy Spirit/Holy Ghost) occupies the life of the Christian and lives within him. The Pauline "in Christ" passages are appropriate to Simpson's concerns, but even more pertinent are the "Christ in us" passages. He cites "Christ is all and in all" (Col. 3:11) to open his study of the Christian life in Colossians, and "Christ liveth in me" (Gal. 2:16) in his study of Galatians.[73] Likewise, Johannine passages work well to support Simpson's thrust: "Abide in me and I in you" . . . "Thou in me and I in them," and so forth.[74] Even the final petition of the Lord's Prayer (deliver us from evil) is, according to Simpson, "a petition for entire sanctification, including deliverance from every other form of evil."[75] "Christ descends out of heaven," Simpson writes in a graphic picture, "and dwells in your inmost being."[76] Furthermore, "Christ Himself is your holiness; He will bring his own holiness, and come and dwell in your heart forever."[77]

The key to Simpson's spirituality is his doctrine of sanctification. The inner core of Christianity he wants to reclaim is the holy life. "He that abideth in him sinneth not (I John 3:6)." This is the goal for Simpson, and the secret of holiness is that it is "not our holiness, but His. Jesus lives in us. This is the secret of sanctification."[78]

The very titles of the Christian and Missionary Alliance hymnals reflect the emphasis on the Christian life beyond salvation: *Hymns and Songs of the Four-Fold Gospel and the Fullness of Jesus* (1890); *Hymns of the*

---

[71] Ibid., 114.

[72] *Four-Fold Gospel*, 39.

[73] A. B. Simpson, *The Fullness of Jesus or Christian Life in the New Testament* (New York: Christian Alliance Publishing, 1890): 216, 172.

[74] *Christ Life*, 58-59.

[75] A. B. Simpson, *The Life of Prayer* (New York: Christian Alliance Publishing, 1925): 26.

[76] *Christ Life*, 55.

[77] Ibid., 69.

[78] Ibid., 21.

Christian Life (1890); and *Songs of the Spirit* (1919). Likewise, numerous book titles—and chapter titles within books—suggest Simpson's concern for a sanctified life, e.g., *A Larger Christian Life, The Fullness of Jesus, Wholly Sanctified, Christ Life, The Holy Spirit or Power from on High.* Finally, the language used to describe the movement reflects concern for developing a sanctified Christian life: "deeper life," "present-truths," "four-fold gospel," and so forth.

One of the most common misinterpretations of sanctification, according to Simpson, is that it is a holy life achieved through effort. But he sees it as a gift of God just as much as salvation is.[79] ". . . [Y]ou cannot sanctify yourselves. The only thing you can do is to give yourself wholly to God."[80] "Sanctification is not the work of man . . . nor of our own strugglings. . . . It is the gift of the Holy Ghost. It is the great obtainment of faith, not the attainment of works. It is the work of God himself."[81]

The sense of the presence of God within the individual is what provides the basis for a morality of separateness from the world. "If we know that God is . . . dwelling in us, we will bow before the majesty of that sacred presence. We will not dare to profane it by sin."[82] The very essence of sin is that it "paralyzes our moral power and leaves us without strength."[83] The holiness leader found many practical applications of the idea of separation. He warned against the temptation of easy money for the church. "We think there is no harm in taking the money of wicked men for religious objects."[84] He warned against Christians marrying non-Christians: "No child of God has any right to intermarry with the ungodly. I would not perform such a marriage ceremony."[85] Dancing must not be permitted.[86] Avoid sinful thoughts, forbidden occupations and worthless and frivolous reading.[87] The list may be extended, but "there is no situation which can arise to which we may not apply the simple watchword 'What would Jesus do?'"[88]

Simpson identifies common stumbling blocks to personal sanctification, and offers solutions to each of these. Some people have

---

[79] *Four-Fold Gospel*, 38.
[80] Ibid., 30.
[81] *Wholly Sanctified*, 10-11.
[82] *Four-Fold Gospel*, 41.
[83] *The Challenge of Missions*, 39.
[84] *Danger Lines*, 10.
[85] Ibid., 11.
[86] Ibid., 117.
[87] A. B. Simpson, *Life More Abundantly* (New York: Christian Alliance Publishing, 1912), 34.
[88] *Christ Life*, 15.

trouble receiving sanctification, Simpson notes, because they (1) cling to their own goodness, (2) stumble and do not see Jesus as their complete Sanctifier, (3) do not completely surrender to Jesus, (4) cannot believe Jesus receives them.[89] But if one abandons his own claim to goodness, sees Jesus as the complete Sanctifier, surrenders to him, and believes that he is received by Jesus, then, "I am certain, dear friends, when you have taken these four steps you can never be as you were before. Something has been done which can never be undone. You have become the Lord's."[90]

Simpson provides useful directives to readers seeking practical advice about living a sanctified life. His experience as pastor doubtless contributed to his attention to these issues. Here Simpson functions as spiritual guide—a significant aspect of the spirituality of any tradition. Simpson's brief chapter, "Abide in Me," for example, provides an eminently practical list of helps in pursuing the holy life. First, recognize that sanctification is for the moment, not once for all. Life is a series of tests. Second, acts of the will are involved. Choices must be made daily. Third, recognize the force of habit—both good and bad—in trying to shape a more holy life. Fourth, look for God's will always. Fifth, watch the outward senses because they are a major source of temptation. Sixth, develop the practice of internal prayer; this is silent prayer expressed in thought not in words.[91] Here Simpson reiterates several themes common in the wisdom of the church's spiritual directors. Separation from the world, personal purification, and being filled with Christ have been venerable themes of Christian tradition. They form the inner essence of the holiness tradition.

Jesus as Healer

Simpson believed that healing is a neglected, but profound dimension of the spiritual life.[92] He conducted healing services in his church and justified the experience in many of his writings. David Harrell writes that healing revivalism was left to others, but that Simpson was honored as a pioneer teacher on divine healings.[93] J. Gordon Melton notes that the Christian and Missionary Alliance was among the first holiness groups to emphasize the place of healing.[94] A succinct statement of Simpson's

---

[89] *Four-Fold Gospel*, 43.

[90] Ibid., 13.

[91] *The Christ Life*, 85-104.

[92] *The Gospel of Healing*, 8.

[93] David Edwin Harrel, Jr., *All Things are Possible* (Bloomington: Indiana U., 1975): 13.

[94] J. Gordon Melton, "Christian and Missionary Alliance," *The Encyclopedia of American Religions* (Wilmington, NC: Mc Grath, c. 1978), 1: 322.

position is found in *The Gospel of Healing*, published in 1915.[95] Healing is
not the whole of the gospel, Simpson argued, but it is a part.[96]

Simpson's teaching on divine healing grew, in part, out of his
personal experience. He placed himself under excessive stress in pursuit of
his studies, and experienced a nervous breakdown at age 14.[97] Simpson
also apparently suffered a heart problem: the act of climbing left him with
a sense of suffocation. Pastoral duties sapped Simpson's energies. After
preaching on Sunday, he did not recover sufficiently until Wednesday to be
able to prepare for the next Sunday.[98] His churches offered him extended
periods of leave for recuperation; his health problem was well known
among his parishioners.[99] All of this is background for a transformation he
experienced.

In 1881 Simpson went to a summer church camp and there heard
many people describe their healings.[100] He began reading his Bible on this
issue and became convinced of the reality of divine healing. This was
Simpson's third major spiritual crisis. He made three pledges: (1) He
accepted that divine healing was part of the Gospel; (2) he "took without
doubting the Lord Jesus for his healing and health;" and (3) "he promised
without fail to use this blessing to the glory of God and for the good of
others."[101] Soon he tested his newfound strength by climbing a 3000-foot
mountain; he was amazed to find that the sensation of suffocating never
occurred.[102] Moreover, the output of his work thereafter was astounding.[103]

Simpson struggled with advocating healing publicly: "I had a great
deal of conservative respectability and regard for my ecclesiastical
reputation. . . . I knew what it might cost. . . . I shrank unutterably from the
thought of having to pray with any one else for healing. I feared so much
that I should involve God's name in dishonor by claiming what might not
come to pass."[104] The former Presbyterian minister suffered personally for
taking this step. Many friends of earlier years did not understand, and left
Simpson feeling abandoned and isolated.[105]

---

95 The Gospel of Healing, 11. See also A. B. Simpson, *The Lord for the Body* (New
York: Christian Alliance Publishing, 1925).
96 *Gospel of Healing*, 8.
97 Thompson, *The Life of Simpson*, 15-16.
98 *Gospel of Healing*, 156-57.
99 Nicklaus, Savin, and Stolz, *All for Jesus*, 6.
100 Ibid., 40.
101 Ibid., 41.
102 *Gospel of Healing*, 147.
103 A. W. Tozer, *Wingspread* (Harrisburg: Chicago Publications, 1943): 81.
104 *Gospel of Healing*, 175.
105 Nicklaus, Savin, and Stolsz, *All for Jesus*, 43.

Simpson preached about his healing experience, and his daughter experienced a healing.[106] Others began to inquire about it, and on May 16, 1883, a number of Christian friends assembled while Simpson dedicated his house as "a Home for Faith and Physical Healing." The healing services which came to be held each Friday afternoon grew rapidly and were later moved to the Gospel Tabernacle. Simpson continued these services uninterruptedly for the last thirty-eight years of his life; the meetings always closed with an anointing service.[107]

Simpson did not use the term "faith healing." He taught that the power to heal was not derived from a subjective state of mind, but from God.[108] Moreover, this power was symbolized in anointing by the elders of the church. Simpson did not usurp the title "healer," a model of ministry that would stretch from Alexander Dowie to Oral Roberts.[109] But the church must also face resistance to recovery of this Biblical practice.

> In spite of the cold, and conservative, and sometimes scornful unbelief of many, this doctrine is becoming one of the touchstones of character and spiritual life in all the churches of America, and revolutionizing by a deep, quiet, and Divine movement, the whole Christian life of thousands.[110]

Simpson sets forth a theology of divine healing. First he argues that the causes of disease are traced to the Fall and to man's sin. Simpson then draws an analogy from the cross and resurrection. The death of Christ destroys sin, but the life of Christ supplies the source of life and health.[111] Thus the very heart of redemption suggests conquering disease and establishment of health. The health of Jesus' body can be shared with the believer: "I am persuaded that His body, which is perfectly human and real, can somehow share its vital elements with our organic life, and quicken us from His Living Heart and Indwelling Spirit."[112]

Simpson develops the notion of a three-fold atonement to respond to man's three-fold nature. Christ atones the spirit of man (salvation), his soul (sanctification), and his body (physical healing).[113] All of man's nature is in

---

[106] *Gospel of Healing*, 176-177.
[107] Thompson, 139, 141.
[108] Thompson, 145.
[109] Harrell, 13.
[110] *Gospel of Healing*, 8.
[111] *Four-Fold Gospel*, 61.
[112] *Gospel of Healing*, 172.
[113] A. B. Simpson, *Life More Abundantly: A Bible Expositor for Each Day in the Month* (New York: Christian Alliance Publishing, 1912): 39.

need of redemption and Christ's atonement addresses every aspect of life.[114]

The doctrine of the Holy Spirit permeates much of Simpson's thought. He cites Romans 8:11 which declares that the Spirit of him that raised Jesus shall also give life to your mortal bodies. Simpson urges that this cannot refer to a future resurrection. Moreover, it is not a quickening of the soul, but of the body.[115] God surely has the power to heal. It takes more of his power to redeem than to heal.[116]

Simpson does not claim to have rediscovered divine healing in the Bible. He credits the German "Pastor Blumhardt as the discoverer of the old doctrine of Divine Healing."[117] But W. M. Turnbull, a Simpson follower, notes that "only a generation ago but few teachers ever touched upon this phase of Scriptural doctrine." He sees Simpson as a pioneer in teaching divine healing for this country.[118]

Divine healing was a controversial subject, and Simpson responded to many objections to the practice. (1) Healings were a sign to help establish Christianity, but that kind of evidence is no longer needed. His response; every new area and every new generation needs visible signs of God's power. (2) God is glorified by our patience in bearing sickness. Response: People do not in fact submit; they all try to get well. (3) If you really believed in divine healing, logic would indicate that you would be healed perpetually and never die. Simpson's practical answer is that healing promotes a full life, but not perpetual life. (4) Doesn't God use "means," i.e., doctors? Yes, he replies, but for believers there is a more excellent way.[119]

In another survey, Simpson spells out what divine healing is *not*: (1) medical healing; (2) metaphysical healing through knowledge or mind as advocated by Christian Science; (3) magnetic healing by a current flowing from one body to another; (4) spiritualism (it is controlled by Satan); (5) prayer cure, as if to change a stubborn God; (6) a faith cure (faith is merely the instrument of healing); (7) will power; (8) defiance of God's will; (9) immortality; (10) a mercenary profession.[120] Obviously a massive number of criticisms were levelled against the practice.

---

[114] *Gospel of Healing*, 21.

[115] Ibid., 26.

[116] *Four-Fold Gospel*, 57.

[117] *The Challenge of Missions*, 70.

[118] W. M. Turnbull, "Preface" in A. B. Simpson, *The Lord for the Body* (New York: Christian Alliance Publishing, 1924): 8.

[119] *Gospel of Healing*, 56-70.

[120] *Four-Fold Gospel*, 47-56.

Divine healing was significant not only for holiness groups in this era, but also for many others in the New Thought tradition, especially Christian Scientists.[121] Simpson wrote to show that these were false interpretations of the Christian faith.[122] Thus he had to justify divine healing on the one hand and reject many expressions of it on the other.

How does one appropriate the gifts of healing?   As with sanctification, Simpson provides practical direction.   Healing is possible only if the believer has faith.[123] There must be full commitment. If one hedges with the common phrase "if it be His will," he should not expect to be healed.[124] Simpson's logic is arresting here. He says that no one uses this phrase when asking for forgiveness. He observes that there is often much subtle unbelief in the prayer 'thy will be done.' Secondly, one needs to prepare for healing. Since sin may be the cause of the disease, it is essential to be rid of sin.   One ought also to do away with medicines, suggesting true reliance upon God. This should be prepared for just as seriously as marriage or any similarly significant step in life. The will is also important during and after claiming the healing. The believer should claim the healing as God's promise and do it in the name of Jesus. Then one must act as if healed. "Don't look for immediate removal of symptoms," he says. And finally, "use your new strength and health for God."[125]

Simpson concludes his major book on healing with an important qualifier. He says that healing should be regarded as part of the gospel, but far more important for him are the issues of "the salvation and sanctification of the souls of men."[126]   There is much discussion of wholeness and health in contemporary religious literature. *The Westminster Dictionary of Spirituality* has no entry on healing or divine healing. Simpson's teaching may raise the question of its place in the study of spirituality.

Simpson found extensive basis for healing in the Biblical narrative. He liked to point to Exodus 15 as an early Biblical example of healing and disease.[127] At the Passover, disease is placed on the Egyptians but not on

---

[121] See Charles S. Braden, *Spirits in Rebellion: The Rise and Development of New Thought* (Dallas: Southern Methodist U., 1963), and J. Stinson Judah *The History and Philosophy of the Metaphysical Movements in America* (Philadelphia: Westminster, 1967).
[122] *Four-Fold Gospel*, 48-53.
[123] *A Larger Christian Life*, 6.
[124] *Gospel of Healing*, 78.
[125] *The Gospel of Healing*, 80-95.
[126] Ibid., 184. His biographer, (Thompson, *Life of Simpson*, 139) however, sees it as his most influential teaching.
[127] *The Lord for the Body*, 11.

the Hebrews. Job is healed by God, not by a physician. The Psalmist declares that the Lord heals all diseases; the Psalmist appeals to God for forgiveness and healing in the same breath. In another of Simpson's arguments, he applies the text "my God shall supply all your needs" to include health. He writes that "good health is the richest material blessing of our bodily life, and as everyone recognizes, is one of our greatest needs."[128] The story of the paralytic is particularly appropriate in Simpson's interpretations of the relationship of forgiveness to healing. "The poor man came for healing, but the Lord saw a deeper need that must be met first." The spiritual life must precede the physical. And so he speaks the word of pardon first. "Son, thy sins be forgiven thee." Then follows his physical healing.

The key healing passage for Simpson was James 5:14. The elders were to pray over the sick and anoint them. Here the authority is given to elders, not to physicians. Moreover, this passage is meant to apply to ages succeeding the New Testament.[129]

Jesus is the supreme healer. Matthew 8:16-17 records that he healed all that were sick. Simpson sees the healing miracles not as isolated events, but as a constant motif in the ministry of Jesus: they were "not occasional, but continual." Jesus spent "three years in deeds of power and love." These healings must not be explained away as mere types of spiritual healing. These were real events of healings. Jesus also said that those who come after him would do greater works than he did. Simpson insists that it is no use interpreting this word to mean that the church would have greater spiritual power after Pentecost; the passage refers to specific deeds of healing.[130]

What happened to the practice of healing after the period of the New Testament? The traditional Protestant answer is that it disappeared with the apostolic age. But Simpson writes, "I see no place in the Bible where we are taught that the miraculous is to cease with the ascension of the Lord."[131] Simpson argues that there are records of healings in Tertullian, Irenaeus, and to the fifth century; it disappeared because of the demise of spirituality; it disappeared gradually in the presence of "growing worldliness, corruption, formalism and unbelief."[132] Simpson believes that healing was being restored in the life of the church because of reviving

---

[128] *Gospel of Healing*, 108.
[129] Ibid., 23-24.
[130] Ibid., 18-20.
[131] *The Lord of the Body*, 18.
[132] *Gospel of Healing*, 10, 53.

faith, deepening of the spiritual life, recognition of the Holy Spirit, and growing awareness of the imminent return of Christ.[133]

Coming King and Missionary Vision

Simpson believed he was living in a unique age. The age had rediscovered and set forth "present truths" of sanctification and healing. But it was unique also in that Christ would return to earth soon. This is the fourth "present truth" of the four-fold gospel.

Simpson accepted the premillennial views of Christ's return, and carefully developed its ideas in some of his longer books.[134] Simpson acknowledges the importance of Darby, but mere correctness in millennial thought is not enough:

> The Plymouth Brethren rose up as the exponents of . . . the blessed hope of the Lord's coming, and when they became too rigid and narrow and substituted a mere state for a living experience, the Holiness Movement was brought to the front to emphasize the indispensable necessity not only of our standing right with God, but our having all that we stand for made living, real and experiential in a purified heart and a victorious life.[135]

Millennialists are preoccupied with calculating times of epochs and providing Biblical descriptions of each. The purpose is to provide clues for the present and to suggest that the second coming of Christ is at hand. For example, Simpson draws parallels between the seven churches of Revelation and the course of church history; he focuses on the final three. Sardis represents "the putrid corpse of Medieval Romanism;" Philadelphia represents the sunrise of the Reformation; but lukewarm Laodicea represents "the church of wealth and pride, languid and lukewarm." It is none other than modern Protestantism. It boasts its numbers, works and resources, but it spends three hundred times as much on liquor and tobacco as on missions.[136] The present situation in the church provides for Simpson ample evidence that the return of the Lord is imminent. Revival and missions he finds as good signs, but also evil influences such as Spiritualism (conversation with the dead), nominal Christianity, greed, self-indulgence and vigorous false religions are equally apparent.[137] Simpson traces

---

[133] Ibid., 11.

[134] See A. B. Simpson, *The Gospel of the Kingdom: A Series of Discourses on the Lord's Coming* (New York: Christian Alliance Publishing, 1980) and a revised edition called *The Coming One* (New York: Christian Alliance Publishing, 1912).

[135] *The Challenge of Missions*, 70.

[136] *The Gospel of the Kingdom*, 99.

[137] *Gospel of the Kingdom*, 214-216; 292, 301 and A. B. Simpson, *Practical Christianity* (Harrisburg: Christian Publications, reprint 1974): 101, 105.

elaborate schemes of interpretation, identifying dates crucial for "prophetic" history and finding significant events which fall on those dates. The major actors in historical reconstruction are the Gentiles, the papacy, the Moslems, and the Jews. He searches for great blows to the authority of each, thus paving the way for a new age and the millennial reign of Christ.[138]

Part of the appeal of Simpson's thought is the interrelatedness of its major parts. Thus he can argue that sanctification, healing and missions are all closely connected to the imminent return of the Lord.[139] The idea of "present truths" suggests that they have been dormant for a long time. They are presumably revived in anticipation of the great event. These ideas do not add significantly to Simpson's spirituality centered on salvation, sanctification and healing. These three are capable of being experienced by the ordinary believer. The return of the Lord serves as a doxology in the four-fold gospel. It provides urgency for holy living and for missions. Simpson says that the doctrine of the Coming Lord "becomes a bright and personal expectation, and the whole world of spiritual things is more real to us in our own conscience."[140]

The doctrine sustains the poor and mistreated. It is "a comfort for life's every trial, something for the housewife amid the poverty of her home, something for the laborer under the scorching sun of the harvest fold, something for the workman robbed of his wages and tempted to fight for his rights."[141] The day of judgment is a day of justice. "That day will make right all our wrongs . . . and displace the sons of pride who have so long trampled on the rights of others."[142] The world will be turned upside down: the oppressors will be punished and the poor righteous will have their day. In short, this doctrine counsels an infinite patience in the midst of suffering and resignation to one's lot in life; it also promises the triumph of good with the imminent return of Christ.

In 1877 Simpson attended a Believer's Conference in Watkins Glen, New York. It included missionary messages. This experience, coupled with

---

[138] *Gospel of the Kingdom*, 218-247.

[139] *Four-Fold Gospel*, 69.

[140] *Wholly Sanctified*, 36. This expectation intensifies the life experience of the Christian. What are its implications? The doctrine of Christ's coming provides impetus for Christian missions. The gospel must be preached to all nations before the Lord returns: "Be diligent, there is much to do. 'You can hasten the coming of the day of God.' The world is to be forewarned. And may this last decade of the nineteenth century mean for you and for this world, as nothing ever meant before, a time of preparation for the coming of our Lord and Savior Jesus Christ." (*Four-Fold Gospel*, 92-93.)

[141] *Practical Christianity*, 100.

[142] Ibid., 109.

a dream of masses of mute Chinese, awakened a missionary spirit in him. He volunteered for missions, but his wife refused to go.[143] Simpson nevertheless acquired a passion for missions which became a fifth dimension added to his four-fold gospel. Since he could not go as a missionary, Simpson conceived the idea of creating a first-rate missionary journal.[144] He produced *The Gospel in All Lands*, an illustrated missionary monthly. He wrote articles, collected pictures, and served as editor. Simpson set very high standards, and the journal received commendation from many people including Harlan P. Beach, missions professor at Yale University.[145]

Simpson argued that Christians must go to foreign fields or else disobey the command of Christ.[146] The task was not optional. He set forth passionate appeals for vast numbers of people and vast sums of money to support the missionary venture.[147] This work could be promoted through vast annual conferences which focused on missions. Simpson used the conventions effectively. He said that the goal of the missionary movement should be to send the full simple gospel by the most spiritual and consecrated people with the most economical and practical methods to the most needy and neglected heathen.[148] This program would set the tone for distinctives in Alliance missionary endeavor: preaching the full gospel, taking the message to the poorest, and living as one with the destitute of the world.

Simpson is usually credited with the formation of the first Bible College in the United States—at Nyack, New York, in 1882. In the following year he established a missionary training college. The first attempt at mission (1884) failed, but missionary work was permanently established in 1887.[149] The missionary movement stimulated organization for training, fund raising, and missionary placement. It made possible an activist form of spirituality: the believer can do something and see some results.

---

[143] Nicklaus, Savin, and Stolsz, *All for Jesus*, 14. Sanctification provided Simpson with a great impetus to help the poor both at home and abroad. The holiness tradition taught that it had tapped a source of power for service and for mission. See Charles H. Lippy and Peter W. Williams, eds., *Encyclopedia of the American Religious Experience* (New York: Charles Scribner's, 1988), s. v. "Pentecostalism" by Grant Walker and "The Missionary Enterprise" by Patricia R. Hill.
[144] Nicklaus, Savin, and Stolsz, *All for Jesus*, 24
[145] Thompson, *Life of Simpson*, 122.
[146] Ibid., 124.
[147] *The Challenge of Missions*, 30-31.
[148] Thompson, *Life of Simpson*, 126.
[149] Ibid., 98-99.

Missions had many values in Simpson's view. First, it would bring salvation to many. Second, it would bring a wide range of humanitarian benefits. Third, it would hasten the return of the Lord.[150] Simpson tied missions closely to his understanding of the return of Christ. It was essential that the gospel be preached throughout the world so that everyone has a chance to respond to Christ before his return. Simpson made a distinction between evangelization and conversion which is common among missiologists. The world could and should be evangelized; that is, everyone should hear about Christ. This, however, is far different from the goal of converting everyone. Simpson counted the number of non-Christians in the third world, pointed to secularizing trends in Europe and concluded that it was unrealistic to think all of these people would actually be converted to Christianity. We are primarily preparing for the return of the Lord. This, not conversion of the world, is our primary purpose.[151] But the Biblical qualification "a great multitude, out of all nations" must be met in preparation for Christ's return.[152] The work of missions is the great means of hastening the end.[153]

The result of Simpson's teaching regarding missions is impressive. Many Protestant groups based in the United States have a small extension of missionaries and converts forming churches overseas. But in the Christian and Missionary Alliance, over eighty percent of its adherents are members of churches organized abroad. The missions rallies are still held, and missions seems to have achieved a central place in the religious consciousness of many members of the Christian and Missionary Alliance. In ranking features of the full gospel one of Simpson's close followers placed missions clearly ahead of healing in order of importance.[154] The foreign missionary enterprise has captured the imagination of many Christians and provides another approach to spirituality today. Missionaries are still "heroes" or spiritual elite in the minds of many people. Simpson's vision of missionary service as part of the fuller gospel has clearly not been lost among present-day followers.

Conclusion

One hundred years ago Simpson provided a fresh model of spiritual life. Protestant piety in the nineteenth century focused on the model of a

---

[150] *Challenge of Missions*, 38-50.
[151] *Challenge of Missions*, 76.
[152] *Gospel of the Kingdom*, 115.
[153] *Challenge of Missions*, 61.
[154] W. M. Turnbull, Preface, in A. B. Simpson, *The Lord for the Body*, 8.

conversion experience in a revival setting. This model was repeatedly shown to be inadequate. At the end of the nineteenth century, revivalism continued unabated. But it could not prevent lethargy in the church. Simpson responded with a program for reform—a deeper life of present truths summarized in a four-fold gospel.

Part of the genius of Simpson was the simplicity and coherence of his message. The four-fold gospel was easy to remember. It began with the Protestant heritage of salvation. It did not try to negate or diminish this teaching. But it added other compelling elements, attractive in its age, and based squarely in scripture; it was both a wider and a deeper Christianity which he advocated.

Simpson taught that a message of salvation was not enough. Divine life, the life of Christ living within the individual was a possibility available to everyone. The followers of Jesus should be both saved and sanctified. This forced new reflection on the Christian life: its goals, its characteristics, its motivation, and so forth.

Methods of formation are always a significant aspect of spirituality. Simpson employed the practice of writing out his commitments to God. This discipline was used extensively in his day. In a modified form the Student Volunteer Movement used it to secure lifetime commitments to missionary work. The temperance societies employed the written pledge to establish abstinence, and so forth. This technique proved its effectiveness; the signed written word appeared to be more binding than the spoken word. Yet Simpson did not prescribe this technique for his followers. Devotional literature was very important in Simpson's own spiritual formation. He refers to Marshall, Doddridge and Boardman with gratitude. However, once again he does not seem to have promoted the reading of these or any other Christian classic among his followers.

Although Simpson did not prescribe devotional readings to his followers, he himself was a prolific author. His books are divided into brief chapters, and provided material that was easy to read. He also produced journals and magazines. The printed word was clearly crucial in the shaping of this denomination. Hymns are a traditional form of spiritual expression. Simpson tried to provide good music for his services and his own hymns clearly express his understanding of the Christian life. Summer conferences were important in awakening Simpson's interest in missions. In the latter half of the nineteenth century conferences were commonly held to promote holiness ideas, dispensational theology, missions, and so forth. This is a key method for recruiting religious personnel today, and it was not neglected by Simpson. The Bible College concept was likewise an important innovation. Here one could shape a different curriculum from that of the seminary, and produce leaders for new causes and new missions.

There is a strong orientation to the person of Jesus or to the person of Christ in Simpson's spirituality. Traditional theological definitions are not so important as the sense of the living Jesus taking up residence within the individual. Simpson wrote often of "Jesus Only" and "All for Jesus." Jesus' presence makes possible the added dimensions of sanctification and healing. The person of Jesus is the center of his spirituality. Similarly, in other writings, Christ is the focus of his attention:

> The greatest movement of today, the greatest movement of the church's history is a CHRIST MOVEMENT; a revealing in our day, with a definiteness never before so real, of the person of the living Christ as the center of our spiritual life, the source of sanctification, the fountain of our physical life and healing, the Prince-Leader of our work, and the glorious coming King.[155]

Here Simpson identifies "Christ as the center of our spiritual life." Simpson does not write merely of salvation, sanctification, healing or the Lord's return. Instead, he keeps the focus on the source: Jesus as Savior, Jesus as Sanctifier, Jesus as Healer, and Jesus as Coming Lord. Simpson had a four-fold gospel, but in the end his spirituality is based on a sense of the presence of the person of Christ in the life of the believer.

---

[155] Thompson, *Life of Simpson*, 153.

13

The Conversion of Mind and Heart:
The Spirituality of John Henry Newman

ROBERT L. FASTIGGI

John Henry Newman (1801-1890) stands as one of the greatest religious personalities of the nineteenth century. His writings have aroused the interest and curiosity of scholars of religion, literature, education and philosophy. The essence of Newman's corpus rests in a convergence of a profound faith with a towering intellect. He is a man of true Christian piety linked to an ever active mind. It is small wonder that Newman's spirituality seeks a common meeting place between faith and reason. Living in a century that embraced the extremes of atheism and revival, John Henry Newman labors to show that the reasons of the heart are in harmony with the powers of the mind.

This paper does not pretend to be an exhaustive study of the spirituality of Newman. Its purpose is more modest. The major focus is on the epistemic issues that run as a thread through life and writings of the great English scholar. The question of the relationship of faith and reason is of central concern to Newman. The issue of the mind's assent to the personal God of Christian faith seems to have absorbed Newman as a young man. It was a topic he could not let go—even in his spiritual writings and sermons. The reason for this lifelong preoccupation are twofold: the first lies in the nature of the age in which he lived; the second resides in the character of the man.

The nineteenth century is an age of great faith and great scepticism. It is an age of religious and anti-religious thinkers. In this single century, religious thinkers like Schleiermacher and Kierkegaard strive to ground the basis of Christian life in the depths of human feeling and subjectivity while thinkers like Nietzsche and Marx raise up moral protests against the very notions of God and religion. Richard Popkin suggests that roots of this turmoil over belief and unbelief can be found as far back as the revival of scepticism during the sixteenth and seventeenth centuries.[1] That may be so, but the nineteenth century witnessed a far greater widening of the gap between those who felt the world is best understood within the context of religious sentiment, piety and faith and those who felt the world is best understood under the parameters of reason, science, and human effort.

The personality of Newman was dominated by matters of the intellect. To picture Newman as a man enchanted by antiquity and romanticism for the Middle Ages is a distortion. The Oxford biographer, Brian Martin, is careful to note the cerebral intensity of the character of Newman:

> Yet although Newman had strong appreciations of the beauties of the natural world, he was by no means a Romantic. His life was above all governed by his intellect. Strong convictions, worked out by hard thought, controlled the decisions which directed his life. His emotions were subject to his intellect. This was true when he underwent conversion in 1845 and in the years leading up to his reception into the Roman Church by Father Dominic Barberi, and in his youth when he made choices about his early religious directions.[2]

In the person of John Henry Newman, we are met with an intellectual filled with piety and a man of faith dominated by the intellect. Perhaps the century and the man were well-tailored for each other. In a lifetime that spans the greater part of the nineteenth century, Newman sets out to explain the logic of religious assent to the rationalists and sceptics and the role of the intellect in religious assent to the fideists and Romantics.

Faith and Reason in Newman's Intellectual Development

Before we explore the central text of Newman's spiritual epistemology, *The Grammar of Assent*, we need to trace his intellectual and

---

[1] See Richard Popkin, *The History of Scepticism from Erasmus to Spinoza* (Berkeley: U. of California, 1979): 247-248.

[2] Brian Martin, *John Henry Newman: His Life and Work* (New York: Oxford U., 1982): 9.

spiritual biography. In his *Apologia Pro Vita Sua*, we find traces of the future scholar already at work in a youth enchanted by books and imagination. As Newman relates:

> I used to wish the Arabian Tales were true: my imagination ran on unknown influences, on magical powers, and talismans. . . . I thought life might be a dream, or I an Angel, and all this world a deception. . . .[3]

Newman also relates that he was brought up to take great delight in reading the Bible, even though he had no formed religious convictions till age fifteen (*Apologia*, 14). Another interesting aspect of his personality is a self-confessed tendency towards superstition, a tendency which resulted in his making the sign of the cross before ever entering the dark.[4]

In the midst of this highly active imaginative life, the young Newman was also exposed to some of the more sceptical writers of the day. As he reports:

> When I was fourteen, I read Paine's Tracts against the Old Testament, and found pleasure in thinking of the objections which were contained in them. Also, I read some of Hume's Essays; and perhaps that on Miracles. So at least I gave my Father to understand; but perhaps it was a brag. Also, I recollect copying out some French verses, perhaps Voltaire's, in denial of the immortality of the soul, and saying to myself something like "How dreadful, but how plausible!" (*Apologia*, 15-16).

Newman's first religious conversion took place in 1816 when he was fifteen years of age. He mentions that at that time, he received into his intellect "impressions of dogma, which, through God's mercy, have never been effaced or obscured." One of the early spiritual influences on Newman was Rev. Walter Mayers of Pembroke College, Oxford who Newman says "was the human means of the beginning of divine faith in me." Mayers was one of Newman's masters at Ealing School and, as an Evangelical, placed into Newman's hands several books of "the school of Calvin" (*Apologia*, 16). Thus, Newman's first conversion was of an evangelical nature. As Newman relates, his initial conversion included the Calvinist doctrine of final perseverance:

> I received it at once and believed that the inward conversion of which I was conscious (and of which I am still more certain than that I have hands and feet) would last into the next life, and that I was elected to eternal glory. I have no consciousness that this belief had any tendency whatever to lead me to be careless about pleasing God. I retained it till the age of

---

[3] John Henry Newman, *Apologia Pro Vita Sua* (New York: W. W. Norton, 1968): 14. Hereafter this work will be cited in the text as *Apologia*.

[4] Ibid. Newman states that he doesn't recall where he learned this practice.

twenty-one, when it gradually faded away; but I believe that it had some influence on my opinions, in the direction of those childish imaginations which I have already mentioned, viz. in isolating me from the objects which surrounded me, in confirming me in my mistrust of the reality of material phenomena, and making me rest in the thought of two and two only absolute and luminously self-evident beings, myself and my creator—for while I considered myself predestined to salvation, my mind did not dwell upon others, as fancying them simply passed over, not predestined to eternal death. I only thought of the mercy to myself (*Apologia*, 16).

From 1817-1820, Newman was an undergraduate at Trinity College at Oxford University. It was during his studies at Oxford that Newman would read a number of important Anglican authors who would move him away from "the detestable doctrine" of final perseverance. Among the writers mentioned by Newman in his *Apologia* are Thomas Scott, Daniel Wilson, William Law, Joseph Milner and Thomas Newton. It was Newton's work on the prophecies that convinced Newman that the Pope was the Antichrist predicted by Daniel, Paul and John. Newman mentions that this latter belief remained in his imagination (at least in its effects) up to the year 1843, even though "it had been obliterated from my reason and judgment at an earlier date" (*Apologia*, 17-18). Newman's reflections on the intellectual effects of such a belief are instructive:

Here came that conflict of mind, which so many have felt besides myself:—leading some men to make a compromise between two ideas, so inconsistent with each other,—driving others to beat out the one idea or the other from their minds,—and ending in my own case, after many years of intellectual unrest, in the gradual decay and extinction of one of them.... (*Apologia*, 18-19).

We can detect in the mind of the young Newman a drive for intellectual consistency and integrity. We can also notice an ability to reformulate positions and to change opinions if the evidence or the logic warrants it. However, we should not think of the developing mind of Newman as solely dominated by logic and investigation. There was a tender and sensitive side to the young scholar that would later express itself in the most gentle prose and moving poetry. Indeed, it seems that as early as 1816 Newman was taken possession by the idea that it was the will of God that he should lead a single life. This impression emerged from an inner feeling that his calling in life would require the sacrifice of celibacy. For some years, Newman felt drawn to the possibility of doing missionary work. However, Newman looks back on this calling as one of the factors that strengthened his "feeling of separation from the visible world" (*Apologia*, 19).

In 1820, Newman was awarded his B.A. degree from Oxford, but he failed in the final examination in which honors would be given. This failure was partly due to the state of exhaustion to which Newman had driven himself because of a very strict self-imposed regimen. As he relates:

> Meanwhile, not only in term time, but in the Long Vacations, nay, in the other vacations also, I read furiously the books in which the candidates for academic honours were examined. I got up in the winters at five, lighting my own fire; and in the summer at half-past four, getting four hours' reading before breakfast. A year or two afterwards I took only four hours, but this was after my undergraduate course was over . . . for the last twenty weeks I read regularly twelve hours a day . . . .[5]

Newman's failure to gain honours he later saw to be providential. Not only did it thwart his father's ambitions for him to be a lawyer but it also moved him towards a decision to take Orders. In 1822, Newman took the examination for a fellowship at Oriel College, Oxford. His success in gaining the fellowship was for Newman "the work of Providence."[6] At Oriel, Newman would meet some of the most influential figures of the Church of England and the later Oxford Movement. Among these people were Edward Pusey, a kindred spirit, whom Newman thought to be "humility itself."[7] In 1824, Newman became a curate of St. Clement's Church in Oxford and was soon ordained a deacon. During this time, Newman came under the influence of Edward Hawkins, the Vicar of St. Mary's, the University Church at Oxford. Newman's credits Hawkins for having clarified many issues in doctrine and belief. Thus, he was led away from his remaining Calvinism and learned an appreciation of Tradition (*Apologia*, 29). Likewise, Newman states that he learned the doctrine of Apostolic Succession from Rev. William James, a Fellow of Oriel (*Apologia*, 21). It was also at this time that Newman read Bishop Butler's Analogy of Religion which introduced him "to the question of the logical cogency of Faith" (*Apologia*, 22).

It should be apparent that the young Newman was moving more and more during this time to the Anglicanism that would later emerge as the Oxford Movement. The influences were coming from people of great learning and devotion. There was Dr. Whately who Newman says took him by the hand and taught him to think and use his reason (*Apologia*, 22). There were Robert Isaac Wilberforce and Richard Hurrel Froude who

---

[5] Newman, "Why I Failed," in *The Essential Newman*, ed. Vincent Ferrer Blehl, S. J. (New York: New American Library, 1963): 22.

[6] Martin, *Newman: His Life and Work*, 28.

[7] Ibid., 29.

would later be part of the Tractarian Movement. However, the man who seems to have made the greatest impression on Newman during this time was John Keble. As Newman writes:

> When the general tone of religious literature was so nerveless and impotent, Keble struck an original note and woke up in the hearts of thousands a new music, the music of a school, long unknown in England. Nor can I pretend to analyze, in my own instance, the effect of religious teaching so deep, so pure, so beautiful (*Apologia*, 27-28).

Newman says that Keble opened his eyes to the importance of the Sacramental system, the Communion of Saints and the notion of the mysteries of the faith. To Keble Newman also gives the credit for making him see that Bishop Butler's idea of probability regarding matters of faith was inadequate. Keble taught that the firmness of assent in matters of religion came not from the probability of the arguments put forward but "to the living power of the faith and love" which accepts the religious teaching (*Apologia*, 28). Thus, we find in embryonic form Newman's own doctrine, enunciated in *The Grammar of Assent*, of real versus notional assent. For Keble, as for Newman, faith and love are not directed towards an idea but towards an Object: in this case, the Personal God.

Newman's career in the Church of England began to move with great promise following his ordination to the priesthood in 1825. He was appointed Vice-Principal of Alban Hall under Whately. In 1828, he became Vicar of St. Mary's Church, Oxford. Soon he was becoming well-known as a preacher. An examination of some of the themes of these sermons reveals a deep concern for the issues of faith and reason which would culminate in *The Grammar of Assent* many years later. Newman is careful to insure that proper respect be given to both the special logic of faith and the proper use of reason. In his sermon entitled "Faith Without Sight," Newman touches upon the theme of conscience as the inner voice which calls the mind to the spiritual Presence of God:

> Every religious mind, under every dispensation of Providence, will be in the habit of looking out of and beyond self, as regards all matters connected with its highest good. For a man of religious mind is he who attends to the rule of conscience, which is born with him, which he did not make for himself, and to which he feels bound in duty to submit. And conscience immediately directs him to some Being exterior to himself. . . and who evidently is superior to him. . . . Thus, a man is thrown out of himself by that very Voice which speaks within him. He looks forth into the world to seek Him who is not of the world, to find behind the shadows and deceits of this shifting scene of time and sense, Him whose Word is

eternal and spiritual. He looks out of himself for the Living Word to which he may attribute what has echoed in his heart.[8]

We see in this passage a sensitivity to the echoes of the heart combined with the inner disclosure of the spiritual Presence of God contained in the voice of conscience. Like St. Augustine, Newman is gifted with an ability to journey inward to the hidden depths of human consciousness. God as the inner voice is more intimate to the soul than the soul is to itself.

In another early sermon, Newman strives to establish the proper use of reason in matters of the faith. This sermon, entitled "The Usurpations of Reason," points out that the opposition between faith and reason takes place only when "either of the two encroaches upon the province of the other."[9] Newman's main thesis is that secular reason has its proper domain, but it should not make itself the judge of matters of religion which operate according to a different sense. However, Newman also criticizes the total abandonment of reason in religious matters. His point is that we should "freely cultivate Reason in all its noble functions" and "employ it industriously in the service of religion."[10] Nevertheless, as important and necessary is the cultivation of secular reason, we must not advance "its influence over the heart."[11]

The theme that begins to emerge in these sermons is a recognition that faith operates according to a different logic than pure analysis of propositions. In his sermon on "Personal Influence, The Means of Propagating the Truth," Newman clearly argues that the spread of religious Truth is not so much a matter of logic and propositions as it is a matter of "the personal influence, direct and indirect, of those who are commissioned to teach it."[12] In his sermon on "Faith and Reason, Contrasted As Habits of Mind,"[13] Newman develops this theme more deeply. He addresses the issue of "evidences" for religion that some philosophers feel compelled to seek. While not opposed to the search for these evidences as a means of bolstering the faith, Newman does not believe that the truths of religion are to be approached with a demand for evidences. For Newman, faith is "a

---

[8] Newman, "Faith Without Sight," in *Parochial and Plain Sermons* (Westminster, MD: Christian Classics, 1966), 13:18.

[9] Newman, "The Usurpations of Reason," in *Fifteen Sermons Preached Before The University of Oxford* (Westminister, MD: Christian Classics, 1966): 58.

[10] Ibid., 73.

[11] Ibid.

[12] Newman, "Personal Influences, the Means of Propagating the Faith," in *Fifteen Sermons*, 79-80.

[13] Newman, "Faith and Reason, Contrasted as Habits of Mind," in *Fifteen Sermons*, 193.

supernatural principle" which has as its object the Supreme and Personal God. Accordingly, the practical safeguard against atheism is not to be found in evidences but in "the inward need and desire, the inward experience of that Power, existing in the mind before and independently of their examination of His material world."[14]

The formative years of Newman's training in the Anglican Church also included a profound and comprehensive study of the Church Fathers. Of course, these historical studies led Newman to his understanding of the historical development of church doctrines. The process of investigating the Christological debates of the fifth century eventually led Newman to question the validity of the "Via Media"[15] of his Anglican Communion. The results of Newman's questioning are well-known. Since he saw the *Via Media* paralleled in the Monophysite position rather than the Orthodox position in the fifth century, the wheels were set in motion for Newman's eventual conversion to the Roman Catholic faith (*Apologia*, 96-120).

The details of Newman's conversion to Rome don't concern us, but the nature of the conversion reveals something important about the mind and spirit of the man. We see his intellectual character at work. Newman's hunger for truth and consistency was all-consuming. He was willing to risk position, friendship and ridicule all for the sake of what he perceived to be the truth. It was a conversion more of the mind than the heart. Yet his affections were so caught up in his life of the intellect that we cannot uncouple them. Newman's reception into the Roman Communion did not change the major intellectual and spiritual concerns of his heart and mind. He was first and foremost a Christian intellectual in search of an adequate language to express the inner geography of the human spirit before its Creator. It is perhaps a testimony to his humility and integrity that he declined an invitation of the French bishop, Dupanloup, to serve as a personal theologian for Vatican I. The nature of the Council with its committees and boards did not excite Newman. He was instead absorbed in the composition of a work which, indeed, he had inwardly been contemplating for some twenty years: *The Grammar of Assent*.[16]

The Spirituality of The Grammar of Assent

In 1833, Newman was visiting the Continent for the first time. In Sicily, he became sick with a fever and felt he was going to die. It was

---

14 Ibid., 194-196.
15 See *Apologia*, 87-96, for a discussion of the *Via Media*.
16 Martin, *Newman: His Life and Work*, 122.

during this time that he wrote the verses of one of his most famous poems, "The Pillar and the Cloud." In the poem, there are these memorable lines:

> Lead Kindly Light, amid the encircling gloom
> Lead Thou me on!
> The night is dark, and I am far from home—
> Lead Thou me on![17]

The words of this poem highlight the main features of Newman's spirituality. God is a Guiding Light, and God is a Sacred Person. Newman combines the intellectual spirituality of the divine illumination of the soul with a personal sense of God as the Sacred Other. Herein lies the richness of Newman's assent of the soul to God. The mind apprehends God simultaneously as the light of conscience in the intellectual sense and as the personal redeemer in the religious sense. However, for Newman, as we will see, the mind and the heart work in harmony rather than tension.

In *The Grammar of Assent*, Newman undertakes what one scholar calls the "contemplation of mind."[18] This work represents an effort of some twenty years of numerous drafts.[19] As Newman himself notes: "I had felt it on my conscience for years, that it would not do to quit the world without doing it."[20] What is strange is that Newman plunges immediately into the subject matter without any sort of introduction regarding purpose or intent. Edward Caswall, an English Oratorian, noted once the gist of what Newman had told him about the *Grammar* in a conversation:

> Object of the book twofold. In the first part shows that you can believe what you cannot understand. In the second part that you can believe what you cannot absolutely prove.[21]

The historical situation of the nineteenth century explains Newman's preoccupation with this issue of faith and reason. As we have already noted, Newman, as a man of faith and intellect, was instinctually drawn into the epistemic problems connected with the assent of the mind and heart to God. Vincent Ferrer Blehl offers this lucid description of the intellectual milieu out of which *The Grammar* emerges:

> The nineteenth century witnessed a great crisis of belief in Christianity, a crisis heightened by the discoveries in the scientific world which seemed to conflict with belief. The intellectual climate was swept by the cold winds of skepticism. In contrast to the seemingly sure methods of science, the

---

[17] Blehl, ed., *Essential Newman*, 42.
[18] See Thomas Vargish, *The Contemplation of Mind* (London: Oxford, 1970).
[19] Charles S. Dessain, *John Henry Newman* (London: Nelson and Sons, 1966): 148.
[20] Ibid.
[21] Ibid.

disagreements on religious matters could only argue, it was said, the inadequacies of faith as contrasted with reason. All views in religion could only attain to the level of opinion. Nineteenth-century religious skepticism was the heir of the deistic mentality of the eighteenth. Newman soon realized that the eighteenth-century defense of faith on the basis of evidences as represented by Paley and the evidential school was hopelessly inadequate to meet the current situation. The entire problem of faith and reason demanded a fresh examination.[22]

Newman begins his investigations with an inquiry into the different modes of holding and apprehending propositions. It is here that he proposes his famous distinction between notional and real assent. Notional assent is given to propositions which are "abstract, general and non-existing," such as "Man is an animal, some men are learned, an Apostle is a creation of Christianity, a line is length without breadth, to err is human, to forgive divine."[23] There are other propositions, composed of singular nouns, in which the terms stand for "things external to us, unit and individual, as 'Philip was the father of Alexander,' 'the earth goes round the sun,' 'the Apostles first preached to the Jews'" (*Grammar*, 10). These types of propositions, Newman labels "real propositions, and their apprehension real" (*Grammar*, 10).

Newman is quick to note that the same proposition may be interpreted in a notional manner by one person and in a real manner by another. Thus, the proposition "Sugar is sweet" can be understood in a notional manner by someone mentally comparing the taste of sugar with honey or glycerine, but it may be understood in a singular or real manner by a child who understands the phrase to refer to the immediate apprehension that "this sugar is sweet" (*Grammar*, 11).

According to Newman, real assent is more "vivid and forcible" than notional assent (*Grammar*, 11). While a real assent doesn't automatically impel a person to action, nevertheless, it

> excites and stimulates the affections and passions, by bringing facts home to them as motive causes. Thus, it indirectly brings about what the apprehension of large principles, of general laws, or of moral obligations, never could affect (*Grammar*, 12).

Thus, we sense the power and strength of the real assent in moving the religious person in a way that an intellectual or notional assent never could. Newman's point is not that religious assent is irrational or merely affective. Instead, he wants to insist that religious assent or true conversion expresses

---

[22] Blehl, *Essential Newman*, 284.

[23] Newman, *Grammar of Assent* (Westminister, MD: Christian Classics, 1973): 9. Hereafter this work will be cited in the text as *Grammar*.

a type of assent that is real, personal and concrete rather than intellectual, abstract or notional. Newman explains it this way:

> Real apprehensions, then, may be pronounced stronger than notional, because things, which are its objects, are confessedly more impressive and affective than notions, which are the objects of notional. Experiences and their images strike and occupy the mind, as abstractions and their combinations do not (*Grammar*, 37).

Newman's main thesis is that the type of apprehension that takes place in religious assent is real rather than notional. He further investigates the quality of real assent by noting its personal character. While we all have the power of abstraction, what really motivates a person towards heroism and passionate action is not an abstract idea but a personal experience which is "peculiar and special" (*Grammar*, 83). Thus, faith and spirituality receive their strength from the moorings of personal experiences which invoke real assents. As Newman explains, these real assents are

> sometimes called beliefs, convictions, certitudes; and as given to moral objects, they are perhaps as rare as they are powerful. Till we have them, in spite of a full apprehension and assent in the field of notions, we have no intellectual moorings, and are at the mercy of impulses, fancies, and wandering lights, whether as regards personal conduct, social and political action, or religion. These beliefs, be they true or false in the particular case, form the mind out of which they grow, and impart to it a seriousness and manliness which inspires in other minds a confidence in its views, and is one secret of persuasiveness and influence in the public stage of the world. They create, as the case may be, heroes and saints, great leaders, statesmen, preachers, and reformers, the pioneers of discovery in science, visionaries, fanatics, knight-errands, demagogues and adventurers. They have given to the world men of one idea, of immense energy, of adamantine will, of revolutionary power. They kindle sympathies between man and man, and knit together the innumerable units which constitute a race and a nation (*Grammar*, 87-88).

Newman wants to flesh out the nature of religious assent as it emerges in the real experience of human life and thought. He is always insisting on the personal quality that accompanies true religious assent and conversion. His approach may be called existential in that he does not wish to talk about religious ideas in the abstract but, instead, wishes to focus on the subjective apprehension of religious truth. Thus, it follows that Newman also wishes to relate belief to action. In this regard, he admits that that real assent or belief does not, in itself, lead to action. Nevertheless, the images in which [real assent] lives, representing as they do the concrete, have the power of the concrete upon the affections and passions, and by means of these become operative (*Grammar*, 89).

It is this quality of concrete, personal experience that places real assent in a different category than notional assent. Rational inquiry and discussion about science, morals, religion, art, etc. can result in a mode of assent in which the terms discussed are to the mind "nothing more than major and minor premises and conclusions" (*Grammar*, 90). Newman observes that

Belief, on the other hand, being concerned with things concrete, not abstract, which variously excite the mind from their moral and imaginative properties, has for its objects, not only directly what is true, but inclusively what is beautiful, useful, admirable, heroic; objects which kindle devotion, rouse the passions, and attach the affections; and thus it leads the way to actions of every kind, to the establishment of principles, and the formation of character, and is thus again intimately connected with what is individual and personal (*Grammar*, 90-91).

We can detect in this passage Newman's comprehensive vision of religious belief. Rather than being a mere intellectual assent to abstract propositions, true belief brings the individual to a transformation in the heart, mind and soul. Real religious assent is inevitably linked to the spiritual, moral and affective dimensions of the human person. The heart and the mind are simultaneously converted in the concrete, personal and real apprehension of religious assent.

In several passages of *The Grammar of Assent*, Newman speaks the language of the heart. At times we are reminded of the passion of a Kierkegaard or the intellectual intensity of a Pascal. Thus, we read:

The heart is commonly reached, not through the reason, but through the imagination, by means of direct impressions, by the testimony of facts and events, by history, by description. Persons influence us, voices melt us, looks subdue us, deeds inflame us. Many a man will live and die upon a dogma: no man will be a martyr for a conclusion (*Grammar*, 93).

It follows from these observations that Newman is not impressed with the detached, logical inquiry into the question of the existence of God. Of such philosophers, Newman writes:

They sit at home, and reach forward to distances which astonish us; but they hit without grasping, and are sometimes as confident about shadows as about realities. They have worked out by a calculation the lie of a country which they never saw, and mapped it by means of a gazetteer; and like blind men, though they can put a stranger on his way, they cannot walk straight themselves, and do not feel it quite their business to walk at all (*Grammar*, 93-94).

Newman is not at all persuaded by the God of reason. His own words on this matter could not be more lucid:

> Logic makes but a sorry rhetoric with the multitude; first shoot round corners, and you may not despair of converting by a syllogism. Tell men to gain notions of a Creator by his works, and if they do set about it (which nobody does) they would be jaded and wearied by the labyrinth they were tracing. Their minds would be gorged and surfeited by the logical operation. Logicians are more set upon concluding rightly, than on right conclusions. They cannot see the end for the process. Few men have that power of mind which may hold fast and firmly a variety of thoughts. We ridicule 'men of one idea'; but a great many of us were born to be such, and we would be happier if we knew it. To most men argument makes the point in hand only more doubtful and considerably less impressive. After all, man is *not* a reasoning animal; he is a seeing, feeling, contemplating, acting animal. He is influenced by what is direct and precise (*Grammar*, 94).

It is at this juncture in his discussion that Newman seeks to describe the nature of the mind's encounter with the Personal God of the Christian faith. In chapter V of *The Grammar*, Newman devotes one section to the belief in the One God. Here he is clear that by the One God, he is not speaking about "a mere *anima mundi*; or an initial principle which once was in action and now is not; or collective humanity" (*Grammar*, 101). Newman leaves no doubt about the nature of the God he is concerned with:

> I speak then of the God of the Theist and of the Christian: a God who is numerically One, who is Personal; the Author, Sustainer, and Finisher of all things, the life of Law and Order, the Moral Governor; One who is Supreme and Sole; like Himself, unlike all things besides Himself which are all but his creatures; distinct from, independent of them all; One who is self-existing, absolutely infinite, who has ever been and ever will be, to whom nothing is past or future; who is all perfection, and the fullness and archetype of every possible excellence, the Truth Itself, Wisdom, Love, Justice, Holiness; One who is All-powerful, All-knowing, Omnipresent, Incomprehensible. These are some of the distinctive prerogatives which I ascribe unconditionally and unreservedly to the great Being whom I call God (*Grammar*, 101).

This Personal God which Newman so eloquently describes is not to be found by means of notional assent. Like Augustine in his *Confessions*, he asks himself how he can attain to the knowledge of God:

> Can I attain to any more vivid assent to the Being of a God, than that which is given merely to the notions of the intellect? Can I enter with a personal knowledge into the circle of truths which make up that great thought? Can I rise to what I call an imaginative apprehension of it? Can

> I believe as if I saw? Since such a high assent requires a present
> experience or memory of the fact, at first sight it would seem as if the
> answer must be in the negative; for how can I assent as if I saw, unless I
> have seen? but no one in this life can see God? Yet I conceive a real
> assent is possible, and I proceed to show how (*Grammar*, 102).

It is at this point that Newman outlines a type of inference by
impression. It is not a proof for the existence of God but an inward journey
into that fine point of the soul where the Divine Presence makes Itself felt.
Newman begins with an analogy taken from sense impressions. As he
explains:

> When it is said that we cannot see God, this is undeniable; but still in what
> sense have we a discernment of His creatures, of the individual beings
> which surround us? The evidence we have of their presence lies in the
> phenomena which address our senses, and our warrant for taking these for
> evidence is our instinctive certitude that they are evidence. By the law of
> our nature we associate those sensible phenomena with certain units,
> individuals, substances, whatever they might be called, which are outside
> and out of reach of sense, and we picture them to ourselves in those
> phenomena. The phenomena are as if pictures; but at the same time they
> give us no exact measure or character of the unknown things beyond them.
> . . . Therefore, when we speak of having a picture of the things which are
> perceived through the senses, we mean a certain representation, true as
> far as it goes, but not adequate (*Grammar*, 102-103).

Newman applies this analogy of sense impressions to the moral sense
we discover within ourselves as a sign of God's impression of Himself in the
depths of human conscience. Just as we gain an impression of the mind
and character of a great author through a reading of his works, so also do
we attain to an inner impression of God within our conscience. As
Newman writes:

> Now certainly the thought of God, as theists entertain it, is not gained by
> an instinctive association of His presence with any sensible phenomena;
> but the office which the senses directly fulfill as regards creation that
> devolves indirectly on certain of our mental phenomena as regards the
> Creator. Those phenomena are found in the sense of moral obligation.
> As from a multitude of instinctive perceptions, acting in particular
> instances of something beyond the senses, we generalize the notion of an
> external world, . . . so from the perceptive power which identifies the
> intimations of conscience with the reverberations or echoes (so to say) of
> an external admonition, we proceed on to the notion of a Supreme Ruler
> and Judge, and then again we image Him and His attributes in those
> recurring intimations, out of which as mental phenomena, our recognition
> of His existence was originally gained (*Grammar*, 103-104).

Newman states that he is not proposing to prove the Being of a God.
Instead, he is only seeking "to explain how we gain an image of God and

give a real assent to the proposition that He exists" (*Grammar*, 105). Newman maintains that in the feeling of conscience, we gain access to God. He describes conscience through various images as "an authoritative monitor," "a voice, imperative and constraining," and "a Supreme Governor, a Judge, holy just, powerful, all seeing . . ." (*Grammar*, 106-110). He also speaks of conscience as a type of human instinct which is analogous to the instincts which operate in animals (*Grammar*, 110-111). Newman finds support for his notion of conscience as an instinct or natural human impulse in the ability of children to understand and experience God as a Supreme Moral Governor. As he explains:

> we shall not be wrong in holding that this child has in his mind the image of an Invisible Being, who exercises a particular providence among us, who is present every where, who is heart-reading, heart-changing, ever-changing, ever-accessible, open to impetration. What a strong and intimate vision of God must he have already attained, if, as I have supposed, an ordinary trouble of mind has the spontaneous effect of leading him for consolation and aid to an Invisible Personal Power (*Grammar*, 113)!

Newman explains that God is far more than a word to the child. He also points out that this instinctual awareness of God found in the child must be nourished and supported or it can be lost. Yet Newman feels it is quite clear that the child

> has that within him which actually vibrates, responds and gives a deep meaning to the lessons of his first teachers about the will and providence of God (*Grammar*, 115).

Newman is not certain to what extent this initial image of God is natural or to what extent it "implies a special divine aid which is above nature" (*Grammar*, 115). He is certain, though, that with proper nourishment this image of God within the soul will grow and expand within the consciousness and life of the individual. The result of this proper spiritual training is the cultivation of one's moral character as well as one's consciousness of God. As Newman writes:

> To a mind thus carefully formed upon the basis of its natural conscience, the world, both of nature and of man, does but give back a reflection of those truths about the One Living God, which have been familiar to it from childhood (*Grammar*, 116).

Newman, therefore, locates spiritual maturity in a type of God-consciousness. For Newman, a religious imagination carries with it a constant sense of God as its own inner voice. As he describes this religious sensibility:

> It interprets what it sees around it by this previous inward teaching, as the true key of that maze of vast complicated disorder; and thus it gains a more and more consistent and luminous vision of God from the most unpromising materials. Thus conscience is a connecting principle between the creature and its Creator; and the firmest hold of theological truth is gained by habits of personal religion (*Grammar*, 117).

We should note here that by conscience Newman is not referring to an autonomous power of the human subject. Rather, he is referring to what he describes in his *Letter to the Duke of Norfolk* as "the aboriginal Vicar of Christ."[24] In more scholastic terminology, Newman understands conscience to be "an impression of the Divine Light in us, a participation of the eternal law in the rational creature."[25] Part of the problem Newman detects in his age is a growing tendency to redefine conscience as "the right of self-will" rather than as the Voice of God (*Grammar*, 264-265).

Conscience, therefore, is more than a moral faculty for Newman. It is the image of God in the human soul which constantly calls each person back to fidelity to God. The result of following this inward conscience is spiritual growth and a deeper awareness of God as a Living Person. As Newman writes:

> When men begin all their works with the thought of God, acting for His sake, and to fulfill his will, when they ask His blessing on themselves and their life, pray to Him for the objects they desire, and see Him in the event, whether it be according to their prayers or not, they will find that everything that happens tends to confirm them in their imagination, varied and unearthly as those truths may be. Then they are brought into His presence as that of a Living Person, and are able to hold converse with Him, and that with a directness and simplicity, with a confidence and intimacy, *mutatis mutandis*, which we use towards an earthly superior; so that it is doubtful whether we realize the company of our fellow-men with greater keenness than those favoured minds are able to contemplate and adore the Unseen, Incomprehensible Creator (*Grammar*, 117-118).

This powerful description of the consciousness of God in every day affairs is reminiscent of Newman's advice on how human beings can attain to spiritual perfection. In his volume, *Meditations and Devotions*, Newman explains:

> It is a saying of holy men that, if we wish to be perfect, we have nothing more to do than to perform the ordinary duties of the day well. A short

---

[24] Blehl, ed., *Essential Newman*, 263.
[25] *Grammar*, 262; the definition is from St. Thomas.

road to perfection—short, not because easy, but because pertinent and intelligible. There are no short ways to perfection, but there are sure ones . . . .

We must bear in mind what is meant by perfection. It does not mean any extraordinary service, anything out of the way, or especially heroic—not all have the opportunity of heroic acts, of sufferings—but it means what the word perfection ordinarily means. By perfect we mean that which has no flaw in it, that which is complete, that which is consistent, that which is sound—we mean the opposite to imperfect. As we know well what *im*perfection in religious service means, we know by the contrast what is meant by perfection. . . .

He, then, is perfect who does the work of the day perfectly, and we need not go beyond this to seek perfection. You need not go out of the *round* of the day.

I insist on this because I think it will simplify our views, and fix our exertions on a definite aim. If you ask me what you are to do in order to be perfect, I say, first—Do not lie in bed beyond the due time of rising; give your first thoughts to God; make a good visit to the Blessed Sacrament; say the Angelus devoutly; eat and drink to God's glory; say the Rosary well; be recollected; keep out bad thoughts; make your evening meditation well; examine yourself daily; go to bed in good time, and you are already perfect.[26]

We see in these lines a man of great spiritual wisdom as well as simplicity. Indeed, Newman's richness may be said to reside in his ability to combine his tremendous intellectual gifts with a constant humility and gratitude before the Living Personal God. However, it would be a mistake to think that Newman ends his *Grammar of Assent* with an appeal to the heart and an abandonment of the mind. While he does acknowledge that the vivid impression of religious objects is independent of books and does not even require any knowledge of Scripture, nevertheless it is important to search for ways of articulating religious experience in notional form. Thus, Newman reasons that

if so much can be traced out in the twilight of Natural Religion, it is obvious how great an addition in fulness and exactness is made to our mental image of the Divine Personality and Attributes, by the light of Christianity. And, indeed, to give us a clear and sufficient object for our faith, is one main purpose of the supernatural Dispensation of Religion (*Grammar*, 118).

In this regard, Newman encourages a study of Scripture, the Lives of the Saints and "the reasonings, internal collisions, and decisions of the Theological School." Newman explains that it has been his purpose in *The*

---

[26] Blehl, ed., *Essential Newman*, 337-338.

Grammar "to trace the process by which the mind arrives, not only at a notional, but an imaginative or real assent that there is One God, that is, an assent made with an apprehension, not only of what the words of the proposition mean, but of the object denoted by them." However, Newman also points out that "without a proposition or thesis there can be no assent, no belief at all; any more than there can be an inference without a conclusion" (*Grammar*, 119). As Newman explains:

> The proposition that there is One Personal and Present God may be held in either way; either as a theological truth, or as a religious fact or reality. The notion and the reality assented to are represented by one and the same proposition, but serve as different interpretations of it. When the proposition is apprehended for the purposes of proof, analysis, comparison, and the like intellectual exercises, it is used as an expression of a notion; when for the purposes of devotion, it is the image of a reality. Theology, properly and directly, deals with notional apprehension; religion with imaginative (*Grammar*, 119-120).

Newman, therefore, argues for the need to bring religion, theology, devotion and dogma into a coherent pattern of unity. He is always the man of balance, and he seeks to avoid the two extremes of pure rationalism and pure fideism. As he explains, notional propositions are "useful in their dogmatic aspect as ascertaining and making clear for us the truths on which the religious imagination has to rest" (*Grammar*, 120). Furthermore, he argues that

> knowledge must ever precede the exercise of the affections. We feel gratitude and love, we feel indignation and dislike, when we have the informations actually put before us which are to kindle those several emotions ... we must know concerning God, before we can love, fear, hope or trust towards Him (*Grammar*, 120-121).

The conclusion is that the objects of devotion "when not represented to our senses by material symbols, must be set before the mind in propositions" (*Grammar*, 121). What this means is that religion stands in need of theology. Newman, the man of faith and religious imagination, is also the man who has studied the subtleties of doctrinal formulations. He is well aware of how much religious experience must be articulated in precise theological language. Therefore, he concludes:

> Theology may stand as a substantive science, though it be without the life of religion; but religion cannot maintain its ground at all without theology. Sentiment, whether imaginative or emotional, falls back upon the intellect for its stay, when sense cannot be called into exercise; and it is in this way that devotion falls back upon dogma (*Grammar*, 121).

In the second half of the *Grammar of Assent*, Newman seeks to illustrate that it is possible to believe with certitude even that which one cannot absolutely prove. He provides many common-sense examples of how we constantly give unconditional assent to unproven facts. As he argues:

> We laugh to scorn the idea that we had no parents though we have no memory of our birth; that we shall never depart this life, though we have no experience of the future; that we are able to live without food, though we have never tried; that a world of men did not live before our time, or that the world has had no history; that there has been no rise and fall of states, no great men, no wars, no revolutions, no art, no science, no literature, no religion (*Grammar*, 177-178).

Newman points out that giving assent to unproven or undemonstrative propositions is too common to be considered illogical or irrational. Life is greater than logical demonstrations. Newman, therefore, suggests that there is within the human mind a certain power or skill directed towards judging and concluding which he calls the Illative Sense (*Grammar*, 353). Newman compares this Illative Sense to the *phronesis* or practical judgment of Aristotle (*Grammar*, 354-57). Since human judgments extend beyond pure logic, there is a need to cultivate "the more subtle and elastic logic of thought." In matters of concrete reasonings like historical research or theology, Newman believes that there is no other ultimate test of truth and error besides this Illative Sense; "just as there is no sufficient test of poetical excellence, heroic action or gentleman-like conduct, other than the particular mental sense, be it genius, taste, sense of propriety, or the moral sense, to which those subject matters are severally committed (*Grammar*, 359). Thus, we are called upon to strengthen and perfect this Illative Sense. For Newman, it is through the range of this Illative Sense that the mind is able to make real assents regarding truths of religion.

The Illative Sense embraces the expanded logic necessary to live in the world of concrete, personal reality. As Thomas Vargish notes: "Only the Illative Sense is elastic and delicate enough to take account of the variousness of reality, the uniqueness of each thing experienced."[27] Thus, Newman sees in the Illative Sense, the use of the word "sense" in a way parallel to "our use of it in 'good sense,' 'common sense,' a 'sense of beauty,' etc." (*Grammar*, 345). Using this Illative Sense, Newman reasons that it is possible to acquire a mental state of certitude regarding one's religious beliefs. This certitude is akin to the certitude of knowing that

---

[27] Vargish, *Contemplation of Mind*, 68.

your parents love you. It is not a judgment based on demonstrable logic but a judgment which emerges out of personal knowledge. Since God is Personal Loving Being, the Illative Sense allows the human mind to have experiential knowledge and certitude about God's love. The reasons of the heart unite with the powers of the mind.

Conclusions

The power, range and depth of the mind and heart of John Henry Newman generate a spirituality which is at once existential, personal and intellectual. Living in a century in which rationalism and romanticism competed for followers, Newman's balance of intellect and affectivity is instructive. At times his writings suggest a soul in allegiance with Kierkegaard in their emphasis on personal knowledge and subjective experience. However, Newman's personality took shape in the midst of ecclesiastical structures and liturgical piety. Kierkegaard was more the outsider and the loner. Instead of an intense involvement in Church and University life, the Dane remained apart from the realms of Christendom.

If one were to attempt to place Newman within an intellectual or spiritual tradition, he would fit in best with his fellow companions of the Oxford Movement like Pusey and Keble. Certainly, Newman was no metaphysical system-builder like Hegel nor a traditional scholastic theologian. His sense of God-consciousness seems to bear some affinities with the thought of Friedrich Schleiermacher (1768-1834), but Newman's intellectual and historical concerns add a dimension that is not so prominent in the German. In the final analysis, Newman is best understood as Christian intellectual and scholar. His concerns, both pastoral and theological, show him to stand in the tradition of the Church Fathers and Christian Humanism (in its broadest sense).

The preoccupation with the issues of faith and reason led Newman into the creative enterprise of *The Grammar of Assent*. Refusing to allow reason to usurp the proper domain of faith, Newman developed the idea of real assent to a concrete, personal truth. Refusing to place faith out of the realm of the intellect, Newman expanded the concept of reason to embrace the Illative Sense. Thus, Newman represents a spirituality of the mind and heart which unite in the conversion of the whole person towards God.

The story that we have not told is of the man of prayer and patience, the tutor, the confessor, the preacher. We must not overlook the inner life of faith that so dominated the soul of John Henry Newman. Perhaps only those who knew him personally could give witness to how well Newman lived up to his chosen motto: *Cor Ad Cor Loquitur*—Heart Speaks to Heart.